MANUFACTURING
BUSINESS

MANUFACTURING
BUSINESS

BY

philip alter crawford

P. W. S. ANDREWS

OFFICIAL FELLOW OF NUFFIELD COLLEGE
OXFORD

WITH A PREFACE BY
SIR HENRY CLAY

LONDON
MACMILLAN & CO. LTD
1949

COPYRIGHT

TO

D. H. MACGREGOR, M.C.

PROFESSOR EMERITUS OF POLITICAL ECONOMY
IN THE UNIVERSITY OF OXFORD
AND SOMETIME PROFESSORIAL FELLOW
OF NUFFIELD COLLEGE

PREFACE

In 1944 the late Samuel Courtauld made to Nuffield College a very generous offer to meet the costs of an investigation into the relation between scale of enterprise and efficiency. He was deeply interested in the Reconstruction Survey, on which the College had been engaged during the War; his own business experience had latterly been confined to very large-scale enterprise, but he had been impressed with the social importance of small-scale business, and, without attaching any narrow conditions to his gift, wished to encourage the realistic study of management in the two contrasted fields. A part of the investigation was entrusted to the Institute of Statistics, which carried out and published a theoretical discussion of the questions involved, and a report on small-scale enterprise in one of its most important fields, retail trade. At the same time the Institute for Research in Agricultural Economics undertook an examination of the extensive material available to it on small-scale agriculture. The main investigation was, however, entrusted to Mr. Andrews.

Mr. Courtauld had made available to the inquiry the experience and records of his own firm, and certain other rayon manufacturers, to whom he introduced Mr. Andrews, gave similar confidential access to their data. Mr. Andrews's first task was to examine and analyse this mass of material. The number of firms in that industry is small, and it is not possible to publish the results of this examination in a form which would not disclose confidential information about particular firms; but the results were recorded in a series of confidential memoranda which provided invaluable new material for an analytical study of the internal organization and external relations of large-scale manufacturing industry.

The study of rayon was followed by a similar study of certain branches of the boot and shoe industry. A general survey of the section selected was made, and this served as the basis for an intensive examination, in the light of actual accounts, of the practice and experience of a dozen representative firms. It is hoped that it will be possible to publish the results of this work; but its primary purpose and value was to provide more material for a general study of the Economics of the Firm, suggested already by the rayon investigation.

In the present volume Mr. Andrews offers such a general study. It is, of course, based on a longer and wider range of reading and investigation than has been involved in the Courtauld Inquiry; but it is doubtful whether it could have been made without some such intensive examination of a large sample of actual firms, and the opportunity of concentrating on such an inquiry, as Mr. Courtauld's generosity provided. It will, I believe, be interesting to other economists. It is primarily a record and analysis of actual practice based on actual records of experience; but it is not loaded with a mass of descriptive data, and aims at distilling from its material such generalizations as it permits of value to systematic economic thinking in general. In particular, the parts dealing with price determination, the relation of average and marginal costs to prices under different market conditions, the relation of costs to scale of operation and volume of output, the relations of a firm with its market, and the extent to which monopoly influences prices and output — will interest them. The study leads to conclusions which seem to me new and to challenge recent theoretical propositions of importance for public economic policy. It links on with, and develops, the theoretical work of Marshall and Macgregor a generation ago.

It has, however, a second and less specialized appeal. It

should interest business men to see how they look from outside to an independent student concerned only to understand their place and function in the present economic system. As such it will, I hope, do something to discourage the common tendency to contrast private and public enterprise as mutually exclusive systems, and to reveal ' private ' enterprise as an alternative social arrangement for attaining agreed public ends.

HENRY CLAY
Warden of Nuffield College

9th December 1948

CONTENTS

xi

INTRODUCTION

SIR HENRY CLAY has explained that this book has its origin in the research which was started on Mr. Courtauld's initiative and financed by his generosity. The two sets of industrial studies, which have been the major part of the research, have involved the detailed investigation of carefully selected businesses in the particular industries concerned. The businesses differed considerably in size, and they and their industries differed sufficiently in their characteristics for them to be a very fruitful nursery for theories of industrial behaviour. In addition, I have, on occasion, made special inquiries into businesses covering a much greater variety of industries.

This mention of a wider experience gives me an opportunity to pay a tribute to a major element in my education as an industrial economist — my association with the pre-war Oxford Economists' Research Group, under its successive Chairmen, Sir Hubert Henderson and Mr. R. F. Harrod. It has been a great privilege to have been allowed to act as its Secretary, and to take part in the questioning of business men. It was the work of this Research Group that developed so strongly the conviction that the behaviour of business men was consistent, and that, accordingly, even though, on many points, it might not seem directly explicable by generally accepted economic theory, there was hope that one would arrive at a consistent theory by studying individual businesses. I owe the Research Group much for its lessons in the technique of interviewing, as well as the results of its researches. The Research Group has been a pioneer in most of the field with which this book is concerned.

Looking back, I do not think that empirical studies, in themselves, would have led to the development of a general theory. In the first stage of this work, the main concern was simply to make such records of the development of the businesses that were being studied, and of their positions during the chosen periods, that it would be possible to make detailed comparisons between them later on. One, naturally, spent most of one's time preoccupied with the details of a particular business, and became absorbed in each in turn. Interviews, the questioning of business men and others concerned with the business, and the recording of relevant data available in the business's records — all these were carried out with the object of getting a consistent account, so far as it was possible to understand it. The next stage of the Courtauld research — making the two sets of industrial studies — made it necessary to think about the inter-relations of business behaviour, and I was impelled to make a stock-taking of the general ideas that had begun to develop.

This book is the result, and the above is the explanation why a work of such a general character has been written before the end of the empirical investigations. The title of the book indicates a deliberate restriction of its focus rather than its range. Most of the problems that are discussed arise in business generally, and it has been necessary to develop some of the theory that is especially relevant to a non-manufacturing business. It seemed, however, that the book would hang together more if each problem was studied from the standpoint of a manufacturer, corresponding to the main focus of the practical research.

This book has deliberately been written as directly as possible, and the details of modern economic theory have been referred to only where they seem misleading. Even that has generally been done so that economists will have some signpost to attract their attention to the change that is being made in emphasis or in conclusions. It has been thought desirable not to obscure the text with any detailed discussion of finer points of economic theory. This is not the place in which to make any general comment on the modern developments of the theory of business. However, during the last twenty years we have indeed wandered far from the viewpoint of Alfred Marshall, and I should like to suggest the need for a re-appraisal of his great achievement as a practical theorist. The achievement of Marshall was to give a generally valid account of the facts of business life. It seems possible that we modern economists have been far too much concerned to give a consistent marshallian theory, and have tried too much to explain Marshall in a higher-critical way than to achieve a better description of the facts of industrial economics.

I must now fulfil the pleasant obligation of thanking all those who have helped in the empirical studies and in the writing of this book. So far as the first part of this obligation is concerned, I must content myself with general thanks. The greater part of my debt is to the business men, trade unionists and others connected with the businesses that have been studied. Within this general thanks, I must stress my great obligation to the business men, not only for the full access that they gave to their papers, but, more important, for all the patience with which they have submitted to investigation, and for the care which they have taken to let the interrogator pursue his ideas to his own conclusions. I regret that this has to be said anonymously, but many of those who have helped me desire that individual names should not be mentioned, lest that should make it more difficult to publish some of the empirical studies that have been made. I should also like to mention especially my debt to my College, for the many facilities which it has given me, and to my colleagues there.

I am glad to be able to make more specific acknowledgements so far as the actual writing of this book is concerned. I am grateful to the Warden for more than his Preface; it will be widely realized how much I must owe to his general encouragement throughout the research. I owe sincere thanks to Miss Elizabeth Brunner, my principal assistant in all the empirical studies, and to Mr. I. M. D. Little, Fellow of All Souls, for their patience in reading and criticizing the book as it was written. I have indeed benefited from the traditional reward of a tutor — the criticism of his former pupils! I should also like to acknowledge the technical assistance of my friends, Mr. J. B. Butterworth, Barrister-at-law and Fellow of New College, and Mr. W. E. Warrington, F.S.A.A. Mr. Warrington read very patiently through the first draft of the chapter upon accounts, as well as its proofs, and gave me very valuable comments and help. Mr. Butterworth, at very short notice and at a very inconvenient time, read through the proofs of Chapter I and the Appendix to Chapter II, and helped to clarify the text as well as ' vet ' the law. Neither Mr. Butterworth nor Mr. Warrington, of course, must bear any responsibility for the use that I have made, or have not made, of their advice. My secretary, Miss B. J. Cooper, has exercised a patience during all the typing, etc., which this book has involved, that has, at least, been equal to that which she showed during the practical work which preceded it.

I wish to thank my wife, not merely for performing the traditional task of reading the proofs — very seriously — but also for putting up with all the inconvenience of my habits of work whilst I was writing.

The dedication to Professor Macgregor is entirely without his permission. I think that all economists will sympathize with my desire to offer my tribute to his work in the field with which I am concerned. The dedication also records a more personal debt, in so far as a chance conversation with Professor Macgregor, when I was a Research Scholar at University College, Southampton, stimulated my first research into joint-stock companies, sending me away fired with a little of his enthusiasm.

I am grateful to the General Editor of *Oxford Economic Papers* for permission to make use of material contained in my article ' A Reconsideration of the Theory of the Individual Business ' (*Oxford Economic Papers*, New Series, Number I : Clarendon Press, January 1949), which contained some of the matter of Chapters III and IV and an outline of part of the argument of Chapter V.

Finally, I should like to place on record my gratitude to my publishers and to their printers for the efforts that they have made to ensure that the publishing of this book, should be a very pleasant experience.

P. W. S. ANDREWS

NUFFIELD COLLEGE
OXFORD
22nd January 1949

CHAPTER I

AN INTRODUCTORY VIEW OF BUSINESS

THE manufacturing business which is the subject of this book is assumed to be a private enterprise run by, or on behalf of, the owners, whose income will come out of the profit which the business earns. It will be convenient to discuss in this chapter the forms of business ownership and the function of the profit motive as a preliminary to the theory of business behaviour which will take up the rest of the book.

(1) INTRODUCTORY: THE CONNEXION BETWEEN PROFITS AND OWNERSHIP

' Control goes with ownership ' and the ultimate control of private-enterprise business rests with those who have put their money in it and own the assets which the business uses. Investors as such seem to play a much more passive part than those who actually work in a business, and it is easy to attack private enterprise as involving working for the profit of those who have ' done nothing except lend their money '. A business, looked at simply as a social organism, appears as a co-operative undertaking in which a number of persons have to collaborate in order to make the product and get it to market. From this point of view, investors, managers and employees alike perform indispensable functions, and, as no business could be completely successful without their full co-operation, it is natural to ask why the owners, in particular, should control the working of the whole.

The subordination of a business to its managers is much more easily understood. It is easily seen that a business must be managed, and that all who are connected with it must act on the basis of a common policy. Further, any policy will have to be continuously reviewed, showing itself in the varying of current decisions about such things as the specification of the product, the methods of production, and the quantity to be produced over any given period. In every business, therefore, there has to be a line of command through which decisions come, and that has to be centred upon a controlling group who are the managers of the business; in the last resort, it will rest upon a dominant personality within that group — the business man who is the real controller of policy. It will be rare that his functions [1] can be shared, and almost never with more than one other person. Granted this necessity for effective management, the question is why the selection and ultimate control of the managers goes to the investors of capital. Why should the managers not be selected by the employees, or controlled by the votes of all those who work in the business ?

The immediate answer, ignoring for the moment all question of social advantage, to be referred to later, is that the right of ultimate control goes to the investors because they bear the risks of their business in a special degree. Their incomes are so vulnerable to wrong decisions that control is necessary to protect their position and to justify the investment that they have made. This is easily over-looked in the artificial and temporary conditions of sellers' markets, when businesses can apparently sell all that they produce at prices which will cover all their costs of produc-tion, but it is a fundamental truth for more normal times.

Our society has developed on the basis of the personal freedom of individuals, and this shows itself in the economic field in the use of money and of money-incomes and is the

---

[1] Which, in the simplest form, consist at least of saying the final Yes or No to the proposals of others.

real cause of business activity being thought of in terms of profit or loss. The normal situation is that a man receives a money-income in return for his economic services, and that he is then free to spend that income as he likes between the goods which are available, or to save it and retain control over his savings, keeping them available for extraordinary expenditure. The needs of the state are normally met in the same fashion; it exacts taxation in money and gets the resources it needs by buying them. The freedom of the buyer in the pricing system has strong popular support. It is kept, as far as possible, even in abnormal circumstances such as those arising during and after a war, when the urgent needs of the state require a very different distribution of resources than would appear if citizens were left free control over their incomes. In these circumstances, the production of many goods is kept far below what people would like at prices based upon costs of production, and rationing has to be introduced, government departments deciding the distribution of such goods as they cannot allow to be produced in sufficient quantities to meet the demands of the market. These are recognized to be abnormal policies, and most people look forward to a time when they will again have greater control over the spending of their personal incomes and resources.

In more normal situations, it will certainly *not* be the case that any business can count on its market taking from it any definite quantity at a given price, or on it being able to get, for certain, a particular price for any quantity. Yet (as we shall see in Chapter III) a business must be planned on the basis of a certain output, and it will need to sell a definite quantity if it is to cover its costs at any given price, or to receive a definite price if it is to justify the production of any given quantity. Even when a business is producing to the order of its customer on a definite contract, and, therefore, knows what it will sell in any particular period, it will have to have committed itself to a large part of its expenditure in advance of the time when the order is placed, and a substantial part of its costs of production will not vary greatly with changes in its output. Land, buildings and equipment have to be purchased at the start, or if they can be had for hire they will be the subject of fairly long leases, and so, in any case, they will pay for themselves only if the business remains sufficiently profitable for relatively long periods.

Thus the capitalists' part in a business is to provide finance for the purchase of its fixed equipment and to carry the working expenditure of the business in wages and salaries and the costs of materials over the period between the start of production and the receipt of the proceeds from the sale of the goods. If the business becomes unprofitable, it will be upon the capitalist investor that the brunt will fall. His partners will have already been paid their wages and salaries ; he can be recouped only from what is left out of the gross income of the business after the costs of the others have been met. If the income is not sufficient to cover the costs, then he will see his assets decreasing as time goes on, and will be powerless to alter the position. The investors as a whole thus get the residual share of the income arising out of the business, and from this point of view it is only natural that they should control the managers. Management, there-fore, will run a business as profitably as it can, in the interests of residual shareholders — it will certainly have to justify any actual loss as unavoidable, in spite of proper foresight and planning.

It is often overlooked that the potential risks of the investor are so great, and it is frequently urged that the broad risks of business life are shared by all — everyone con-cerned with business suffering in the slump. It is also argued that, by reason of their relative poverty and their dependence upon relatively restricted ways of earning a living, the employees of business are often hit harder by bad times than the business owners who suffer a loss of income. Each of those contentions is true, and a lot of political capital has sometimes been invested in them, but it is equally true that the persons employed by a business can work elsewhere, and that various social devices (such as unemployment insurance, removal grants and retraining facilities) can be used to facilitate any such transfers and to minimize the personal hardships that are involved. On the other hand, a good deal of the investment that has been made in a business will literally be sunk in it and its owners' fortunes will sink with the business if it goes down. The efficient management of a business, in preventing this, will also avoid the corresponding disturbance to employees.

Granted that persons parting with their money for the purpose of business investment can refuse to do so if they do not like the terms on which it is required, it can, therefore, easily be understood that they will retain control over the business at least to the extent that they can appoint and dismiss the principal managers. It follows that those managers will have regard to profits when they take their decisions and, in private enterprise, it can be taken for granted that those who run a business will look at its profitability as the criterion of its success and of the success of their efforts. It does not follow, as we shall see in the following section when we discuss the forms of ownership, that where the investors are most remote from the actual operation of the business the managers will necessarily maximize the incomes paid to the investors.

This section of this chapter has quite deliberately been restricted to the consideration of the way in which ownership brings control and to an explanation of why the managers will have regard chiefly to profitability when they make their decisions. Any question of the social function of profits and profit-seeking private enterprise stands a little outside the analysis which is the main purpose of this book. At the same time, it seems desirable that some comments should be made on the bearing of the analyses of this book on the wider question, and these are given in the last section of this chapter. Meanwhile, we turn to the question of the legal forms taken by business ownership and their economic significance.

(2) THE FORMS OF BUSINESS-OWNERSHIP

The possible remoteness of the proprietors from the detailed control of a business and the desirability of protecting the interests of its creditors have been the two primary considerations affecting the development of the various forms of business ownership recognized by the law. Indeed, in the earliest stages, the business owners were thought to be able to take care of themselves sufficiently through the type of control which it was both usual and desirable for them to exercise, and the law was mostly concerned that business practices did not develop in any way likely to weaken the position of creditors.

(a) THE SINGLE PROPRIETOR

The simplest type of business is that which is run by a single proprietor. It is also the most primitive. In this case the distinction between ownership and control which was made in the first part of this chapter is purely formal, for both functions will be performed by the same person, who will manage the business for which he will have provided the bulk of the finance. It is quite clear that he will be in the strongest position to protect his interests as owner in the day-to-day management. Further, the whole of the income will accrue to him personally; he will be able to withdraw what he likes, and to invest or reinvest what he chooses. The assets will be his personal property and he can make what use of them he likes, having complete freedom to dispose of them.

It was natural for the law to take the view that the creditors in such a business were entitled to the maximum protection and that the owner should be responsible as a person for any debts incurred in so personal a venture. Until accountancy had fully developed, it would, in any case, be difficult to draw a distinction between the trading assets of the business and the private fortune of the owner, for one will shade into the other, and if any dividing line were established it would be difficult to make it a boundary for the owner's conduct. The law, therefore, declines to draw such a distinction. It recognizes that creditors are, in effect, making personal loans to the proprietor, and that they will be influenced by his resources and standing generally. To leave the owner completely responsible for the debts which he incurs gives him the strongest motive for being careful that any commitments into which he may enter are likely to justify themselves. Accordingly, the position of the sole proprietor in his business will be the same as in any other of his activities which involve him in debts — his creditors will have the right to recover what is due to them from any of his personal assets, whether actually ' in the business ' or not. His liability to his creditors will, therefore, be limited only by his resources as a whole ; hence it is sometimes said that the liability of such a proprietor is ' unlimited '.

The resources which its proprietor can put in will be the chief factor limiting the size to which such a business can grow. He will usually be able to get extra resources by borrowing from others, but the extent to which he can do this will depend upon the security which he can offer. It may be easier to borrow if either his business or personal assets include real estate or other property which can easily be mortgaged or pledged, but he will, in any case, be unable to borrow more than a certain proportion of the total resources which he will need. The security of creditors will be weakened in proportion as their loans represent a significant part of the total assets with which the business is trading. If too great a proportion of the assets of the business are pro-vided by the creditors, they will have come to bear a good deal of the risks proper to actual ownership in the business, without the opportunity for detailed control which an owner would require. It will be true for all businesses that the amount that an owner can put in will exercise an effective restriction on their size. This restriction will be most serious for the sole proprietorship and for its close relation the partnership, which will be considered next, because the possibility of getting extra funds from the owner, with a consequent increase in borrowing powers, will generally be limited by the nature of the business.

(b) THE PARTNERSHIP

When a business is, as imagined, run by a single owner, it follows that it will be necessary for him to introduce new proprietors who will put permanent finance into the business and share in the full risks of ownership, if the business is to grow beyond the limits otherwise imposed. Until the mid-nineteenth century, such new proprietors would have had to become partners. Partnerships are still important in some industries today, but generally speaking they have been replaced by the limited liability joint-stock company, which first became a generally available legal form in 1856. Today partnerships of any size are most important in commerce and in certain professions such as stock-broking, the law and medicine, where the personal responsibility of the partnership remains attractive.

In the case of a partnership the law still deems the business to be the personal responsibility of the proprietors. They can make what arrangements they like between themselves concerning the amounts that they will put in the business, the way in which they will participate in the running of the business, and the manner in which they will divide up the income or bear the burden of any failures, and the law will enforce these rights as between themselves. It will not allow any arrangements of this kind to prejudice the position of a creditor. A partnership is presumed to trade so that the partners are sufficiently in touch with each other for each to bear full responsibility for the conduct of the business as affecting outside persons. If any partner is, or appears to be, acting on behalf of the firm, it will be possible for creditors to hold the partnership responsible. A partner can thus bind his fellows, and they will be liable to meet the debts of the partnership to the full extent of all or any of their personal fortunes. Further, a creditor can get satisfaction of any unsettled claims from any member in the first instance, leaving it to him to get what satisfaction he can from his partners.[1]

Not only is it the case that the liability of a member for the debts of a partnership will not be limited to the money which he has put into the business, he will naturally be restricted in his freedom to dispose of his property in the business and will not be allowed to transfer his rights to others without the consent of his partners. The conduct of this type of business is an intimate affair and the partners will require to approve of the entry into their business of anyone who can commit them in so extensive a manner. Further, the withdrawal of a partner cannot take place without some formality, since creditors also have an interest in the exact composition of the firm, and, although any partner will remain liable for the debts of the business up to the moment when he quits it, it does not follow that the new partnership will be so acceptable to the creditors, and they are entitled to know of the change — failing which his liability will remain. The personal nature of a partnership also means that it has no independent life outside that of its members. It will be

---

[1] English law was very reluctant to recognize the fact of a sleeping partner, who merely provided funds and acted as an owner taking no active part in management, since it was difficult to prevent any recognition from becoming a bolt-hole in misfortune. In 1907 the law did permit the creation of limited partners, but the possibility is so hedged about with restrictions to prevent abuse that it prevents such a partner from exercising even that degree of control over a business which he may legitimately want. In any case, the new provision came too late; by then the joint-stock company form had become firmly established, and the privileges given to private companies were so attractive that they tended to supplant partnerships in any case where a partner wished to be inactive, as well as in most other cases where the partners were all active. Nowadays, a partnership is usually only a stage in the growth and management of a small business until it is stabilized under the form of a joint-stock company.

legally broken by the death of a member, when the business will have to be reconstituted and may face serious loss of resources through the withdrawal of the estate of the dead member. Similar difficulties will arise if a partner becomes bankrupt, when his creditors will have a right to call on that part of his personal assets which is invested in the business.

The size which a partnership can attain, although greater on the average than that which is likely for a sole proprietorship, will necessarily be limited by its legal characteristics — that its members are jointly and severally liable for its debts, that shares in the business cannot be freely transferred, and that its life has to bear the uncertainties which may be caused by the death or withdrawal of any of the partners. There must be some limit to the number of persons that can effectively act together in the running of such a business, and the number of proprietors cannot grow beyond the number who can keep an effective eye on what is going on, which means a virtual participation in the management to some extent. (The law has now come to recognize the limitation in numbers as fundamental to the successful working of a partnership; it is illegal for it to have more than twenty partners. If a business gets to such a size it must be incorporated as a company.)

There will also be an effective limit on the capital which the partnership can raise. No new partner will come lightly into a business about which he knows little, or join up under the risks of partnership with persons of whose character, ability and resources he is ignorant. The existing partners in their turn will have identical reasons for being chary of the new-comer. This restricts the circle from which new capital can come to those who are already in fairly intimate contact with the business — or the business must offer a high enough probable reward to repay the expense of all the inquiries which the newcomer will wish to make and to leave him in the opinion that it is worth running any personal risks that he cannot estimate.

(c) The Joint-stock Company

Industry and commerce could never have developed on the scale that we know, so long as business was confined by the restrictions of partnership law. There would have been a consequent failure to derive the full benefit of modern technical knowledge, and, in many cases, even, an incapacity to develop that knowledge to the extent that it has developed today. Any venture that required more money than could be got together by persons who were in fairly intimate contact, or which required a greater number of proprietors than could effectively take part in the government of the business, would be frustrated for lack of funds. Such needs arose early in the development of capitalism, and to meet them the company form of business was evolved.

The essence of this form of organization is (1) that the owners delegate the conduct of its management to a specially designated group of directors, whom they appoint for the purpose, these being the only people who can bind the company, and (2) that their rights as owners to share in its income are expressed in some standardized form so that they may be transferred to others. This development met the needs of the new industrial circumstances by permitting (1) the effective separation of ownership and management which was required if the business was to expand beyond the limited resources available from those who would effectively be running it; (2) the emergence of a specialized class of managers who need not be substantial proprietors; and (3) an increase in the funds that could be tapped for business purposes as soon as the ownership in business could be expressed in standardized units capable of being dealt in by an organized market, so that an individual was less permanently committed to retaining his interest in the business, despite any change in its fortune or in his personal circumstances.

It should further be noted that the rapid development of accountancy in connexion with such ventures was one of the factors making it possible effectively to distinguish the assets of a business from the personal wealth of the owners, thus paving the way for the later development of the separate legal ' personality ' of a business, whose property could be accounted for in a form which might readily be understood by creditors.

The new form of business, however, ran into the great obstacle that the law, when it could not definitely prohibit the creation of this type of enterprise, insisted on treating as partnerships any companies which did not have very special legal authority. The proprietors were thus left with full personal liability for the debts of the business, and the law refused to recognize any device for limiting their liability to money which they had put in, or had undertaken to put into the business. Where the interest of the state required it, or the prerogative of the King demanded it, as with companies established by Special Act of Parliament or by Royal Charter, companies might be expressly given the privilege of the limitation of the personal liability of shareholders. This facilitated some of the great early enterprises for the development of overseas trade and commerce, and the development of public utility companies at home. Otherwise the law gave no protection, and the legislature resisted any proposal to make the privilege of limited liability of shareholders more widely available.

It was held that this privilege took away an important safeguard, making a man fully responsible for the affairs of his business, and was only to be granted on clearly established overriding public interest. Companies not granted this right, therefore, suffered from the penalties of the simple partnership. It followed that they would not be able to get capital from any very wide circle unless they offered countervailing attractions in the possibility — real or fancied — of speculative gain, as in the case of the notorious ventures of the South Sea Bubble period. Meanwhile the needs of ordinary industry went unrecognized, although it was here that the company form was less likely to be used for purely speculative enterprise, and the delay in the recognition of the new need must have led to an undesirable diversion of resources away from productive industry.

In the end, the needs of developing industry, some considerable experience of the unnecessary hardships involved in the operation of unlimited liability, and the development of accounting techniques protecting the interests of shareholders and creditors alike in existing companies, led, first, to the full legal recognition of the company type of business, and then to the general grant of limited liability. It is to this that we owe the full development of industrial enterprise on the modern scale, which could not have come into being unless businesses had been able to acquire an existence which continued independently of and beyond the lives of individual owners, and unless these latter had been able to take shares in a business purely by way of investment.[1]

The Public Company

As the law has developed, two forms of joint-stock companies with limited liability have become recognized — the private company and the public company. Each of these possesses the essential features of company organization which have already been referred to on page 11. The differences between them are based upon their different relationships to the general public. The characteristic of the public company is that it obtains capital by general subscription, that its shares are freely transferable, and that there is no limit on the number of persons who may own shares. It is the development of this type of company that has removed any legal limitation on the area from which a business may

[1] Even in the matter of borrowing, the new type of business brought a benefit extending the possibility of its growth. A company can issue debentures to its creditors, and these recognitions of shares in *debts* due from the company, rather than formal ownership of its business, thus came to be as freely transferable and available to be dealt in on the stock markets as shares themselves. This enabled the full development of a specialism among investors which will be referred to at the end of this section, when we shall describe the types of investment which have developed among joint-stock companies.

get the investment that it needs, and has thus permitted the development of the modern large company, which at its largest is almost an industrial state in miniature.

It was early recognized that the privilege of seeking so far afield for capital necessitated special protection of the shareholders, who necessarily became much more remote from the actual business of government and much more liable to be misled as to the nature of their investment than would have been possible under the older forms of enterprise. The law, therefore, enforces provisions designed to keep the sovereignty of the shareholder against the otherwise all-powerful executive that he nominally appoints to manage his business, to provide him with a certain minimum of information (which has gradually become very extensive) and to require that a certain code of conduct is followed by those who would seek control of other people's money. It has also been realized that there is a paramount public interest in the affairs of the large businesses, which could not have come into being without the privileges which they enjoy under the law. It has, therefore, increasingly been recognized that they may fairly be required to give far more information about their affairs than would be defensible if they were *merely* the business of the shareholders. The final consequence of this has been the Act of 1947, which not only requires very full information about the income and capital accounts of public companies to be published and available where it will be accessible to interested members of the general public, but also gives a government department very full powers of special inquiry.

In the full development of this type of large company, the interests of the shareholders are fully recognized to be not quite synonymous with the interest of the company. The directors have come to have increasing power, and to a large extent it is they and not the shareholders that really control the business. Their views as to the proportion of income that should be distributed to shareholders must prevail unless the shareholders are sufficiently of one mind to upset the management — with the risks involved — and to appoint new directors. At the same time it is not true that companies are generally irresponsible towards the shareholders, and that the directors will have regard to the shareholders' opinions only when things go wrong. A very important unwritten part of the ' Constitution ' has grown up in the financial press and in other public agencies, which use the increasing amount of information which has become available to constitute a bar of public opinion, serving not only the interest of the shareholders but also the wider interests of the public. With all the talk of the disenfranchised shareholder and the ignored general public, the power of the modern press in this matter, and the responsibility with which it is exercised, have not been sufficiently recognized. An important part has also been played in these unofficial controls by the wisdom of the Council of the Stock Exchange.

The directors of the larger public companies have themselves come to recognize this informal but representative constituency to which they have to address themselves, show a great sensitivity to its opinion, and have, in the form of the advertised Chairman's speech at the annual meeting of shareholders, not only addressed themselves to the absent shareholders but provided the student of economic affairs with one of his most valuable sources of information, strangely neglected though it is to some extent. If shareholders do leave well too much alone for the taste of some critics, it is because they have reliable organizations seeing that all does appear to be well, and it is not for want of a continuous reminder of the interest of the shareholder in the business which is his legal responsibility — such reminders being given by business leaders as well as by the press which reports them.

The Private Company

The private company developed because, since the privilege of limited liability had been granted, private busi-

C

nesses which otherwise would have been simple partnerships took advantage of the opportunity to become incorporated companies. But they were otherwise unchanged. The capital would still come from the persons who were associated with the management or from their families or from other close associates, and they would in their own interest take steps to restrict the freedom of shareholders to transfer their shares and to bring other persons into the intimate management of this family type of business. The usefulness of this type of company proved itself sufficiently for the law to give special powers to the private company — which achieved special legal recognition in the Act of 1907 — whilst it tightened up the requirements on the more public type of company. It is not required to publish the same amount of information about its affairs so long as it does not raise capital from the public, and so long as the number of proprietors (exclusive of any employee-shareholders) is less than fifty, and provided that the right to transfer shares is expressly limited in the constitution of the company. In such a company, the shareholders are free to give to their directors just such powers as they think are necessary for the good management of the business in its special circumstances.

This law of the private company thus gave the privilege of limited liability to small businesses — where the partnership type of organization is appropriate — without imposing legal requirements which would have been to the serious disadvantage of that form of organization without effectively increasing the safeguards already given by the close association between ownership and management in this form of business. With these privileges it will be obvious that there still goes, to some extent, the disadvantage of the partnership proper — that the legal requirements, as well as the implied nature of the business, will limit the amount of capital which can be raised to that which is forthcoming from the small circle of those in immediate contact with the business. Since this is suitable for many industries and for the early stages of business growth in most industries, the private-company form of business was a valuable invention of the English legal system. It has occasionally been abused by big companies seeking to conceal their affairs more completely than the law would otherwise permit, through the operation of fully owned private companies, but company law has now been tightened up so that the privileges can go only to the businesses for which they are intended, and suitable in the public interest as well as in that of their owners. In this last century the advantages which limited liability offered to the owner developing a small private business have been of undoubted advantage to this country.

In both forms of companies the owners will get shares in the ' capital ' of the business in exchange for the investment that they have made, and with the transference of the owner-ship of their shares will go the transference of their rights as owners. An explanation of the ' capital ' of a business is given in an Appendix to the next chapter, which explains accounts, and accordingly the present discussion will be con-fined to matters more closely affecting ownership as such. The main point in this connexion is that the shares to be issued need not be all of the same class, but that different classes of shares may be given different rights to share in the income of a company.

Classification of Share Capital

The simplest case is where a company divides its share capital into two classes — preference and ordinary shares. In this case, the preference shares will usually be given the right to a fixed income, expressed as a percentage of the nominal value of the shares ; this must be paid before any income can go to the residual ordinary shares. This simple division of capital is the most usual, and in it the ordinary shares will be entitled to all the income which the company earns after the preference shareholders have received their fixed dividend, subject only to the directors' decision as to how much should be distributed.

Ordinary shareholders thus bear the first incidence of the risks of business and, as against the right of the preference shareholders to the fixed preferential dividend, they have the benefit of the results of any increase in the prosperity of the business, in compensation for the extra risks that they run in taking the right to an income which may well fluctuate considerably more sharply than the profits of the business as a whole. Increasingly, the special nature of the risks run by such ordinary shareholders has been recognized by companies giving them a greater voting power per share, the preference shareholders having no votes (or reduced voting powers) unless any proposal before a company directly affects their interests. This development has been much attacked, but where the rights of the preference shares and the position of the company are such that they have the virtual certainty of a fixed income, come rain come shine, it does not seem to be unjust in principle.

This classification of shares into groups dividing up the risks of the business in different ways has been very useful, both to shareholders and to companies; to the former in so far as it enables them to select the degree of risk which they will bear, and to the latter in so far as it widens the circle of the public from which resources can come, since many people will invest in relatively safe preference shares who will avoid the speculation of ordinary shares, while the possibility of substantial earnings on the latter attract the more speculatively minded. The recent tendency for public opinion and the Government to enforce a limitation on the dividends going to ordinary shares may, in the long run, prove to be disadvantageous. Investors in them are being relegated to the limited-income status of the preference shares without the compensation that the latter have of preference in the payment of dividends. The new tendency may, therefore, result in a discouragement of investment in more risky industries and enterprises, although it may be to the public interest that these should be carried on.

The possibility of issuing preference shares has enabled sound businesses to raise capital at difficult times, when investors are only prepared to invest with a limitation of the risks that they run. In industries where the profits tend to fluctuate rather sharply, so that, in bad times, even the preference dividend may not be covered by profits, the preference capital sometimes takes the form of preferred ordinary shares — the shareholders having the right to a fixed preferential dividend and then to a limited share in the extra profits so far as these are distributed. Similarly, there has sometimes been created a special class of residual shares which carry the right to a high share of the profits if and when the business does exceptionally well, but to a much smaller share in other circumstances. Occasionally such shares are retained by the original founders of a business when investment in it becomes more widely available to the general public.

In these ways, the original simple distinction between preference and ordinary shares has been developed into what is sometimes a very subtle differentiation of the rights and risks of ownership, and in any individual case it will be necessary to consult the constitution of the company to ascertain exactly what rights belong to the owners of any particular class of shares. The general principles which will apply will still be that some shares will have relatively less risk of fluctuations in income, with or without the right to further participation; and that the classes of shares which rank after them in the right to an income from the profits of the business will have a more fluctuating income but the chance of greater earnings, having the greater claim on whatever is left of the profits after the favoured shares have received their dividends, and usually receiving special voting privileges.

The full development of the company form of organization has thus led not only to the separation of the functions of ownership and management, and to the businesses of this type developing specialized managers without which modern forms of management would have been impossible; it has also led to the possibility of extensive specialization between shareholders, who divide up the general risks of ownership between themselves so that it is possible for investors who wish to have only a certain degree of risk of fluctuations in their income to make investment over a much wider field than would have been possible had this differentiation of share-capital not occurred. In a footnote on page 13, reference was made to the use of debentures which make it possible for *lenders* to have a readily transferable form of investment while keeping their right to a fixed rate of interest, failing which they have a creditor's rights against the business. This has made possible the maximum degree of differentiation of investment according to risk.

At this point the reader who is interested only in the positive theory which this book will develop, may turn on, omitting the next section of this chapter, which discusses the social function of profits and would be out of place in a book of economic analyses were it not that opinions on this topic have been so frequently supported on the basis of wrong or misleading economic doctrine.

(3) SOME COMMENTS ON THE FUNCTION OF PROFITS

Thus far, the argument has been entirely in terms of the advantage and interests of the investors of capital, and we may fairly be held to have explained how the association of ownership with the control of business has come about, but not to have attempted any justification of it from the wider point of view of the society in which private enterprise works. Yet it can be shown to have a social rationale; even if it should be thought that an alternative system would have greater social advantages, the system does at least work in the direction of the social interest, and much more so than contemporary discussion of the subject would suggest.

There is a purely negative justification which will probably be accepted by most people, so far as it goes. The efforts of the managers will at least ensure the avoidance of loss in so far as that lies within their power. They serve their society in this, for even though the assets which they control are private property, they represent potential producing powers which might have gone elsewhere and been worth at least their cost-value at the time of the original investment. The value of their product should, therefore, not be less than their cost-value, if the usage of them in a particular business is to be justified socially.[1] If a loss is made, then there would appear to be *prima facie* a waste of social resources and the investment ought not to have taken place.[2] It will also be accepted without any question that the working of the profit motive will tend to result at least in the maximum internal economy in the running of the business. This again seems of clear social value.

It is the positive side of the case — the search by private enterprise for maximum profits — that most troubles people

[1] This applies to nationalized industries as well as to private enterprise. Special justification should always be required for the working of a publicly owned industry at a loss.

[2] The force of this argument has lately appeared to be denied because in normal times, so far as our generation has known ' normality ', there has usually been fairly heavy unemployment. It may, therefore, be argued that, since it is better that the unemployed persons should produce something than that they should stand idle, the social cost of employing them will be less than the figure of the money-costs in business accounts, and that, consequently, a strict adherence to the no-loss criterion would lead to a waste of resources from society's point of view. It is true that the avoidance of cyclical unemployment is not within the power of private enterprise acting on its own, and that it is worth while for society as a whole if its unemployed members are set to work. But this does not mean the abandonment of the profit criterion, certainly as between individual possibilities of employment, and the possibility of state action to maintain employment will not lessen the need for economy in the operation of individual businesses. In fact, that will be one condition for full employment remaining compatible with a rising standard of life — an objective of social policy which is sometimes overlooked in some of the contemporary advocacy of full employment at any cost, when employment is in danger of being accepted as an end in itself, rather than as the necessary means to as full a life as possible for the members of our society.

nowadays, although it was the one most stressed in the days of economic liberalism. It will be useful to suspend the argument for a moment and to state in a simple — and therefore rather crude — form the case for the profit motive as it used to be put, even though modern economic theory has come to doubt it, and although many modern economists have come to lead political attacks upon private enterprise explicitly on the basis of theoretical conclusions about the way the profit motive actually works.

According to the older view of profits, the business man, following his own interest in the maximization of profits, served society by ensuring that those goods were produced which it was to the greatest social advantage should be produced, thus leading to the optimum distribution of productive resources between all alternative uses. The maximization of profits would lead to the maximum economy within the business, and (since enterprise would tend to flow wherever abnormal profits were to be had, and to leave employments where profits were abnormally low) the final result was thought to be that the rate of profits everywhere tended to a normal level, allowance being made for any special risks involved in a particular kind of investment. It was thus argued that goods tended to be produced with the maximum economy from society's point of view, the normal prices of any products coming to be determined by their costs of production.

The capitalist pricing system was thus thought to justify itself broadly by its results. Of course, it was recognized that the social interest also had to have regard to non-economic ends, and that it might, therefore, be necessary to interfere with the system by taxation and subsidy, in the same way as the taxation system might be used to correct any inequalities of income that were too great, transferring income by way of social services to the poorer members of the community. Similarly, it has recently become recognized that there is room for social action in order to give a greater stability to the income which the economic system creates, lessening the force of the evils of trade depression which have hitherto been the recurrent companion of private enterprise.

THE MODERN VIEW

Modern economic theory, however, has tended to argue — or has become disinclined to argue against the proposition — that the rate of profit which a business gets is not even mainly determined by the competition of business men in response to the stimuli of costs and prices. The business man is regarded as having control over his price through his control over his own output, and he is thought to exercise that control, and to maintain his profits at their maximum level, by restricting output, regardless of the community's interest in greater production. The theory upon which this has been based has been misleading in its description of price determination, in its account of the behaviour of the demand for the product of an individual business, and in its view that the effect of individual businesses tending to possess their own market was that they became monopolists intent upon restricting output. The argument given later in this book, especially in Chapter V, contends that the gross margin on the basis of which a business man determines his price is very much determined by competition and the threat of potential competition, and, accordingly, that the broad description given in the older theory of profits is correct, and that the capitalist pricing system has, therefore, its social rationale.

This is not to deny that individual businesses will differ in the extent to which they are exposed to competition; it merely asserts that competition is much more important than modern economists tend to recognize. This is shown by the fact that the rate of profit, when expressed as a percentage of the total capital which has been actually invested in one way or another in businesses, does not tend to vary to great extremes, as far as the data of actual cases have become available, and that, even in cases of large businesses which tend to be most naïvely referred to as typical monopolies, the average rate of profit over a period of years does not appear obviously and grossly excessive when account is taken of the risks of business.

Further, on the basis of the theory developed in this book, the competitiveness of business could be greatly increased by social action. This is more important than would be suggested by the statement that really excessive profits appear to be rarer than is generally assumed nowadays. For any lack of competition will bolster up inefficiency, and may be compatible with modest margins of profit. Although business men may not be in a position to exact excessive margins, they may yet quietly continue less efficient than they would be forced to be if it were made easier for new businesses to get capital, or for the prosperous business, run by a vigorous man, to get the additional capital which its growth requires. Recent experiments in the development of finance corporations may be expected to work in this direction and might be encouraged.

The polemical tone in this part of the present chapter is not due to any desire on the part of the author to argue *for* a *laissez-faire* society, but it is caused by the fact that so many of the present-day attacks on private enterprise have been conducted on false premises in economic theory. A political case has been argued as though it were simply a matter of economics. Lest it be thought that we are too stringent and unfair, it will be interesting to examine the case of one concept of modern economic theory which has begun to have considerable political importance among younger economists and the fairly large audience which is interested in elementary expositions of economic doctrine, whether derived from pamphlets or the adult-class room; this is the idea of the ' degree of monopoly ' in our economic system. It is an example of the use of technical terms without scrupulous regard to their emotive force, and without making sure that that force really goes the way of the economic argument.

THE 'DEGREE OF MONOPOLY'

The term ' degree of monopoly ' was originally applied [1] to the ratio between price-less-marginal-cost [2] and price, because price would equal marginal cost in the case of ' pure competition ' on the basis of the usual theoretical assumptions about the behaviour of demand and costs — assumptions which the argument later in this book will dispute, and which certainly do not directly correspond to the facts of the case. The definition of pure competition need not detain us here, but it should be noted that it could exist subject only to the fulfilment of some rather severe and impracticable conditions. Given the basic theory, it followed that the degree of monopoly ratio could be used to measure the relative advantage to be got by a monopolist behaving in the manner assumed by economic theory. The new concept had, therefore, great technical convenience for the theory for which it was invented, whatever the degree of correctness of the theory itself.

Next, in his *Essays in the Theory of Economic Fluctuations*, Mr. Kalecki showed, as a statistical fact, that the share of the lower-paid workmen in the national incomes of Great Britain and the United States had been approximately constant for a considerable period. As part of the process of finding an approximate theoretical explanation of this, use was made of the difference between the prices of commodities and their average direct costs (in the sense discussed in Chapter III). It happens that in certain special conditions this ratio would correspond to what had been called ' the degree of monopoly ' — although, as already asserted and as will be justified later in this book, the way in which prices

[1] By A. P. Lerner. ' The Concept of Monopoly and the Measurement of Monopoly Power ', *Review of Economic Studies*, June 1934.

[2] Marginal cost is the change in total costs due to the production of an additional unit of output

are actually determined does not correspond to the assumptions which would justify the original naming of the concept. Anyway, as an easy shift of language, the term ' degree of monopoly ' came to be applied to the direct-cost ratio. Ignoring the effects of any change in the prices of direct materials, the share of labour in the national income would vary with the difference between price and direct costs, i.e. it would depend upon the ' degree of monopoly '. The consequence of this theory has been the spread of an unjustified belief that the extent of actual monopoly in our economic system holds constant the share of the national income going to labour. Mr. Kalecki is not responsible for this — the misconceptions that have arisen come from sources where the terminology and the argument have been loosely repeated, but the statistical figures have been given clearly enough. Often it is simply asserted, especially in verbal discussion, that this constancy of the share-out of the national income is due to the degree of monopoly.

The difference between price and average direct costs in fact represents more than the share of the national income going to business men and to shareholders ; it also includes the wages and salaries of all managerial and office staffs, all the labour which is not actually employed directly in the processes of production (a substantial part of the labour-force in many modern industries) and all the money which is needed to replace machinery and equipment when it wears out, as well as all the costs of distribution and other services apart from actual production. In actual fact, the statistics which are explained by the ' monopoly-ratio ' refer to the share, not of direct labour, but of all sorts of lower-paid and manual workers. The use of the emotive term ' degree of monopoly ' has stood in the way of all discussion as to how far the constancy of such ratios represents the working of necessary or even beneficial economic forces. The layman stops short at the view that a large fraction of the national income is entirely maintained by the operation of monopoly tendencies, which he further translates as the cunning of business men.[1] In fact, a very great part of this share of the national income will be made up of the wages of workmen and managers who would still be thought worthy of their hire in any system, capitalist or no (managers, in fact, appearing to have rather enhanced values under state enterprise), and part of the rest will be payments for property which would still be charged for.

All this is not to argue that it is not possible to envisage a completely planned society of an authoritarian kind, administering social resources as a whole and completely planning their use in accordance with some objective criteria of the social advantage, but it is not yet true that the working of such a society has been adequately explained from the economic point of view. The economic case for a fully ' planned ' society has been conducted too much in terms of pictures of the defects of private capitalism. It can at least be argued that there is a possibility of a reformed capitalism, which would avoid the worse evils of the trade cycle and might be even more competitive than it has been so far, and that it would be a rational economic system. Further than that the argument cannot go.[2] In any case, this book is not the appropriate place to add a single square yard to the battlefield between the ' planners ' and the ' anti-planners '. It will restrict itself to economic theory of an objective kind and will comment on the political aspect of the matter only where there has hitherto been a mistaken use of economic theory, or where other factors may have led to the public being misled as to the exact implications of the economic

[1] He is frequently surprised and indignant when he is told that his own income is included in the share ' going to monopoly ' — which will be the case if he is not a lower-paid worker !

[2] The fact that capitalism tends to create inequality of personal incomes has not been discussed, because, once more, there is a social technique for dealing with this through taxation and redistribution via social services, etc. It is desirable, if the degree of equality of personal incomes is to be further increased, that a sharper distinction be drawn between profits which are ploughed back into business and those which are distributed as personal incomes, since the former can only be of social benefit.

theory of business. The planning issue is really a political one and must be settled on political grounds, for its issues involve the very stuff of which a democracy is made. It cannot be settled even approximately on the basis of economics, for, at the present stage of our knowledge, it is not possible to weigh up the pros and cons of the possible systems so that a rational choice may be made on economic grounds.

The attack on the business man has, of course, been largely political in origin, and it is unfortunate that it should have appeared so strongly reinforced by economists if, as I believe, their theory was wrongly grounded. For the view that the business man was a monopolist grinding the faces of the poorer classes, and that all profits are at least suspect as the result of a monopolist racket, has been especially unfortunate, leaving, as it has done, the business man under the force of a theoretical attack which he cannot understand. It does not explicitly fit the facts of business life as he finds them, but, if he queries the assumptions, the experts say that his denials are not evidence, since the rationale of the economic doctrine is so soundly established that he *must* behave in the theoretically determined manner, and that he must do so unconsciously, if he is honestly not conscious of so doing and has not explicitly got the data in terms of which theory assumes him to behave.

If it is true, as this book tends to argue, that private enterprise does work broadly to the benefit of the society in which it exists, despite the possibility that another system of business might be devised which would work better from that point of view, then we might at least acknowledge that usefulness, even if only pending the construction of the better system. At the present time, this country depends not less, but more, upon the energy of the business man, and he will continue to be important until the time, if ever, when he is replaced. The very thing which hinders his playing his part and which reduces his efficiency is the niggling denigration which tends to make him ashamed of his way of life merely because success brings profits and enriches his business as well as his country. Profitability must remain an important test of efficiency, and, other things being equal, it is a guide to the social importance of production. Some recent discussions would almost lead to the conclusion that business men would benefit society more if they made a loss, and may well leave the consciences of any inefficient business men too much unwrung at a time when the maximum efficiency is called for.

CHAPTER II

THE RECKONING OF BUSINESS INCOME

(1) INTRODUCTORY

THIS chapter explains the form and content of Profit and Loss Accounts and Balance Sheets. We shall be concerned only with the general principles involved in the drawing up of accounts and with the general practice of accountants. Accountancy practice is not uniform in every detail, but such differences as are to be found are more suitably discussed in a text-book of accounting rather than in a general book of this kind. It should, however, be said that the practices of the accountant are not necessarily explained according to the principles to be found in the professional text-books. In fact, accountancy does not appear, so far, to have developed any generally agreed corpus of theory. There are a number of points on which accountants, while they have a uniform practice, seem to hold differing views as to the reasons for that practice, and accountants have occasionally urged changes in particular practices (e.g. depreciation and stock-valuation) which would appear quite inconsistent with the general principles upon which they seem to work. The general line taken in this chapter was developed as most consistent with what accountants actually do, as seen by an outside observer; it does, however, agree with the views put forward by Mr. Harry Norris,[1] an accountant who has written upon accounting theory, and the present author was

[1] Harry Norris. ' Profit : Accounting Theory and Economics ', *Economica*, August 1945.

thereby encouraged to hold firmly on to the principles which are here set forth.

It is worth taking the trouble to know at least the main features of business accounts, because they have an important place in the minds of business men, who are used to thinking of their activities in terms of the ways in which their accounting position will be affected, and look to their accounts for a summary of the results of those activities. It is for this reason that all students of economics should at least be able to read business accounts and understand the story that they tell. Such knowledge will enable the approach to business problems to be made in a more realistic manner than would otherwise be possible. Further, significant differences in the economic characteristics of businesses often show themselves in the accounts.

From the accounting point of view, a business is engaged in buying and selling goods and services for money or money's worth. A purely trading business will not alter the physical characteristics of the goods that it buys, and performs the service of supplying the goods in different places, in different quantities, or at different times, from the place, quantities or times that belong to them at the source from which it gets them. The manufacturing business with which this book is mainly concerned also turns the goods that it buys into what are expected to be more valuable physical forms (as steel — plus other things — plus labour, into razor blades). Any business thus acquires goods and services at a financial cost, and sells them, when suitably changed in time, space, quantity or form, in exchange for its financial revenue.

This is reflected in the Double Entry system of the book-keeper's accounts, which treats every transaction as involving either (1) the getting of valuable things, the cost value of which is recorded in *one* account as acquired by the business, and, in *another*, as a corresponding liability simultaneously incurred to the source of the valuable things, or (2) the disposal of valuable things, the charge for which is similarly entered in

D

one account as value passed over to the destination, and recorded in *another* as a corresponding liability simultaneously due from that destination. The book-keeper records in this manner all the financial transactions into which his business enters, and analyses them in summary forms of accounts suitable for the various uses to which they are put. We are treating book-keeping as the hand-maiden of accountancy, and shall be concerned only with the use which the accountant makes of the book-keeper's products.

At prescribed dates, the book-keeper will balance the accounts. It will be realized from the description of the double-entry system that every account must have two sides, showing separately the amounts debited against it or credited to it during the period since the last balance was drawn. The book-keeper makes his balance by setting off the total of the credit side of each account against the corresponding total of the debits, and he then enters the resulting balance, which will be a debit or a credit according to the nature of the account and according to what has happened in the period. The books can be balanced at any dates, and the balances for any one date will then summarize the transactions that have taken place over the period since the last date that the balances were struck. For this reason, profits *could* be estimated for any period, no matter how short it may be.

When it is remembered how precisely profits are stated in accounts, the implication of the previous paragraph — that profits are estimates — may at first be queried, but, generally speaking, this is the case, and the apparent precision of the figures in profit and loss accounts is always to some extent illusory. It merely reflects the preciseness of the original book-keeping recording the transactions of the business and the definiteness of the operations that the accountant performs on the basic figures that the books give him. The definiteness of these operations does not alter the fact that, as we shall see, some of them involve estimates of the ultimate effects of transactions which are incomplete, in the sense that there has not been time for the business to get the full benefit, or to discover the full liability, arising from them.

The shorter the period for which the accounts are drawn up, the heavier will be the relative weight of these uncompleted transactions and of the uncertainties which go with them. So long as the business still goes on, the accountant will always have to include *some* estimates in his accounts, however long the period for which the accounts are drawn up — that is why an accountant is not just a book-keeper, for it is his business to make the rules that have to be applied. The longer the period, however, the less will be the relative importance of the uncompleted transactions, and the more precisely the accountant can estimate the profits. But the convenience of the persons concerned will set a limit to the period. In accounts, as in so many other things, men usually ' reckon time by the year ', and annual accounts have become the general rule in business. The fact that the accountant's task must be done before the owners of the business can know their income would probably be sufficient to explain annual accounting — a year being long enough to smooth out some of the worst uncertainties affecting shorter periods, and about as long as the owners would generally tolerate. In any case, the tax-gatherer has to be reckoned with, and the Inspector of Taxes needs a copy of the accounts on which to base *his* calculations. Joint-stock companies have also legal obligations requiring the meeting of shareholders and the presentation of accounts, with a report from the auditors who inspect them in the shareholders' interest. Quite frequently, businesses do prepare some sort of accounts for the six months intermediate to the main dates, but these are generally straws to test the flow of the financial current. They are, moreover, usually unofficial documents, drawn up for internal use only, in accordance with the practice at the annual accounting, but with such things as stock-taking done in a more rough-and-ready fashion that is adequate for their purpose.

(2) THE ESTIMATION OF PROFITS

We may now turn to get a more definite view of profits, and to take a general glance at the problems which are involved in their estimation. The idea of profits may be realized most clearly in the case of a ' business ' coming into being for a single transaction and ending with it. Suppose, for example, that a man buys an oil painting for £100, intending to resell it. There may be some other expenses that he will have to incur; say, £20 for cleaning and 5s. per week for storage and insurance. If he sells it for £150 at the end of a month, and the above amounts were his only outlays, £121 will repay them, and his profits will be £29. If, on the other hand, he cannot sell the painting so readily and gets only £110 for it, his outlays will exceed his receipts by £11, his ' profits ' will be negative, and he will have incurred a loss of £11.

That example is so obvious that it may be thought to be hardly worth stating, but it will be useful to have begun with a case which is so clear of complications just because the profits in a continuing business are not so much a matter of simple arithmetic. In all cases, however, the principle behind the accountant's practice will agree with the simple case that we have just given, and may still be put simply as *the profit for a period is what is left of the revenue from the business's activities when the financial outlays properly attributable to that period have been made good.*[1]

From our point of view, the serious difficulties arise in the second part of the accountant's work, seen in terms of the above definition. What is revenue is usually pretty clear, in view of the character of the business concerned. A

---

[1] A more usual way of putting the matter would be something like — profit is what is left after maintaining intact the financial value of the assets. This is valid, so long as it is understood that ' value ' there implies merely the total of the sums of money laid out, i.e. it is a *cost*-value, and not value in the sense of market valuation.

business's outlays, however, normally include money spent on property (in a general sense covering other possessions besides bricks and mortar) needed and used in the business but not obtained and used entirely within one income period. These possessions will all have played their part in helping the business to earn its revenue — either by being converted directly into the finished goods whose sales enter into revenue, or by helping as instruments in the processes of earning that revenue. Most items in any list of a business's property will disappear from that list in the course of time, either because they will have been sold or because they will have gradually worn out or otherwise become useless to the business.

The accountant tries to ensure that the money that the business has spent on any property will have been entirely recovered by the time that it has ceased to be owned by, or to be useful to, the business. Property coming directly into the normal sales of a business — *Floating Assets* — will have the whole of its expense charged as a cost against the revenue from those sales. In the case of property which earns revenue more indirectly by its use *in* the business, and whose useful life is a matter of forecast and conjecture, current cost-charges will be imputed to it by the accountant on some basis which is expected to have covered all the money originally involved in its purchase by the end of its useful life.[1]

---

[1] This is a valid account of present practice. There has recently been a strong move to promote a change in the principle on which the accountant acts. After a period of inflation, such as we have recently gone through, the values of capital equipment rise to a *permanently* higher level. It follows that the provisions by way of the depreciation charged as a cost will not suffice to maintain the physical capital intact, as distinct from the sum of money originally spent on it. It has accordingly been suggested that the depreciation charges should be increased, in order to take account of the rise in replacement cost, and that the Inland Revenue should recognize such charges as costs for income-tax purposes. The present author feels some temerity about intervening in a dispute properly the business of another profession, but it seems to him that those accountants who resist the change on the ground that it would give a false statement of the profit that the business man has in fact earned, are correct. Surely, while such provisions should be made by a prudent business, they are properly a charge against profits and would constitute a specific reserve made from those profits. The question of the extent to which the Inland

The second part of the accountant's task may, therefore, be seen as estimating the current costs of the business's operations. He classifies the balances of the accounts prepared by the book-keeper accordingly, dividing them into *revenue* balances, which are those whose credit balances are wholly suitable to be brought into revenue, or whose debit balances are wholly appropriate to be charged as current costs, and *capital* balances, relating to receipts or expenditures not entirely applicable to the current period (henceforward referred to as the ' year '). Revenue balances enter directly into the accountant's estimation of profits, while capital balances will affect the profit figures only by the accountant's estimates of the current costs and revenues attributable to them in the year with which he is concerned. Capital accounts are recorded directly in the balance sheet, and remain open from year to year, the balance of one year appearing at the start of the account for the next. Revenue accounts, on the other hand, are opened and closed during the year.

It is now time to look at the accounts which emerge as a result of this accounting process, and to study in a little more detail what the principles of the accountant come down to in practice. An illustrative set of the two chief accounts is appended to this chapter. They are purely illustrative and do not come directly from any single business, but they are by no means simply imaginary, since they have been drawn up on the basis of experience, and are such as might have been produced in the year in question for a medium-sized, fairly well-established business producing men's boots and shoes and selling them partly to large multiple stores, partly

Revenue should recognize those reserves as qualifying for income-tax relief is a separate issue which cannot be discussed here. While businesses are feeling the effects of the transition, the existing income-tax law makes it more difficult for them to make proper provision for physical replacement, and there may be a good case for asking the Inland Revenue to grant some relief from income-tax for some such special provision, but that does not call for a major change in the concept of profit as such. Prices will ordinarily be fixed to cover depreciation on any new machinery. The enhanced value of this reflects its higher earning powers, and so, in the long run, the new price level should make possible the replacement of capital.

to factors (wholesalers) and partly direct to independent shops. It will be noted that the business has been assumed to be a joint-stock company, but, from the present point of view, the question of the legal form in which the ownership is embodied is not very important. What the business does is more important.

(3) PROFIT AND LOSS ACCOUNT

The profit and loss account [1] gives the calculation of the year's profits in a summary form. It is essentially a summary document even as drawn up for those operating the business and other ' insiders '. Published accounts are always still more summary.[2] The profit and loss account of our example is divided into two parts — the Trading Account and the Profit and Loss Account proper. (The Appropriation Account is a distinct document which records the effects of the decisions about the *disposal* of the profits.) Other divisions occur, and the exact form taken by the profit and loss account varies to some extent with the type of business. Our example shows the most general form and suits the type of business that has been presupposed.

(a) THE TRADING ACCOUNT

The purpose of the trading account is to state the gross profit resulting from the year's manufacturing and trading

[1] Mr. W. E. Warrington has suggested to me that it would seem more logical to call it the Profit *or* Loss Account, since it results in a statement of the profit or loss attributed to the period. J. Mellis's *Brief Instruction*, 1588 — the earliest reference of the *Oxford Dictionary* — does indeed suggest that this was the case originally : ' Of the famous account called Profitte or Losse, or otherwise Lucrum or Damnum and how to order it in the Leager '. The dictionary's definition is, however, ' an account . . . to which all gains are credited and losses debited, so as to strike a balance between them and ascertain the net gain or loss. . . .' This suggests that the modern name may have arisen as a result of all credit items (' gains ') being loosely regarded as ' profits ' and all debit items as ' losses '.

[2] A mild statement of the previous practice of most public companies ! The new Companies Act, however, enforces a great improvement, and now, generally speaking, secrecy stops after the trading account.

activities. Gross profit may be defined as what is left from the revenue that those activities have brought in after *prime costs* [1] or *direct costs* have been deducted. The right-hand side of the trading account is the revenue side. It will be seen that it shows the total amount of revenue from the year's sales (the balance of the sales account, after deducting any allowances for returned goods, etc.) and adds to this a value for the stocks in hand at the end of the year. The left-hand side is the prime cost or direct cost side, and it will be noticed that this includes a value for stocks at the beginning of the year. This treatment of stocks as a revenue for the year whose accounts end with the stock-taking, and as a cost for the year then beginning, will be justified later. Meanwhile, it will be convenient to examine the idea of prime costs in more detail, and, for the moment, it is merely pointed out that, consistent with the definition which has been given of gross profit, this item is given on the left-hand side of the account, balancing with the other items on this side the total of the items on the revenue side. If our business had done so badly as to suffer a loss on trading account, the figure for this loss would, similarly, appear on the revenue side and balance that against the total of the costs side.

The term, direct costs, is useful as giving a more immediate idea of these costs, since they may be defined as those outlays which are *directly linked to production*: (1) direct materials costs — for purchases actually going into the product; (2) direct labour costs — for labour actually engaged in the process of production; (3) direct expenses — the other outlays which have been incurred similarly in the actual processes of manufacture (e.g. the renting of any machinery used in production and the running cost of motive power). It may be noted that all other outlays are *indirect costs* or *overhead costs* (*alias* oncosts and supplementary costs) and arise from

[1] This term has not the precise meaning which traditional economic theory has found convenient. Since I wish to conform to business usage in the classification of costs, I shall generally prefer to use the second term — direct costs — as not carrying theoretical associations which I wish to avoid.

what we shall later call the general organization of the business, as distinct from the actual task of production, to which they contribute only indirectly.

If anything goes by two names, we may generally be sure that there are at least two ways of regarding it, each sufficiently important to be kept alive in the language. It is so here; the 'directness' of direct costs arises as follows: first, as directly attributable to the product, they can, given a specification, easily be calculated in the light of past experience; second, direct costs are the part of total costs that is most likely to vary directly with the level of production. For these reasons they will play an important part in the theory of price determination, which will be discussed in Chapter V. The idea of 'prime' costs as such embodies the notion that they are the first costs that the revenue of the business must cover, if the production is to be at all worth-while, since they could be avoided by stopping production.

The precise nature of the items charged as direct costs in the accounts will vary, but two items will always be there, the costs of the purchases of direct materials and wages of direct labour.[1] Strictly, the wages of labour not directly concerned with production (e.g. foremen and workers not engaged on process work) should not be included in direct cost wages. In practice, especially in smaller businesses, it may not be worth bothering about small items and some wages of this sort are frequently included. Again, the wages cost of direct labour includes the employers' contribution under social insurance schemes, but it is often charged separately in overheads where it suits the business man for the purpose of costings (it not being thought worth-while to split the insurance account between manufacturing and non-manufacturing wages) — which is the case in the sample accounts.

Strict practice would also require that the cost of carriage on purchases should be treated as a direct cost. For the type

---

[1] Shown as 'Manufacturing Wages' in the sample accounts.

of business to which the sample accounts relate, the cost to it
of carriage inwards would only be about 0·1 per cent to 0·2
per cent of the total cost of purchases. It is, therefore, not
separated out from the general carriage account but charged,
together with carriage outwards, among the overheads and
general expenses of the profit and loss account. Motive
power is similarly not charged as a direct cost here, although
it would be in a business where it was heavy enough to be
worth separating out.

The item ' Royalties ' calls perhaps for special comment.
It represents payments made for the hire of machines. This
is important for the majority of the businesses in the Boot
and Shoe industry, for they hire nearly all the machinery
that they use for the actual ' making ' of the shoes. Where
such machines are owned, the direct costs would be lighter,
because of the absence of this charge, and the other expenses
charged in the profit and loss account would be heavier.

It remains to justify stocks appearing as revenue in one
year and as cost in the next. The stocks so entered consist
of raw materials, partly finished goods (goods in process) and
finished goods. These are, of course, held in order to be
sold in the ordinary course of business, and at the date of the
stock-taking are assets acquired in the course of one year
and handed on for sale in the next. They are a revenue
addition for the year in which they were held as stocks, since
the business could have let its stocks run down to nothing
(with corresponding benefit to its costs of purchase and of
manufacture) without failing to make the sales that it made,
in fact, to its customers. It has improved its trading position
beyond this by the acquisition and retention of these stocks.
Equally, such stocks are an addition to costs from the point
of view of the next period, because the business still has to
recover expenditure upon them, and because, without them,
the business could not have made the same sales to its
customers without increasing its other costs.

The direct-cost entries proper are simply totals of money

that has been spent, but stocks involve the question of valuation — the accountant has to value them so that they will be fairly credited as revenue in one period and fairly charged as costs in the next. In accordance with the main principle on which the accountant acts, the whole of their costs must be recovered by the time that they are sold. The actual money costs that will have been laid out on such stocks will, however, have been incurred over an interval of time up to the date of the stock-taking. If market values have fallen during this period, the costs expended on the stocks at the beginning of the next accounting year would be greater than the costs at which the business could *then* acquire similar goods. Now, it is essentially the purpose of the business to hold such goods for ultimate sale and to take the risks of the market. If they were carried at outlay-cost into the balance sheet at the end of the year, the next year would be saddled with what would be the consequences of financial risks which were really incurred in the earlier period, and the year in which the business acquired them would be avoiding one of the costs of its having done so — the fall in prices that has taken place. Stocks are, therefore, valued at market prices at the date of the stock-taking when such prices are falling. This procedure thus correctly deducts the fall in values from the money-costs of the stocks before they are credited to the year's revenue and, thence, carried on as costs to be recovered in the subsequent year. *Rising* market prices do not affect the valuation of stocks, for these cannot be valued at other than a cost basis. To value at market prices when prices are rising would falsify the cost position and cause the following year to be charged with costs which had not been incurred in fact. The reduction in stock-values when market prices fall, far from falsifying the cost position, makes a just apportionment of cost between two adjacent periods so that each has a profit figure which will reflect its share of the risks of trade that are proper to the business.

The text-books know this principle of stock valuation as

the rule of taking stocks 'at the lower of cost or market values'; it is often referred to, however, as an example of the accountant insisting upon estimating income 'upon a conservative basis'. In our view, it is nothing of the kind, and the accountant's rule here is a strict application of the logic of his principle of charging as costs the money outlays that have been incurred during any period. This is quite different from the accountant quantifying his principle in such a way as to minimize estimates of gains.

The gross profit which finally emerges in the trading account is the sum earned in the year which has just closed, and available to pay all the non-direct cost expenses of the business and to provide an income for the owners — our imaginary business has the sum of £26,600 for this purpose. From the income viewpoint, gross profit emerges as we have described it, as the balance remaining from the revenue of the business after total direct costs have been deducted. In the later part of the book, however, we shall be especially concerned with the idea of a business as a *producer*, and shall make a good deal of analysis in terms of its output of finished goods. It is useful in this connexion to think of gross profit as the difference between the value to the business of its output of finished goods and the total of the direct costs incurred in order to get it. For this purpose, the stocks held by the business must be classified into raw materials (i.e. stocks of goods still held by the business in the form in which it acquired them from other businesses) and finished goods (stocks of goods in the form in which the business will sell them) with the intermediate class of 'work in progress' (goods in process of production but unfinished at the date of the stock-taking).[1] This classification has been made in the sample balance sheet. For present purposes any writing down of stocks, with the consequent reduction of the value

---

[1] It would be relevant here to discuss the precise basis of the valuation of work in progress and finished goods, but that question is deferred for convenience until the balance sheet is discussed.

of output, should be ignored — i.e. it must be charged separately after the calculations which we are describing, since the cost and output position of the business as a producer is a different question from the losses it makes on the stocks which it holds in trade. However, this need not complicate our arithmetic here, since we may presume no write-off for the specimen accounts which we are using.

The total value of the finished goods produced during the year will equal the total sales less any decrease in the stocks of such goods, to the extent that such sales have been met out of stock, or plus any increase in stocks, to the extent that a part of the year's output has not been sold. In the specimen accounts, stocks of finished goods have *increased* by £2000, and, therefore, adding this to the total sales, the output must have been £152,000.

The *usage* of raw materials during the year will equal the purchases less any increase, or plus any decrease, in the stocks of raw materials. The X.Y.Z. Company will be seen to have consumed £82,450 worth of raw materials (= £82,000 purchases plus £450 decrease in stocks). The other direct costs of the year's production are wages and royalties, which together amount to £42,900, and this, added to the usage of raw materials, gives a total of £125,350 as the total direct costs of all goods produced, whether finished or unfinished. To get from this to the costs of the total output of *finished* goods we must deduct the amount of any increase in the value of the stocks of unfinished goods (work in progress), or must add the amount of any decrease in such stocks. In the case of the X.Y.Z. Company, we must *add* £50 for this reason, and thus get £125,400 as the direct cost of the finished goods actually made during the year 1937. Deducting this from the £152,000 value of finished goods produced, we once again get the gross profit figure of £26,600 (this is identical with the figure reached by the earlier — revenue — approach, because goods until sold are valued on a cost basis, and because in the particular case discussed we have assumed no writing down of stocks on account of falling values).

This concept of gross profit will be very important in our theorizing later. We have said that it is the fund available for the payments of all the income and expenses not directly associated with the processes of production. The proportion of gross profit to total output will later be used as a very significant magnitude in the analysis of the economic circumstances of particular businesses and of industries.

(b) The Profit and Loss Account Proper

The second section of the revenue accounts, the profit and loss account proper, brings in, as revenue, the gross profit from the trading account, and adds to it any remaining revenue (i.e. other than sales revenue) obtained in the normal way of business. Against this total is then set all the expenses not already charged in the trading account as prime costs. The resulting balance between the revenue and the expenses is the year's *net profit or loss* — the income reckoned as accruing to the business during the year covered by the accounts. The most important items that are here added as revenue to the year's gross profit will be any interest earned on bank balances, etc., and ' discounts taken ', which last item is matched by ' discounts allowed ' on the other — expenses — side of the account, and we may explain these together.

As industry has developed, it has become normal for businesses to allow their trade customers a reasonable time in which to settle the accounts sent to them for goods supplied or for services rendered. This ' trade credit ' plays an important part in the financing of the movements of products through the successive stages from the original raw materials produced by the extractive or agricultural industries right down to the finished goods sold to the final buyer. Such credit is usually freely allowed where a business has no reason to distrust the customer, but it does involve some cost to the business which grants it. To be paid in prompt cash reduces the amount of money locked up in book debts, and sets it free to finance other sides of the business's operations, or to reduce *its* obligations to others — and, of course, it also means avoiding all the risks involved in the debts themselves. Prompt settlement is, therefore, encouraged by the creditor business giving a cash discount of so much per cent off the invoice value when the debt is settled within a stipulated period of time — which is, of course, equivalent to charging interest on debts not settled within this period. In the boot and shoe industry before the war, for example, it was usual for a manufacturer to allow his customer $6\frac{1}{4}$ per cent off the invoice value for payment within 10 days, 5 per cent within 30 days, and $2\frac{1}{2}$ per cent within 60 days. Beyond 60 days, the account became due at its invoice value, and was expected to be paid in full within 90 days. The business itself would similarly be allowed various discounts by the suppliers of its leathers, etc.[1]

Discounts taken and discounts allowed are, thus, the totals of the amounts by which the invoice values of the goods supplied to the business or by the business, respectively, have been reduced on account of prompt settlement of the debts involved. It is a natural question to ask why these are not entered in the trading account, the one reducing the cost of purchases and the other diminishing the revenue from sales.[2] The main reason is that the precise incidence of discounts depends upon business policy, and that, in turn, will be affected by the financial position of the business concerned. From the point of view of business strategy, therefore, the entries for discounts come most naturally in the profit and loss account.

It will be prudent for a business to settle its debts promptly

[1] Cash discounts are, of course, quite different from the secret discounts that a business will sometimes allow to favoured customers, thus practising discrimination whilst trying to avoid the wrath of those less favoured.

[2] It will be realized that the time-lag between the date of an invoice passing through the purchases or sales accounts and that when it is settled, means that the discounts shown for any one year will not relate entirely to the transactions of that year.

and to take all the discounts to which it is entitled. The saving in costs is always a good return on the money involved. For example, a boot and shoe retailer, making the maximum use of trade credit and settling his bills only after 90 days, would really be paying 6·7 per cent over the cash that he would have paid if he had settled within 10 days — a heavy rate of interest. A struggling business that is short of ready cash may reluctantly have to put up with the costs of trade credit, so long as it is allowed to have it. Any business may find it convenient to use trade credit in busy times in order to meet a temporary increase of trade by expanding beyond the resources that would otherwise be available. Trade credit thus becomes of increased importance in an industrial boom, and makes the industrial system more elastic than it could otherwise be. During the building boom of the 1930's many of the smaller building firms were financed in this way. A builder with some standing in the trade (in evidence given to the Oxford Economists' Research Group [1]) said that trade credit was the chief explanation of the mushroom growth of small businesses which then took place. As soon as boom conditions passed away many of them became bankrupt. With a recession in trade, their trade credit made their current expenses high in comparison with businesses with a stronger financial basis, and, at the same time, it added to the weight of their short-term obligations, so making it more difficult to get any fresh finance.

Whatever the rates of discount that a business may quote to its customers, they will, of course, normally be included in with other costs when it fixes its prices. With the rational preference that a business man will have for prompt cash payment, the rates of discount are fixed at a level which will encourage the customer to pay promptly, and which will give reasonable compensation if he should fail to do so. Businesses will, therefore, normally refuse to allow discounts which have been forfeited through late payment. Of course, when times

[1] *Oxford Economic Papers*, No. 3, Feb. 1940, p. 46.

are bad some businesses may be too weak and anxious for continuing orders to resist pressure from customers who try to secure a relaxation of terms. ' Discount snatchers ' of this kind will have little chance with most businesses in normal times, but weaker businesses will always have to reckon with them unless they are in a general seller's market, such as we have recently passed through. When markets slacken in falling trade, the higher the rates of discount the easier it will be for what is really disguised price-cutting to appear with the weaker firms, thus weakening the market for the industry in general. For this reason, one sometimes finds an industry discussing the reduction of rates of discount.

The expenses charged in the profit and loss account cover all the outlays of the business not deemed to be direct costs, and, therefore, consist mainly of the overhead costs of the business. They will be shown in sufficient detail to enable the business man to exercise the effective control over his overheads, which is an important part of business strategy. The analysis in the profit and loss account is necessarily summary, but it will be carefully inspected as a first guide to reasons for any changes in the fortunes of the business. The groupings of items will vary from industry to industry, and to a lesser extent from business to business. Where businesses rent their premises, the expenses will naturally include these costs and will tend to be higher than those shown for businesses which own their buildings. There will, of course, be some partial offset for this in the absence of any charges for structural repairs and for reserves for the depreciation of premises. The incidence of ' Light, Heat, Power and Water ' will vary in importance both with the industry and with the methods of manufacture (e.g. the cost of power is nil for hand-processing).

In general, the expenses arising on the purely selling side of the business will be kept separate from the other expenses, but a complete separation cannot be made, for marketing cannot be completely disentangled from production. The

E

commissions which are paid and the salaries of specialized sales staff will be separated, but at least some aspects of the sales policy will be the concern of other people. It will be quite usual for the head of the business to have a good deal to do with at least some of the more important customers, and in a small business quite a large part of the selling costs will be merged in salaries of persons performing other functions. Advertising will normally be shown separately where it is important, but in the type of business to which the specimen accounts refer, advertising is not important (its importance for manufacturing businesses generally has been greatly exaggerated) — press advertising would normally be negligible, and advertising expenses would consist mainly of the cost of circulars, show-cards, price-lists, etc. They are, therefore, frequently lumped together with stationery and similar expenses.

The relative amounts shown for directors' remuneration and for other salaries will depend largely on the type of business. In private companies, the directors will generally be working directors, and their remuneration will include amounts which would otherwise have to be paid to salaried staff. In large public companies, it is quite usual for at least some members of the Board to be only part-time, and management is much more frequently done by salaried staffs. In the family business, moreover, it will be to some extent a matter of indifference whether the directors are remunerated through the profit on their shareholdings or through their salaries as directors. Since there are some advantages from earned income relief for incomes of moderate size, smaller businesses may, therefore, tend to have rather heavier expenses for salaries and consequently smaller profits than they would if the ownership of the business were more diffused among ' outside ' shareholders.

The profit and loss account expenses will normally include any bank charges, interest on overdrafts, etc. Where an overdraft does not exist, and where bank charges are small enough, these will often have been set off against part of the interest received from the bank before that is entered as a credit on the other side of the account. It may be noted that businesses differ considerably in the extent to which they use the lending facilities of banks. Generally speaking, there are strong prejudices against using bank credit, and, for this reason, manufacturing businesses come some way down the list of borrowers from banks in order of the importance of the total loans to classes of borrowers. Since banks will lend more readily for such things as the purchase of materials, bank loans, and the charges for them, will tend to vary between industries, according to the importance of raw materials and the extent to which these are held in stock. In times of rising trade, therefore, when businesses' own resources may be strained, and when there will usually be an increased desire to add to stocks, there will tend to be greatly increased borrowing from banks, to be cut down in times of falling trade.

It will be noticed that the expenses in the profit and loss account have been grouped so as to put first expenses which have actually to be paid out in cash — these are the *paying-out costs*, to which reference will be made in a later chapter. It will be seen that they play an important part in the analysis of business behaviour. At the end of the list come charges for depreciation. This, as we have seen, is an apportionment of past expenditure and does not involve current cash payments. Together with the previous item, general repairs, it will naturally be relatively more important the greater the importance of capital equipment, although the actual size of the annual charge will depend upon the business's policy in the matter of depreciating equipment. Depreciation is, of course, a real cost which has to be borne over the life of the capital equipment if the original expenditure is to have justified itself, but the effects of not bearing it are rather different from those of default on the other expenses. It is quite possible for a business to run for a number of years without putting by cash resources to cover all the depreciation that will, in fact, have occurred. Similarly — as war-time experience has shown — repairs are extremely amenable to postponement until the ' rainy day ' makes them necessary, although they will more urgently need to be covered than will all the depreciation charges. We shall pursue some of the implications of these facts in a later chapter.

(4) THE APPROPRIATION ACCOUNT

The balance of the gross income brought in to the profit and loss account, after the expenses have been deducted, is the business's net profit — or loss. This is the income that is properly creditable to the owners of the business as having been earned for them during the year. This net profit or loss will be brought into the appropriation account, and there will be added to it any balance of net profits earned previously but not distributed or otherwise disposed of. Income that has not been earned directly in the business, such as interest on investments or dividends from subsidiary companies, will also be added here, as a rule. The total of these amounts thus credited to the appropriation account gives the total of income earned but not already disposed of. Out of it, the owners of the business will have to settle all payments which are really disbursements of income. The first claim will be that for income tax and profits tax.[1] If dividends are paid, the business will deduct tax, at the standard rate, from the gross dividends which it declares and will actually pay the shareholders the net amounts. Since such dividends will be paid out of income which has already paid tax, the cost to the appropriation account will be only the net dividends. Where, as sometimes happens, the account shows dividends at their gross values, the amount *shown* for income-tax separately will

---

[1] The 1937 specimen of accounts, of course, does not show any deduction for profits tax.

accordingly be reduced, but this will not affect the real position.

After income tax, certain payments to the owners of the business may arise as a matter of course — this will normally be the case with preference dividends. The balance after charging such prior payments is the amount over which those owners of the business who are entitled to it will have an unfettered discretion. It does not follow that they would be prudent to take out of the business all the income which the account shows to have been earned for them,[1] nor that they could *get* it without inconvenience, for, as we shall see, the balance may very well not be covered by cash or by other easily cashable assets. This will be appreciated when we have completed our study of the balance sheet to which we now turn.

(5) THE BALANCE SHEET

The balance sheet for any given date is a summary statement of the balances of the business's books of accounts at that date. These balances will, of course, be of two kinds, those due to persons in a legal sense outside the business itself, and those due to the business. For this reason it is often referred to as summarizing the assets and liabilities of the business at its date. It is certainly convenient to regard the right-hand side as a statement of the assets or property owned by the business. Before turning to consider that side of the balance sheet, it will be useful to emphasize the fact that *the balance sheet refers to the accounting position at a given date*, in contrast to the revenue accounts which we have just been discussing, which cover the affairs of the year which ends with the date of the balance sheet.

In any business it is necessary to distinguish between Fixed and Floating Assets. *Fixed Assets* are those which do

---

[1] In a joint-stock company, the directors will determine the extent to which the earned income is distributed.

not enter directly into the course of business. They render the business a more or less lasting service in the form in which they were originally acquired, and enter into its income only indirectly, by the help that they give to the production and sale of the goods with which the business is concerned. The money that has been invested in their acquisition is, therefore, said to be 'fixed capital'. Factories and land, or the leases for them for a period of years, machinery and plant, and the 'intangible asset' goodwill (to be explained later) are examples of fixed assets.

Floating Assets, on the other hand, are those which come directly into the course of trade. They consist of such things as the stocks of raw materials, work in progress and finished goods, the debts that are currently owing to the business, and cash (including, for this purpose, investments which have been made outside the business in order to invest spare cash until it is required — i.e. marketable investments generally).[1] They thus consist of cash and the assets which the business expects in the normal way to exchange for cash. They get their name because the money that has been invested in them is a floating sort of capital. Thus stocks when worked up and sold are converted into debts, debts similarly becoming cash on repayment, and the cash is likewise continually being spent on the current expenses of production and sale, thus getting temporarily embodied in stocks and debts.

Precisely what assets are fixed and what floating will depend upon the nature of the business. For example, sewing machines are fixed assets to a garment manufacturer, but they are floating assets to the maker of sewing machines. We shall find it useful later to remember that goods which are fixed assets from the point of view of one business may be of exactly the same kind as those that will be reckoned as floating assets in the hands of its suppliers. It will be appreci-

[1] Investments in subsidiary companies or other 'trade investments', together with even marketable investments when these are held for purposes implying a relative permanency of the investment, are really fixed assets.

ated that fixed assets are usually more at risk than floating assets, just because they are more firmly embedded in a particular business. For this reason, the owners of the business themselves will usually have had to provide the bulk of the resources that are needed for the purchase of fixed assets, outsiders not being very willing, as a rule, to see their loans covered by such hostages to fortune.

The accountant, in accordance with his rules, will look at the assets of the business as representing the sums of money that have been laid out on them. The cost of them will be charged against the appropriate account, and will accordingly enter into the balances in the books of the business. The accountant will ask if the particular assets may be expected, in course of time, to cease to be useful to the business, or if they will be permanently available for its purposes. In the former case, which will be true for the majority of the fixed assets, he will require that the business shall charge, as current costs against the annual revenue, sums that may be expected to have added up to the total expense incurred by the time that the assets are expected to have ceased to be useful. Each year the sums that have been charged as current costs in this way will be deducted from the original cost of the assets as shown in the books, and the balance will be carried into the balance sheet as costs still to be recovered. The fixed assets which are judged to be permanent will not give rise to any costs, and will be carried into the balance sheet at original cost.

Apart from the writing-off due to such current-cost deductions, a business may at any time ear-mark some of its profits to cover the expenses that it has laid out on fixed assets. In such cases, the sums involved will be deducted from the balance of profits which would otherwise be carried forward in the appropriation account, and will be written off the value of the fixed assets concerned, which will then be brought into the balance sheet at values that have been written down — reduced — accordingly. Such writing down will, of course, be in addition to any deductions from their values on account of current costs.

The values at which fixed assets are carried in the balance sheet are, therefore, their money costs, less any amounts which have been charged in the profit and loss account as current costs and less any specific allocations from profits. It follows that the balance sheet value of fixed assets has no general significance apart from its accounting use of recording the balances of the original expenditures which have still to be recovered. Since the balance sheet value is derived from the original expense when the asset was acquired, which may be a long time previous to the date of the particular balance sheet, it will have no necessary relation to the then current market values of the assets, nor will it be purely a total of the sums expended on them, since they will have been written down either as costs or out of profits. Accordingly, the balance sheet values of the fixed assets owned by different businesses cannot be compared : (1) the original expenses may well have taken place at different times, and in different ways, and thus will represent real assets of possibly very different values at any one time ; (2) there is no reason to suppose that any two businesses will have written down the values of their assets in the same way or to the same extent.

In future, the provisions of the recent Companies Act will require businesses to show the original cost of their fixed assets and to state separately the amounts by which they have been written down. So that eventually it will be possible to make comparisons of the total sums of money laid out on the assets, but those values will still not be comparable in any other sense by reason of (1) above. It follows that all attempts to relate profits to the total of the balance-sheet values of the assets, in order to compare the profitability of different businesses, will be essentially meaningless, since the uncertainty of the real meaning of the values of the fixed assets will affect the total of which they are a part. Such calculations appear meaningful just because each part of the calculation will employ figures from the accounts which appear comparable simply because they are expressed in pounds sterling. It may be noted that, in so far as successful businesses will have tended to have written their assets down more quickly than less successful businesses, such comparisons will probably tend to exaggerate the profit ratio of the more successful businesses. Equally, if two businesses are equally successful, the one that writes down its assets more quickly will, in the end, appear as relatively the more profitable.

Having outlined the general accounting position of fixed assets, it will be useful for later analysis if we consider in a little more detail the current cost-charges which are made on their account. One of the principal reasons why the useful life of these assets will be limited is simply that they will deteriorate through use. Even factory buildings, which may last for a very long time — as will be evident to anyone passing through older manufacturing areas, such as Lancashire or Northamptonshire — deteriorate continuously. This will be due partly to the working of natural forces, such as wind and weather, and partly to the actual wear and tear of the use to which the business puts them. Some of this deterioration can be met and made good by the repairs that will be carried out from time to time. There will, however, be a balance which cannot be recovered in this way, and, year by year, some of the money which was sunk in purchasing the building must be regarded as having been lost by reason of this deterioration. The calculation of the sums that should be charged against revenue as current costs [1] on this account will be very much a matter of conjecture. Something should ordinarily be charged, and the business man will charge what he thinks reasonable. In practice, there are, in many trades, conventional allowances for the depreciation

---

[1] It should be noticed that accounting practice varies and that some businesses do not charge depreciation against buildings specifically but allocate sums to a ' Properties Reserve ' or other reserve account.

that should be written off the values of buildings used for particular purposes.

The same considerations apply to machinery. Here, however, the incidence of wear and tear can be more easily calculated, and it is quite usual for the business man to be able to say how long a life such and such a machine should have when used for a certain purpose, at a given average rate of output. He could, therefore, easily allocate a definite proportion of the cost of the machine as the amount that should be recovered as an annual cost. If we put it this way, however, a business man would at once say that it was unrealistic, and that merely replacing the actual machine that he has bought would not be enough. To give an example where the reasons for this attitude will be obvious : a business, whose founder was a pioneer user of a motor-car to get round to see his customers, would not now regard that car as a business asset, no matter how completely its physical wear and tear had been made good. Machinery becomes out of date or obsolete as well as wearing out physically.

Obsolescence is just as much a cost to the business as wear and tear, for, if it is to maintain its revenue against the competition of its rivals, it must be at least as up to date in its equipment. An obsolete machine will have higher costs than one which is of newer design, and its value on the market will, therefore, decline for this reason. Such wastage of value is known as obsolescence. The business man, therefore, charges against the book value of physical assets (and brings in as costs to be met out of current revenue) sums that are intended to provide for the impact of obsolescence as well as the depreciation due to purely physical wear and tear, when taken for each class of asset as a whole, and over a reasonably long period of time. Obsolescence, of course, will not apply only to machinery. It certainly occurs in the case of factory buildings, but its impact is more considerable in the case of machinery and similar plant. The fact that it is provided for by definite charges must not mask the equally definite fact that its incidence is uncertain, and that such charges contain a large element of reserves against possible costs rather than provision for costs which have materialized.

Industries vary greatly in the relative importance of depreciation charges. They will be lightest where the physical deterioration is relatively slight and where technical changes are relatively rare, as in textile weaving. They will be heavier where the opposite conditions apply, as, for instance, in the making of rayon fibre. In many cases in some of the newer industries, the charge made for depreciation, although heavy, is almost entirely a reserve against obsolescence. A large part of the plant used in some of the heavier chemical and allied industries is quite adequately maintained by repairs, being more usually scrapped because it is obsolete than because it has significantly deteriorated. In any individual case, the charges made in the profit and loss account, and hence the values at which the assets stand in the balance sheet, will reflect the judgment and caution of the business man concerned, as well as conditions which are common to all businesses in the industry in which the business man operates.

It should be obvious that if the current charges for depreciation, including obsolescence, are cautiously estimated — as they normally will be just because of the difficulty of making precise estimates — then the over-deduction that will be made on this account may give rise to an element of hidden reserve, the asset still being used by the business although perhaps completely written off or having a market value if sold that is greater than its book value. The costs of repairs carried out will usually be written off from current profits, and, in this way, they may also lead to hidden reserves, since the advantage of such repairs will frequently not be exhausted in the year in which they are made.

These references to the business man as making reserves by writing down the values of his assets may be misleading unless we stress that there will not necessarily be any corresponding reserves of cash put by. All that necessarily happens is that the writing off will reduce the amounts of profit shown as available for distribution. The corresponding sums of money may well have been invested in the business. There is a tendency nowadays to decry this and to suggest that the business man should put by such reserves and invest them outside the business so that they will be available as cash when the assets have to be replaced. This view is really mistaken. The assets will normally earn far more for the business inside, and, if the price of its product really does cover the charges that it makes for such replacement, the business will usually be sufficiently profitable to be able to get money as and when it wants it, even if only temporarily, until it has saved it out of current revenue. The usual practice of the business man appears to be right — that he should decide, as an independent matter, how much of his resources should be kept in liquid form, and that he should invest the annual additions to his liquid resources as seems best. However, it should be said that the weight of opinion in the accountancy profession appears to be hardening against this practice.

The balance sheet thus carries fixed assets at values which have been derived from their original cost values. If any fixed assets are sold, the next balance sheet cannot still give them their book value, since they will no longer exist in the business. At the same time, the money value that they have fetched will not necessarily be equal to their book value. In this event, writing off the book value will leave the business either with a capital profit or with a capital loss, according as the receipts on sale exceed, or are less than, the value of the particular assets on the books. This question of capital profits and the use that is made of them involves many nice points both in law and in accounting. The position may be summarized as follows. Legally, a business is usually free to distribute as dividends to its shareholders any capital profit that will appear as genuinely realized when a reasonable view is taken of the values placed upon the assets generally. In fact, however, business practice, and the advice of auditors generally, is against the using of capital profits for revenue purposes. Normally the profit will be put to a special reserve, thus balancing the increase in the value of the total assets in consequence of the profit, or it will be written off the values of all or any of the assets. A capital loss will generally be provided for out of profits. If small, it will tend to be written off from current profits. If large, it may be met by a transfer from reserves (so reducing the ' liabilities ' side of the balance sheet correspondingly with the reduction in the value of the assets) and if severe it may be carried forward as a charge against the profits realized for a number of years. In that case, the value of the loss will appear as a fictitious asset, counterbalancing the ' liabilities ' side of the balance sheet until it has in due course been written down by appropriation of profits.

Before we turn to consider floating assets, we should perhaps explain briefly what is the ' goodwill ' which some balance sheets show as an asset. Goodwill is the sum over and above the current market value of the assets considered separately, that the owners of the business get on its sale to someone else. A going concern that is at all successful is worth more than the market value of its assets, just because it is in existence, with its own connexions with customers and suppliers — and the extra value is named from the goodwill that has thus been built up. A successful business is not to be had merely by buying the right physical assets, and a going concern must be paid something for the value of its market. In the first balance sheet of the new owners, the physical assets will be shown at their then market valuation, as the cost to be recovered by the later accounting charges. The remainder of the capital that has been put into the business at the time of purchase will be represented by the intangible asset, Goodwill. This will not have any costing significance. It is a once-for-all payment for the abnormal profits (from the point of view of a mere owner of the physical assets) that the business is expected to bring in. It cannot be used up merely by the working of the business, and its current value, in the sense of what the new owner would get for it in the event of resale, will be maintained or increased according to the profits that he achieves, calculated without any allowance for goodwill.

There is a prejudice against a balance sheet containing an asset whose value is so peculiarly irrelevant to current operations — especially as in the pathology of public joint-stock companies, its value has frequently been known to reflect the fraud of the previous owners as well as their business success. For this reason goodwill is frequently written down by occasional appropriations of profits (sometimes not entirely down to zero, a nominal sum, such as £1, being left as a reminder) in the same way as other fixed assets.

Floating assets — because, as we have seen, they enter so directly into the business's current transactions — are not subject to such notional deductions from their original book values as are fixed assets. A detailed discussion of the valuation of stocks was made during the explanation of the trading account and need not be repeated here. The upshot was that stocks are entered at the value appropriate to the fact that they figure as a cost to be recovered in the next year's trading, i.e. they are taken at their original cost less a deduction, if current market prices are falling, to allow for the effect of such a fall up to the date of the balance sheet.

It is perhaps worth noting that differences exist in the way that businesses value their stocks of finished goods. They will always be valued at their prime costs at least (with any reduction due to falls in the values of their materials), but some businesses value them at figures covering their share of the year's overheads as well. This would seem logical so long as *selling* expenses are not included. Some businesses frown on this practice, however, because the reckoning in of overheads will mean that, if stocks go up, the revenue and, therefore, profit will be given at a higher figure than if they had been valued at the lower, prime-cost figure. This looks like taking account of profits before they are realized, and many businesses, accordingly, like to value only at prime cost, regarding the goods as liable to bear overhead expenses only in the year in which they are sold. There would, however, seem to be good reason for valuing such goods in such a way as to recognize the factory costs at least which have been incurred in getting them. However, so long as a consistent practice is maintained from year to year, there will not be any very great difference in the results, and this is perhaps a matter which should be left to be resolved by the accountants whom it concerns.

Debts are valued at their actual ledger values (i.e. according to the invoices where they originate). It will, however, be certain that the business will not receive cash to the full extent of that value. First, it will have to allow any cash discounts that may be due on prompt payment of invoices, and, second, some of the debts may later turn out to be ' bad '. The first contingency will usually be provided for by making a special reserve for discounts, to be deducted from the total value of the debts. The second may similarly be met by a reserve for bad debts, but, where the amount is small and infrequent, it is quite usual to meet it as it occurs, by a charge against profits in the year when the debt is adjudged doubtful or is condemned.

It is important to distinguish debts arising from the business's trade (invoiced for goods supplied) — ' trade debtors ' — from others. They will be more immediately affected by trading conditions. Their total should normally go up in proportion to sales. If they increase more than in proportion, this will indicate a deterioriation in the financial position of the business, in so far as more of its circulating capital is going to finance payments which are taking longer to come in. If, at the same time, sales are going up, this may mean that the market has been widened to take in business that will not be so satisfactory on the average as the old, and an inquiry into possible optimism in accepting new accounts in the sales department might be desirable.

Cash, and bank deposits, of course, will always be entered at the face value. In some industries, businesses will accept bills of exchange in payment of debts, holding them until they mature or discounting them for ready cash. If such bills are held, a reserve will normally be made against the contingency of default, the total going into the balance sheet at a correspondingly reduced value. Where the total of such bills is small it may be included with the cash in hand.

The treatment of marketable investments varies, but the general rule is to enter them at the lowest of their cost- or market-values, since they will be regarded as much as a reserve of cash as a source of income. The original cost-values will, therefore, usually be written down by an appropriation of profit whenever the market-value falls below them. On the other hand, once they are written down, it is not usual to write them up again if market-values rise. When such investments are sold, any profit that may be made because market-value exceeds the book value will normally be treated as a capital profit.

Clearly, the values of floating assets may well contain hidden reserves, in so far as the assets may be worth more than the values at which they are shown when they are eventually turned into cash. In fact, the values shown in the balance sheet for such assets must be regarded as minimum values, but, even so, the total of floating assets does have a real general significance, in contrast to that of the fixed assets. It will provide a minimum estimate of the only resources available within the business for getting cash to meet any liabilities or to finance any new development without disturbing the general organization of the business (as would happen if it sold off some of its fixed assets). Apart from this, it would have to call upon outside sources of finance. Both business men and creditors, or possible creditors, therefore, do well to attach some importance to this total. Further, this total will probably be roughly comparable as a minimum between businesses, since we may expect that the £ sterling unit of account will be more comparable than in the case of fixed assets, and the total of floating assets can be taken as at least a minimum of their current worth at the date of the balance sheet. This quantity can, therefore, be used, for rough comparisons, at least, when one is looking at the accounts of different businesses.

We now consider the ' liabilities ' side of the balance sheet. The total of this is merely the sum shown by the books of the business as having been invested in the acquisition of the assets, after those assets have been written down either through current costs or by appropriations of profits. As a matter of book-keeping, it follows that the total must equal the total of the asset values on the opposite side of the sheet. It, therefore, will be equally devoid of general meaning, and we shall not discuss it further.

The separate entries made on this side of the account may be divided into those relating to persons other than the owners of the business, and those which relate to the owners. The latter will be represented by a single item — ' capital ' — in the case of a private, non-joint-stock company business. This will be the total of the sums directly invested in the business plus the accumulated profits, in so far as these have not been drawn out by the owner or allocated to writing down assets, and minus any losses that have been incurred. In the case of a joint-stock company, the *total* amount shown as liabilities to the shareholders will have a similar meaning, but because the ' capital ' of a joint-stock company has a special legal meaning and cannot be increased or reduced on account of accumulated profits or losses without special procedure, the total will be divided into three accounting entities : (1) the issued capital, which will be the nominal paid-up value of the shares which have been issued — the precise significance of this is explained in a note appended to this

F

chapter, since it is frequently misunderstood; (2) the share premium account,[1] if any; (3) any formal reserves of accumulated profits; plus (4) any balance of profit not added to capital, nor allocated formally to reserves, nor written off the values of assets (and similarly minus any balance of losses not written off from reserves or from capital).

As was explained in the previous chapter, the total capital shown as issued in the form of the various classes of shares will have a significance for the shareholders concerned, as affecting their rights against one another in the event of the company being wound up, etc. Popular opinion attaches to the figure for total capital a significance which is illusory. It has no economic significance, and, accordingly, we do not need to make any detailed study of it for the sake of later analyses. At the same time, since it is misunderstood, and since the operations of writing capital up and down play an important part in contemporary mythology of the joint-stock company, it seems undesirable just to leave the matter here. A fairly full explanation of ' capital ' has, therefore, been given in an appendix to this chapter.

The rest of the liabilities of the business will be in the ordinary sense liabilities due to persons other than as owners. Here it is important to distinguish loan creditors from current liabilities, which are the sums due to short-term creditors. Loan creditors are those who have lent money to the business for more or less long periods, including lenders upon mortgage, and, in the case of a joint-stock company, debenture holders. The value shown for these will normally be the sum which will be due on repayment, or which will be recoverable by the creditors in the event of default in the payment of interest. The liability on account of such loans will not represent any need for cash in the short-run — the need to make current payments on account of interest will

---

[1] This states the total amount received in premiums on share issues, i.e. the difference between the money paid for the shares and their nominal value. Since 1947 these have had to be specially segregated, and, in effect, will form a kind of quasi-capital.

be met by entries in the current liabilities. They are thus of a different class from the latter, which will be the debts due at the date of the balance sheet, or at fairly short notice, at the option of the creditor.

Bank loans and overdrafts are usually considered to be current liabilities, together with any interest which may have accrued on them, because banks will not lend on a long-run basis, and retain the right to request payment at short notice. Such loans are normally used for the day-to-day finance of the business, and, therefore, take the place of the cash which would otherwise appear among the floating assets. It is worth noting that sometimes a bank loan may be used to obtain temporary finance for longer term investment, pending the provision of longer term finance through shares, mortgages or debentures.

Trade creditors (or ledger creditors) are normally kept distinct from other current liabilities. They consist of debts due to those who have supplied the business with goods or services, and their total indicates the extent to which the business is being currently financed by its suppliers. Trade credit, as we have already seen, will normally vary with the purchases, but the proportion will usually rise in busy periods. If it increases unduly, especially in times of falling trade, it will be a danger signal, in so far as the business is probably becoming slacker in the matter of paying its bills. The cost of such additional credit is the discounts which would have been taken on prompt payment, and it should be regarded as too costly for normal use.

The rest of the current liabilities will be of a miscellaneous character, including such things as amounts owing for taxes, for wages, for dividends declared or otherwise due, for interest on loans — in short, for all other obligations that have accrued but not been met at the date of the balance sheet. The total of these will not necessarily have any close connexion with the current trade of the business.

All current liabilities will be valued at the full amounts

known to be due, and, at the same time, the business will make specific provision for any contingency that is expected but has not formally arisen (e.g. for income tax due but not settled) and may make a general provision for ' contingencies ' to cover any unexpected liabilities which may present themselves. All such provisions will be added to the current liabilities, properly so called, just as the making of them initially, or of any increase in their amount, will be represented by charges somewhere in the profit and loss or appropriation accounts. If such provisions are excessive, then, this will be equivalent to making reserves out of profits, and these will be completely hidden if the amounts provided for such contingencies are not separately stated.

When provisions for contingencies are included, the total of the current liabilities may be taken as a conservative estimate of the extent to which the business may have to find cash at relatively short notice, and it has, accordingly, a significance parallel to that of the total floating assets on the other side of the balance sheet. The difference between the totals of floating assets and of current liabilities, frequently known as the ' surplus floating assets ', will give a minimum estimate of the solvency of the business on current account. In the same way, the difference between the more liquid floating assets — cash and marketable investments — and current liabilities will give a minimum estimate of the current financial strength of the business, in so far as it has or has not got free capital available for any expansion. The extent to which such surplus assets exist will depend upon the financial policy of the business, and the position, therefore, varies between businesses. Apart from this, it will vary with the state of trade. Rising trade will tend to deplete the business's cash resources, perhaps to the point where its increased activity is being financed entirely out of trade credit or bank loans. Similarly, a fall in trade will set free liquid resources, with the result that many businesses' balance sheets are in a stronger position on current account during a slump.

The above completes our review of the balance sheet as such. It comes out as much less significant for our analysis than the revenue accounts that were considered earlier. Taken as a whole, it is merely the accounting document that it purports to be. The only parts of it which have any general significance are the statements of the values of floating assets on the one side and of the current liabilities on the other. The other items will have analytical importance only in so far as they result in revenues, or give rise to charges which affect the revenue accounts, and they are directly taken into account there.

APPENDIX TO CHAPTER II

THE CAPITAL OF A JOINT-STOCK COMPANY

WHEN we read that 'the Issued Capital of Imperial Chemical Industries Ltd. is £84,655,830 ', the mere fact of its being stated in terms of a definite sum of money seems to give it an objective meaning, and it becomes tinged with the reality of the value of the sum of money which would be stated in exactly the same way. The fact that dividends are customarily reported as so much per cent of the nominal value of the shares instead of as a particular amount per share encourages this. It is, therefore, easy to be misled into reckoning the dividends or earnings of a company as a percentage ' on capital ', thence possibly deriving conclusions about the exorbitant rate of profit which a particular company earns for its shareholders — exorbitant it may be, but the only correct basis of such calculations must be either the sums of money which have actually been invested in the business or the estimated current value of the assets which are currently employed in the business, according to the exact purpose of the comparison and the data available. While, therefore, it is quite common in political argument to hear references to a company paying ' 40 per cent ', etc. on its ordinary shares, the plain man perhaps being left to draw his own conclusions about the reasonableness of dividends of this size,[1] such comparisons are devoid of any essential meaning, because of the impossibility of attaching any significance to the nominal capital of a company, of the kind which is required. For the nominal issued capital is only a legal entity ; the only firm economic significance which it has being as a total from which an individual shareholder can derive his proportionate interest in the assets and earnings of the company.

Everyday experience also shows that it is found bewildering to see reports of companies writing the value of their share capital up or down, with all the appearance of a juggling with ' real ' money values, and, in short, of just the sort of financial manœuvring which the ordinary man in the street instinctively suspects. The

[1] In comparison perhaps with the $2\frac{1}{2}$ per cent interest which is paid on his deposits in the Post Office Savings Bank.

writing up of capital, with the consequent issue of bonus shares, has proved to be particularly suspect. The reason seems partly to be that the transaction looks like giving shareholders a genuine ' bonus ' of extra shares for which they have ' done nothing ', and partly that the increased nominal capital will reduce the nominal rate of dividend which is declared. Just as a high nominal dividend rate of, say, 40 per cent, is readily taken as *a priori* proof that earnings are exorbitant (so that employees of the company may legitimately claim that their earnings should be increased, or the public that prices should be reduced) so the writing up of capital — say, doubling it in the case that has been imagined, when the same money dividends would now be stated as 20 per cent — is easily regarded as a near fraud to conceal the high earnings, and make it less easy for employees and the public to see just what is going on.

The above discussion has referred to the plain man or the man in the street ; it should be admitted that, in recent times, he has apparently been supported, or rather led, by a Chancellor of the Exchequer who had, at one time, held acknowledged rank as a professional economist, and who apparently shared all the plain man's misunderstandings ; but misunderstandings they remain. It seemed accordingly desirable in a book of this kind to try to answer the questions which many readers will ask themselves when they see a reference to the capital of the company in the accounts studied in Chapter II : What exactly is the capital of a company ? What is implied in the operations of writing it up or down ? and, How do those operations come about ? Since the answers to these questions would not be directly relevant to the analysis which was the main purpose of this book, and since Chapter II had become long enough anyway, it was decided to put the discussion in this appendix.

To take the first question first, the capital of a company is, as has been said, a legal entity and is rather an abstraction. It will be easier to explain it if we make an indirect approach and see how this special sense of capital came into being. We shall have to start with the case of the unincorporated business — the sole trader or partnership as distinct from the limited company — for here the term ' capital ' has a precise meaning which led to the crystallization of the legal form of capital, as applied to a joint-stock company, when the legislature became obsessed with the possible dangers involved in the granting of limited liability.

The sole trader starting up in business will have bought certain assets and will be using a certain sum of money in the day-to-day operations of his business by way of providing for its circulating capital. He will regard as his capital the sum of money which he has thus invested in his business, and, if a balance sheet were drawn up for the day when he commences business, the assets which he is using, valued at their cost to him, would be exactly counterbalanced by his ' capital ', after deducting any sums that he had borrowed from other people. If, in the course of his operations, he has made a profit at the end of the next accounting period, and does not draw out the whole of it, the balance of his profits will automatically be added to his capital — a recognition of the extra money that he has really invested in the business — which will then balance the total balance-sheet value of his assets (which must have increased by the amount of the profit). Similarly, if he makes a loss, the value of his capital will automatically be reduced by the amount of the loss. The capital of such an unincorporated business, therefore, may be said to represent the total money investment that the owners have made in it, less any losses that they have sustained.

When Parliament decided to introduce the system of limited liability, that meant that the shareholders in a company would have their liability limited to paying the sums of money or other consideration that they undertook to give in exchange for the shares that were issued to them, and, once the shares were fully paid up, or issued as fully paid up, no further liability could fall upon the shareholders. The business had accordingly become a distinct legal person, with its own assets and liabilities ; its liability to meet its debts was limited to the assets that it possessed — a great difference from the private business, where there was no distinction between the business assets of the owner and his other wealth, all that he had being liable to be called on to meet his business debts. The law was thus conferring a big privilege which the development of modern business had made necessary, but it tried to remove the possibility of certain misuses of the new system, the prospect of which had, in fact, delayed the granting of limited liability for a considerable period.[1]

In particular, the law was concerned about the possibility of creditors being defrauded through shareholders withdrawing

---

[1] It is a great pity that one of the casualties of the recent war was Mr. H. A. Shannon's manuscript of his London lectures, wherein he told the fascinating story of the way in which the legislature at last took this very big step.

from the business the capital which they had put into it, so that it was no longer available to meet the claims of creditors who might well have had dealings with the company solely on the basis of the assets which it had. The incorporated company was, therefore, required to state its paid-up capital, originally conceived as the sum of money which the shareholders put into the business at the start. Dividends were not allowed to be paid out of capital, but had to come solely out of profits — the income of any individual shareholder being determined by his share of the capital invested in his class of share. Originally, until experience had shown that some change in the law was desirable, the paid-up capital could not be reduced at all. Nowadays a reduction in this capital can be effected, but almost exclusively such a procedure requires the consent of the Courts to ensure that the possible interests of creditors are protected. The consequence of the law is that a company starts with a definite figure for its legal capital, and — disregarding the case where some of the capital is uncalled, where the shares are not fully paid-up — this will simply be the sum total of the nominal value of the shares. Two sorts of capital are recognized — ' Issued ' and ' Authorized '. We shall generally be concerned only with the Issued Capital — the total nominal value of the shares that have been issued. The Authorized Capital is simply the limit to which the company can issue capital without fresh authorization and the payment of percentage duty.

Shares can be issued only for cash or other consideration (i.e. in exchange for non-monetary assets). As a general rule, shares will be issued only for at least their face value in money, or for assets whose value *in the balance sheet* will appear as at least equal to the nominal value of the shares, but even at the time of issue the total nominal value of the shares *need* not correspond to the sum of money or the genuine value of the other assets contributed to the business by the original shareholders. They may be worth considerably more or considerably less. The former is quite definitely the case with many private companies, where the details of the original capital transactions may not greatly concern outsiders, and where a low nominal value of the capital may be fixed in order to escape the duty payable on a higher value,[1] the assets in

---

[1] An extreme case was that of a private estate company whose file was shown to the author at Somerset House. The assets were unquestionably of some considerable value, but the authorized capital was £100, the issued capital being ½d. in two farthing shares !

the balance sheet being either written down accordingly, or the rest of the shareholders' investment being represented by loans.

Shares may quite well be issued at a premium, even in public companies, and will correspondingly fall short in nominal value from the total value of the assets given in exchange. When a successful company issues new shares, they will almost certainly be issued at a premium,[1] in so far as the stock market may value their right to the expected income of the company at more than the nominal value of the shares. Equally, cases have been known of the promoters of new companies fixing a high value on the assets which they have brought into the company (intangible assets such as goodwill have been especially liable to over-valuation, as have such things as patent rights). It has also been known for new businesses to value their assets at a high level with a view to impressing outsiders.

These instances justify the contention that the total nominal issued capital of a company has no necessary correspondence with the money values of the assets. What values were, in fact, actually handed over as consideration for the shares can rarely be determined, because of the difficulty of deciding the reasonableness of the value placed upon the intangible assets. But, even when the initial nominal value of the shares does correspond to the actual sum of money, or to a fair valuation of the other assets, which the shareholders gave the business for the shares, it will not continue to correspond to the total money which they have invested in the business. For, as has already been stated, the capital of a company cannot be changed except by special process, failing which it must remain at its original figure. When the business makes profits, these will appear, as was seen in Chapter II, in the profit and loss account, from which they will be brought into the appropriation account. If these profits are not wholly distributed as dividends, there will remain a balance to be carried forward in the accounts, either as a free or as a specific reserve,[2] and these will be quite distinct from the company's capital. If

---

[1] As already stated (p. 64) the amounts of any such premiums now have to be placed to a special reserve shown separately in the balance sheet, and, generally speaking, will have to be treated as capital. From 1947, therefore, the additional money invested by shareholders will be segregated here.

[2] Including, in this case, any use that may have been made of them to write down the fixed assets beyond the amounts written off by way of costs, since, if necessary, these amounts could be written back into the balance sheet.

losses are incurred, they will at first be written off against any balance of unallocated profits, and may be reduced by writing them off against other reserves. In that case they will reduce the total of liabilities correspondingly to the reduction in the value of the balance-sheet assets which will accompany the loss, but the nominal value of the issued capital will still be unchanged. If the available reserves from previous profits do not exist, or are not sufficient to counterbalance the loss, then the balance of loss to the date of the balance sheet will have to be shown as a fictitious asset to counterbalance the — unchanged — nominal capital. Subsequent profits will, of course, result in the reduction or cancellation of the balance of loss.

If a business's losses are heavy, or continue for such a period that the total balance of losses carried forward becomes heavy, it may be a long time before the deficit would be wiped out by subsequently earned profits. The fact of the balance sheet carrying a loss balance will entail one certain consequence for the business ; even though it may subsequently have turned a corner and begun to earn profits, it may not pay any dividends to shareholders until the balance of loss has been extinguished. To pay a dividend when there is no positive balance of undistributed profits available against which that dividend may be charged, will mean reducing the assets available to the business when these are not sufficient to counterbalance the ' capital ' of the company. In the eyes of the law, this involves the payment of a dividend ' out of capital '.[1]

No business would ordinarily wish to pay dividends in such circumstances, for, unless its basic economic position has changed, it will normally be desirable that it should restore its assets and recover the position that it had formerly. There are, however, some circumstances in which it may be highly desirable that the company *should* be able to pay a dividend. Suppose a company to have had such a period of losses but that it could now make a good use of additional capital resources in order to restore its profitability — it may, in fact, be already making profits *before* writing down its balance of loss carried forward. Existing shareholders or other investors will find that the company would, apart

---

[1] It should be stated that this is a very simple statement of a difficult legal position. The position is complicated by the question of the extent to which the law will allow the depreciation of fixed assets to go uncovered by reasonable provision, but where the law may be doubtful auditors are not.

from the necessity of writing down its balance of loss, be able to make them a fair return on the additional capital that it requires, but the fact that no dividends may be paid until the loss is extinguished, which may take a long time, will mean that the extra capital will not be forthcoming. Yet it will be to the interest of all connected with the business, whether they are shareholders or creditors, that the additional capital should be obtained, and accordingly that the ' capital ' should be written down by the amount of the loss, so that the balance of loss no longer gets in the way of paying dividends out of current profits.

A second rather similar case, where it would be reasonable to wish to avoid this consequence of the accumulated losses, will be where the previous losses have reduced the company's scale of operations but where the company has become profitable at that smaller scale. It may be quite unreasonable that the company should seek to restore its assets to the previous scale. In that case, it would be reasonable that it should carry on as it is, and, if the accumulated losses did not stand in the way, it might reasonably make some dividend payments to the shareholders out of the current profits. The denial of this income to the shareholders in such circumstances may very well not involve any real benefit to the creditors of the company.

In either of these cases, the company can apply to the Court to sanction its reducing the value of its issued capital. Should that be granted, the loss balance will be written off against the corresponding reduction in the total of the nominal issued capital on the other side of the balance sheet, and any profits that are earned in the future will appear in the appropriation account as available for the payment of dividends, the shareholders thus getting access to the income which is being currently earned.

For completeness, one other case where the reduction in the issued capital may be desirable should also be mentioned. It sometimes happens that through a permanent reduction in the scope of its business as it has been run so far — e.g. through the closing down of a department with the consequent release of its assets — a company will become possessed of greater resources than it would wish to employ in the changed circumstances. The directors may properly decide that the company should not expand into some other line of activity, and that it would be preferable to pay out to the shareholders some of the money that has become surplus to the company's requirements rather than hold it for reinvestment by the business. Such a repayment of capital may only be provided by writing the capital down.

Devoid of essential meaning though the nominal capital of a joint-stock company may be, its position in company law thus accounts for a company wishing to write it down when it would, otherwise, suffer an undesirable restriction on its freedom to dispose of currently earned profits, or of redundant capital resources. It is difficult, at first sight, to understand why a company should wish to write up its capital out of its reserves. The position before such writing up will be that the company has previously reinvested, in the assets of the business, profits, which its accounts have shown as earned for the shareholders, but which have not been distributed to them as dividends ; in consequence, corresponding amounts will be shown by the balance sheet as having been accumulated among the reserves on the liabilities side.

These reserves are legally available to be distributed as dividends, if the company should have sufficient cash resources and wish to make such a payment, but such dividends cannot be made without the recommendation of the directors, and, until that has been made, the savings must remain invested in the business. When it writes up its capital, the company, on the basis of an appropriate resolution by the shareholders, issues the desired amount of shares as paid-up, as a bonus to the shareholders which is payable out of the accumulated reserves. A corresponding transfer will then be made from the reserves in question and they will be reduced by the amount of the increase in ' capital '.

Such a writing-up is thus purely a book-keeping transaction. No money leaves the company ; all that happens is that the nominal value of each shareholder's holding has been increased, the balance sheet will show the nominal issued capital as having increased, and the other reserves on the liabilities side as having decreased, but all this does not affect the size of the real assets which the shareholders own in the business. Neither does it increase at all the money which is available through current profits for dividends. The company has exactly the same assets as before, and its earning powers will, therefore, be quite unaffected.

There will, however, be one consequence of the reserves having been translated into ' capital ' in the legal sense — it will not be so easy to use the new ' capital ' to offset any trading losses that may subsequently materialize, nor will they be available, as they were when they were legally reserves of accumulated profit, to offset any dividend payments not covered by current earnings. However, as has been stated, in strict law a directors' decision to withhold such reserves — or, indeed, any of the profits which the business may earn currently — does not need the support of this legal sanction which is given by the reserves having become ' capitalized ' in this way, and the other consequence, if it materializes, will have the disadvantage that any loss which would have been ' met ' out of the reserves will have to be accumulated obviously in the accounts.

With one difference, the situation is exactly the same as if the company had paid out a cash dividend equal to the amount of the share bonus, and as if the shareholders had then promptly re-invested the money in the business, without exercising any option to retain such a cash dividend for themselves.[1] The *real* investment of the shareholders in their company remains the same, for they have already reinvested these accumulated profits, and any earnings from that investment will appear in the form of current profits available to them as dividends. Why then should they make this sham investment ?

There are, in fact, a number of reasons why directors may wish to capitalize reserves, and why shareholders may welcome them — we shall consider later the reasons why other people may attack bonus issues. The main reasons for directors wishing to capitalize reserves is that it makes the position of these reserves quite clear. They will always have been reinvested in some way or another, and a successful business which has for a period ploughed back its profits in this way may come to accumulate substantial reserves. Unless something special is done with them, they will appear in the balance sheet and appropriation account as if they were available for the payment of dividends. In fact, of course, their use in this way would reduce the scale of the business, since

---

[1] The difference is in the income-tax position of the shareholders. Any dividend out of past profit will rank as current income with them for tax purposes. The company's position is not affected, since these profits will already have borne tax, and it will pay out only the net dividend. Shareholders not liable to tax at standard rate, however, will be able to get a tax refund, and those liable to surtax will have to pay on this addition to their income. These latter are thus enabled to make a bigger (apparent) investment in the company than they could have done out of their net receipts from a corresponding cash dividend, but their beneficial share of the investment which the company has, in fact, made will not have been affected.

they could only be paid by depriving the business of assets which it has been using up to now.

Nevertheless, the appearance of such reserves may act as a strong inducement to shareholders to press for a more generous dividend policy, even though it is against the interest of the business, as the directors see it. The directors can prevent such larger dividends being paid, but will experience pressure for a bigger payment. That can only be avoided by using the reserves so that they no longer appear as free. They could, of course, be used to write down the balance sheet values of the assets, but, in a business which is prudently run, those assets may have already been written down so that their values are already well under the true figure. In that case, the directors may be reluctant to write down further and by any substantial amounts, such as we are discussing. That would apparently reduce the value of the assets held by the business, and, although the real position will be unaffected, the balance sheet will appear that much weaker, to the possible disadvantage of the company. The only other thing that they can do is capitalize the reserves. The values of the assets will be unaffected and the reserves will no longer appear as available for the shareholders. Such a capitalization, then, makes the company's ' capital ' conform more nearly to the true situation. Of course, the directors are not likely to transfer all the available reserves ; it may be inconvenient not to have some reserves available to offset dividends or to meet any losses.

Another reason which may influence the directors arises really from the popular misunderstandings of the true position of the company's capital, to which we have referred earlier. They may wish to pay the shareholders larger dividends. This may be quite justified, in so far as the shareholders have ploughed back into the business in the past the profits which, appearing separately in the company's reserves, have added to the assets of the business and hence gradually added to the profits. Auditors have, in fact, been known sometimes to exert a strong pressure on directors in very cautiously run businesses, where the enforced saving of shareholders has resulted in great increases in the income of their business but where the directors are still ploughing back. In such cases, the dividends going to the shareholders may not have altered for a long period, despite the increase in profits. The argument that the shareholders are entitled to see some return from their savings would not appear obviously immoral. It certainly does not result from immoral conduct on the part of the shareholders, for it is generally in the public interest that profitable businesses should expand, and shareholders, by not withdrawing for their own purposes all the income to which they have become entitled in the past, have performed some public service.

So long as the nominal capital remains the same, such an increased dividend will result in the rate at which the dividend is declared — as a percentage on the nominal capital — being also increased. But this rate of dividend is the one thing that the ordinary man sees quoted, and it is very easy to use it for political purposes — ' the shareholders in X are getting 15 per cent now, when they only had 10 per cent last year ', etc. The directors will correctly see the dividend as resulting from the investment which the shareholders have made but which is not represented in the capital of the company. If they declare a share bonus, not only will that make the ' capital ' increase in some way to correspond with the investment that has taken place, they will also be able to avoid declaring so great an increase in the nominal rate of dividend, thus making it less easy to attack them. Lest the reader should regard this increase in capital as just a financial manœuvre to avoid justified criticism, it may perhaps be pointed out that the capital bonus can only be made if, in fact, profits have been reinvested which legally could have been paid to the shareholders as dividends.

Shareholders like having capital bonuses : there is no doubt about that. There are several reasons, not all of them irrational, but none of them making the capital bonus affect the real investment position. First, as has been said, no directors will declare such a bonus if they think it at all likely that a reversal in the company's fortune will make it incur losses or reduce dividends which could have been met if the reserves had continued to be free in the balance sheet, instead of being legally tied up as ' capital '. The making of capital bonuses is thus one sign of the directors' confidence in the strength of a growing business. Second, because capital bonuses, which certainly imply that the dividend position should not become weaker, have frequently heralded the decision of directors to pay higher dividends, they may be welcomed for that reason, and will increase the value of the shares. If the capital bonus misleads the market about the position of the company, then the improvement will not be maintained, and the shares will fall back in value to a level justified by the business's real position. The improvement will only persist if the business does become stronger or if the shareholders do get extra dividends, and the strength of the business's position will not be improved by the capital bonus, as such, just as the dividends could have been increased without the bonus.

There is one way, not mentioned so far, in which the making of a capital bonus may benefit the shareholders. It will increase the total number of the company's shares available on the market. They will thus tend to become more ' marketable '.[1] The effect may well only be slight, but if it is at all important, then, even for the same total dividends, the total market valuation of the increased nominal share capital will be greater than it was for the smaller capital. Even here, however, the share bonus is not necessary for this result to occur. The same effect would follow from a simple subdivision of the existing shares — e.g. each £1 nominal share being divided into two worth nominally 10s. and the subdivision would be facilitated normally for a successful company by the shares being worth more in the market than their nominal value.

What about the objections of the plain man, as expressed by politicians' reactions to share bonuses ? We have seen that it is quite true that the making of such issues will, if attention is paid only to the nominal rate of the dividend, disguise the paying of a larger dividend. There is this to be said for the common attitude of suspicion : it is the law of limited liability which has made it possible for the great modern company to appear, and, with the growth in the scale of business, it has been made more possible for monopoly to appear. It seems that the ordinary man in the street is justified in demanding that businesses do not make unreasonable profits, or that shareholders do not get unreasonably high incomes. Increasingly the legislature has compelled public companies, in return for the privilege of limited liability, to make disclosure of the profits that they are making. The

[1] In the sense that a larger number of shares of smaller cash value will gradually tend to become more widely held and more frequently dealt in. They will, therefore, tend to be subject to rather less extreme fluctuations in market value than a smaller number of higher-priced shares for the same company. The advantage of the greater ' marketability ' will tend to be reflected in the average price ; it must not, however, be thought that there will be any sensational difference in the total market value of the shares before and after the bonus issue.

political advisers of the plain man, especially since the recent Companies Act, will have a lot more information from which they can reach those decisions about company profits which are rightly a concern of democratic politics. They should abandon the simple naïve quotation of the rates at which dividends are declared, for the level at which these stand proves nothing. Further, after the new legislation, it will be a lot easier to calculate what exactly has been invested in the business, although it may not be possible to distinguish the sums which have been properly put by for depreciation from other write-offs which really consist in a ploughing back of profits.

Companies themselves could do something to meet this, and should recognize that it is not sufficient for them to believe that their rates of profits and dividends are fair. They owe something, in the spread of correct information, to the democracy which has given them their legal powers. It would, in the course of time, be a quite simple matter for the great public companies, on which the attention of the man in the street is largely focused, to provide audited statements of the capital which is really employed in the business, stating the total sums of money which their shareholders have actually put into it, after deducting depreciation, and possibly, also, before such deductions have been made.

It would then be possible to see how far such companies are making excessive profits on the capital which has been put in, and the case could be argued for changes in the price policies of the companies concerned, if, over a long enough period to take care of the usual variation in trade, the companies were making excessive profits. More important, perhaps, it would be possible to calculate the dividends of the shareholder as percentages of their real investment. It should be said that, in the author's experience, many of the large nominal dividends which are quoted against some of the large companies loosely attacked as monopolies (with the implication that they exploit their monopoly position) would come down to a much more reasonable figure.

Whatever may come of this suggestion for more light of the right kind to be thrown on the position of companies and the shareholders in them, it is still true that the nominal rate of dividend on share capital means nothing in itself, and it is undesirable that it should be loosely used for the political argument of a democracy. It also remains true that, in itself, the making of capital bonuses, resulting from peculiarities of the law relating to joint-stock companies, is politically neutral, and is not inherently good or bad from the social point of view. It only recognizes one thing which is socially good in itself — the accumulation of capital by the saving of shareholders.

CHAPTER III

COSTS OF PRODUCTION: PART I
THE EFFECTS OF CHANGING OUTPUTS

(1) INTRODUCTORY

WHEN studying business behaviour it is convenient to follow the pattern suggested by the accounts, making separate analyses of the factors affecting costs and revenue before proceeding to the discussion of the factors affecting the net profitability of a business, which will result from the balance between the two previous sets of factors. The business's revenue will, of course, depend upon the price of the product as well as upon the amount which is sold at that price. Price accordingly plays a central part in the theory of revenue. In traditional analysis it has become usual to begin with the theory of demand and prices, since the sales of a business are usually regarded as dependent upon price. The change in the order of approach adopted in this book reflects a changed emphasis in its theory.

In particular, prices are thought of as dependent upon costs, and output is not considered to be the result of any balancing of marginal revenue against marginal cost. A knowledge of the behaviour of costs of production will be essential before the theory of prices can be discussed, and the theory of prices and of other factors in marketing strategy is accordingly postponed until Chapter V. It will be desirable to defer with these any consideration of one sort of expenditure — the costs involved in selling the product to the customer (including any expenditure which is intended to influence his demand in favour of the particular business). The present chapter is, therefore, restricted to considering how costs of *production* will vary as a business changes its output.

All theory involves abstractions, and, therefore, the use of assumptions. The first two assumptions that we shall make are essential, for a rational discussion of our question would be impossible without them. It must be assumed: (1) that the product remains unchanged, in the sense that it will still be possible to sell it at the same price as the same commodity.[1] Secondly, output, like most economic quantities, is a flow, and the time in which a given output is produced is of the essence of its description; it will be assumed (2) that the production period is uniform, all outputs being per ' week ', for example.

The remaining assumptions are made as a matter of convenience, in the sense that it would be possible to do without them, but at the cost of more cumbrous reasoning. The first two of these are: (3) that the business is producing a single product only; and (4) that that product is being produced in a single factory or productive establishment localized in a single place. Each of these assumptions involves some departure from typical conditions. Most businesses are, in a sense, multi-product, for it is rare that a business's output will consist entirely of a single product, rigidly defined. It will typically produce at least a ' range ' of the ' same ' product, and it is not unusual for a business to be producing a number of quite dissimilar products (even within the same factory) — in fact, that is the usual case with many large modern businesses. It is not so unusual for a business to be operating a single factory, but it is quite

---

[1] It should be recognized that *some* change in the technical specification of the product may be made necessary if there is any substantial change in the methods of production, as is shown by a commodity being spoken of as re-designed for mass-production; this assumption merely sets some limit to the re-designing that may take place, so that the generalizations about cost may be considered always to refer to the ' same ' commodity.

common for a large business to have several factories, each producing quite similar goods. Speaking generally, businesses become multi-product or multi-factory on account of factors arising on the marketing side, and the ways in which such situations come about will be discussed later on. Meanwhile, the analysis of costs on the basis of these assumptions will be applicable to each product considered separately, and to each factory also, if the make-up of its output is taken as given.

A further desirable assumption is that the prices of the factors of production, to use the convenient technical term which economists apply to the goods and services used by a business in order to produce its product, are not affected by any changes in output. In actual fact, the prices of at least some of the factors of production might well be affected by changes in the output, and hence in the business's demand for these factors, if a large enough change is assumed to take place. The formal making of this assumption will, however, enable us to isolate the consequences of changes in output as such. Consequential changes in the prices of factors of production will be considered when the markets of the business are being discussed, which is where they logically belong. It will, therefore, be assumed (5) that the prices at which a business buys or hires its factors of production will *not* be affected by changes in its output.[1]

In this chapter, also, the fact that it is common in the actual world for changes in output to take place in the same direction simultaneously for a number of businesses will be ignored, and it will be assumed (6) that only the individual business changes its output. If this assumption were not made, then the previous one — that the prices of the factors of production remain unchanged — might be quite absurd.

---

[1] This does not mean that the cost of labour will be unaffected if output is increased by getting workmen to work overtime. In that case, they will generally have to be paid at a higher rate for the extra hours (e.g. one and a quarter times the basic rate), but this overtime rate itself will depend upon the basic rate and will be assumed to remain constant with it, whatever the level of output.

Anything approaching a general change in the outputs of businesses using the same factors of production will tend to affect the prices of these factors. In fact, a good many of the typical features of the trade cycle are due to systematic changes in the prices of factors of production induced by simultaneous changes in, or attempts to change, outputs by businesses generally. Such inter-relations between businesses' outputs, costs and prices will concern us later on, of course, but it will first be necessary to know how costs may be expected to vary, simply on account of changes in the output of the individual business considered separately.[1]

It will be convenient to begin with the case of a factory which is being newly planned, and imagine it first as producing the output which was intended when it was first laid out and the organization of the business was set up, going on to consider the effects of changes in output from that level. Given the prices of the factors of production, the average cost of production will depend upon the rate of physical usage of the factors relatively to the output which they produce. The leading question of this chapter, how will costs change as output varies, thus may be asked alternatively as, to what extent will changes in output require a more or less than proportionate change in the physical quantities of the factors of production needed in order to produce the output? Business accounts, as we have seen, draw a sharp distinction between direct and other costs; the corresponding distinction between the factors of production giving rise to those costs is an important one from the point of view of the behaviour of costs (and also from that of the determination of prices).

[1] At any given time, of course, the exact level of a business's costs will be affected by other factors besides the output which the business is producing, but these may be regarded as accidental circumstances from the present point of view. A particular delivery of a raw material being unusually good or bad, the effects on the attitudes and efficiencies of all persons working in the business of such things as changes in the weather, political news, or personal circumstances — such things may mean that costs will vary even if output remains constant, but they may be ignored for present purposes as tending to be random in their nature, so far as changes in output are concerned.

(2) CLASSIFICATION OF SHORT-PERIOD COSTS

The direct factors of production are those which are directly engaged in the productive processes and may, in a sense, be seen as more strictly embodied in the actual product which, given the specification and the method of production, will require definite amounts of the direct factors for each unit that is produced, whereas it may not be affected by changes in the other factors of production employed by the business. As seen in Chapter II, the main classes of direct factors are : (a) direct labour — the employees who are actually engaged in the processes through which the product passes on its way from raw material to being finished ; and (b) direct materials — those which are included in the specification of the product, for the most part forming the physical stuff of which it is made. Direct costs, as we know, are entered in the trading account. The costs of the other factors employed by the business come into the profit and loss account. They consist of the costs of the factors engaged on selling the product, which do not concern this chapter, and the costs of the indirect factors of production. These latter may conveniently be thought of as constituting the physical and personal organization of the business so far as production is concerned.

The indirect factors of production thus include all work-people not involved in the actual processes, the office staffs and all grades of management from the lowest grades of supervisors upwards,[1] the machinery and equipment used in production, the premises in which production is carried out, and the land on which the premises stand. The initial planning of the business man mainly consists of his deciding on his complement of indirect factors of production. When

---

[1] We may here disregard the fact that some members of the management in a small business may be directly engaged in production and that some of the managers, and the office staff also, will be concerned with the sales side as well, so that their costs cannot easily be divided between the two sides of the business.

he has decided this, he will have decided how the business is to be organized and the size and character of the organization. The direct factors, of course, also impose some limitation, in so far as a business man will not contemplate setting up a factory to produce an article unless he thinks that he will be able to get all the direct factors that he is likely to require, and also that he will have, or will be able to obtain, enough working capital to carry him over the interval between his paying for them and his receipt of the proceeds of the sale of their product. Since, however, these costs will be recovered by the sale when it takes place, it will usually not be difficult for the business to obtain short-term finance to carry an increase in output which its sales justify. So the main consideration in the case of direct factors will be their physical availability in the area in which the factory would be localized, and, because labour is the most rigidly localized factor, it will be the availability of direct labour in the area that will chiefly concern the business man. He will not, however, have to commit himself to any long-term employment of direct factors, and, accordingly, his decisions here, unlike those on the indirect factors, will not tend to restrict his future decisions about the specification of the product, the methods by which he will produce it, and the quantity of it that he will produce.

The business man, of course, will usually start his planning with a figure for the output for which his factory will be effectively laid down, and it will be on that basis that he will plan his organization. That figure will, naturally, be larger than the *average* output which he would produce if he actually achieved his expectations. He must plan to have something in hand. He will know that seasonal fluctuations or the trade cycle will cause some variation in his actual output, and will have to plan to meet his market at the peak at least as reasonably as other producers can meet theirs. It is not only that such periods of temporarily high demand will be needed to offset the periods of low demand that he can likewise expect, and that such demand, being temporary by its very nature, will not be there to be met in slacker times ; the customers themselves may very well not come back, even with their reduced orders, but may transfer them where they found that they could get deliveries at the more difficult time. To some extent, it may be possible to help out in such periods by the use of stocks which have been carried over from times when the pressure for output was not so great, but there will be only a limited possibility of this wherever the specifications are liable to change.[1]

Having fixed the basic output on which the factory is to be planned, the business man will first think of the equipment which will be needed to produce that output. He will almost certainly have to choose between alternative techniques of production for at least some processes, and each technique will involve differing equipment and organization. The business man will choose the method of production which he thinks most suitable, but it does not follow that he will choose that method of production which would give him the basic output at least cost. If he did choose his equipment on that basis, he would usually be committed to producing more nearly to that output on the average — and to continue producing just that particular product in that particular way — than he would like, or indeed than would be wise. In fact, he will know that he will normally produce less than the planned output, that his output will fluctuate, that he may very well have to alter the precise nature of the product in order to meet some change in the market or because he can get an advantage by so doing, and that minor changes in the technique of production, at least, are always likely, and that the effect of these may be important taken cumulatively.

The business man being assumed to have chosen the methods by which his product is to be manufactured, the types of machinery and equipment that are to be put into

---

[1] The financial burden entailed by locking up working capital in such stocks, with the accompanying risks, will also impose limits.

the factory will also have been decided, and the next question to be settled will be how many of each type are to be installed. Each machine will have a fairly definite average capacity as used in the particular factory and on the particular product which is planned. The business man will normally be able to make reasonable estimates of what the capacity of each machine will be when the factory has really got going.[1] The estimates that he makes will give him a schedule of the expected capacities of his machinery, and he will then have to install sufficient machines of each type for their total capacity to add up to the through-put for that class of machine when the factory is producing the total output for which it is planned.

The exact amount of machinery which is required will depend, of course, not only on the capacity of the machinery and the planned output but also upon the number of hours for which that machinery will be in use in each production period. A given output will imply the heaviest demand for capital equipment if the business man intends to work single shifts (i.e. only one productive shift per day) and if he does not intend to work overtime. He will be able to plan to tighter limits, so far as his machinery is concerned, if he intends to work all or any of his departments on a two- or three-shifts-per-day basis.

The consequent economy in machinery will be shown in the reduced charges in the profit and loss account for obsolescence, i.e. the non-wear-and-tear part of the depreciation provision, which will fall in the case of double-day shifts to 50 per cent of their amount for single-shift working, and to 33 per cent in the case of treble-shift working. There will, of course, be other factors to be taken into account. Wear and tear, and with it the repair bill, will rise with the extra utilization of machinery and equipment, and, at the

---

[1] He will probably have to expect some initial period of lower output until all concerned have had sufficient experience, quite apart from any period that may be required to work the new machinery in.

same time, the opportunities for doing major repairs outside production hours will be more restricted, and not available at all in the case of treble-shift working. At the same time, there will be some difficulties with labour, unless workpeople in the district where the factory is being set up are already used to working on that basis. When a third shift is worked, higher labour rates will have to be paid for the night shift, and there is a good deal of evidence that the efficiency of night-shift workers is lower, thus further increasing the labour cost. Further, female workers are not allowed on night shifts.

When these factors are taken into account, three-shift working will be thought to be profitable only where capital costs are large in relation to labour costs, and where obsolescence makes up a larger proportion of those costs than pure depreciation due to wear and tear. In many industries the working of two day-shifts will appear as likely to be worthwhile, if one does not reckon in the opposition from the workers, the pattern of whose lives has to be altered.[1]

As already indicated, the business man may also plan to finer limits in his capital equipment if he intends to take care of part of his anticipated peak output by working all or any of his departments overtime, which will not be possible where he plans to have three-shift working. The economy in capital here will be balanced by the heavier wages payable for overtime. Whatever he plans to do in the way of overtime or shift working, the calculations made solely on the basis of his machines will give him only the minimum equipment which he will require for his planned output-capacity with his given methods of production, and this, it must be stressed again, is not enough. He will have to reckon with the possibility of breakdowns and of machines consequently being idle for repairs. The extent of this repairs allowance and the precise form in which it is made will vary for different

[1] Note, in any case, how much smaller the proportionate saving in obsolescence costs is for an extension from two to three shifts as compared with that from one to two ; they are halved in the latter, but only further reduced by a third — or by a further one-sixth of the single-shift costs — in the former.

types of machinery.[1] It will be relatively large, for example, in the case of process machinery with fast moving parts, but there a considerable part of the reserve may be in the form of stocks of spare parts, reducing the size of the necessary reserve of complete machine units.

Of course, not all the repairs that have to be done are of immediate urgency, and the reserve capacity to be installed need not take account of all the possible incidence of such deferrable repairs. For the business man may, to some extent, plan to meet his peak output by working his equipment for longer periods without overhaul, meeting the (probably increased) bill for deferred repairs later, when he will not be so busy. A visit to a factory which is short of resources for new capital equipment, and a comparison of the condition of its equipment with that in a business where the policy is to repair and replace as occasion arises — with adequate resources to implement that policy — will frequently result in the investigator being surprised just how long some machinery will keep running (at a cost). To the extent to which such a policy is intended to be adopted, the planned capacity of the factory need not include a full allowance for repairs, but, even so, not all repairs are deferable, and on some machinery no repair can be postponed, or even ' botched up '.

Apart from repairs, there is another factor making for some, at least, of the machinery and equipment being larger in nominal capacity than its planned through-put — the business man's initial investment will tend strongly to limit his future policy. In particular, he will wish to take advantage of any opportunity to expand that a rising demand for his product may bring him. All business men hope for growth (and frequently that will be the only thing which will justify the foundation of a really new business and make it profitable). They will know, in any case, that any opportunity

---

[1] The point should perhaps be made that, where machinery is rented with a contract for service, some of the provisions for repairs will fall on the machinery supplier and need not be given any explicit consideration in the costs of the business which uses that machinery.

which comes must be taken, if possible, and that to let any demand go to their rivals, when it would otherwise have come to them, may threaten, in time, their hold on the demand which they have.

The business man will generally be most limited by his investment in the machinery which has the largest capacity per machine in relation to the planned output of the factory, and the larger the output of a machine or other piece of equipment the more likely it will be that the business man will plan to have reserve capacity over and above the repairs allowance.   Several factors operate to make this so.   It will not be easy to make piecemeal extensions to such equipment. Such plant is usually bulkier and needs special care in its siting in the factory.   When an addition is called for, short of major reconstruction of the premises or of the lay-out which is being operated, it may be necessary to put it in just anywhere where it will go, with a possible decrease in the speed of the internal flow of goods in process.[1]   Its installation will often take considerable time, during which the extra business for which it is wanted may well be lost.   One instance may be given of the sort of thing which comes to mind in this connexion : anyone who has seen a really large press being installed will understand why, where the work calls for such equipment, the business man tends to allow a fairly generous margin of reserve.   The excavation of the site for the foundations is not a small job — like an iceberg, there is a lot more below than is visible from the surface — and then follows the delicate job of installing and adjusting the great machine, bedding it in and trueing it up so that it will work properly.

Frequently, too, machinery and plant, whose capacity is large in relation to the typical output of a business in the industry which uses them, are either made specially to the

---

[1] The output of such machines, when it is not itself bulky, frequently needs bulk treatment, whereas the output from the smaller process machinery is usually more made up of separate articles which can be handled relatively efficiently in batches.

requirements of the business or produced only to order — small stocks possibly being kept by the manufacturers but soon disappearing when busy times produce an expanded demand. In such cases, the probable production delays have to be added to any that may be expected during the installation, correspondingly lengthening the period which must elapse before a new machine which is wanted can be put into operation. It must also be remembered that this heavier sort of equipment will usually have a relatively long life and, therefore, it will not pay to scrap it; whereas with process machinery it can often be scrapped, and expansion may be made the occasion for thoroughgoing new investment in more up-to-date machines.

All the previous factors simply make for reserve capacity. The nature of this type of plant, however, frequently has consequences for its design. It has already been stated that most businesses will not expect to have a steady output when once they have settled down in their market, but will expect to share in the normal fluctuations of that market due to the trade cycle, and, in many cases, they will have to reckon with seasonal fluctuations as well — in some consumers' goods industries seasonal fluctuations may well be larger than the expected trade cycle fluctuations. In such cases, the business man, when he is planning the design of his equipment, will frequently prefer each unit of such equipment to be somewhat smaller than he would otherwise like on the basis of his planned capacity, provided that doing so does not add disproportionately to his costs. Any decrease in output can then be met by closing down a complete unit, instead of working a larger unit at low output, and this may bring a saving in labour and other costs. He may, in such circumstances, plan to get the capacity that he wants with, say, three machines where he might otherwise prefer to have only one.[1]

---

[1] Subject to the addition of an appropriate repairs allowance in each case — in fact, of course, working with such smaller units may enable him to economize in repair capacity as well.

There will, however, be a limit to the possibility of designing such smaller scale plant, for the fact that such machinery is designed for relatively large outputs per unit, as compared with other machinery or plant, often means that its costs of operation rise fairly sharply with any reduction in its scale. In some cases the diseconomies of small-scale designing may be so great that the business man will find it desirable to plan a single unit to accommodate at least the bulk of his output capacity, and this (plus any stand-by for use in case of repairs or emergencies) may mean that he will have a big reserve of capacity in this particular part of his equipment in normal times.

At the other end of the scale, the machinery with the smallest capacities will be dominated by what may be called process machinery. This may need the largest relative allowance to take care of repairs, but it will often be of least importance as a limiting factor in case of any future increase in production. For one thing, an increase may be met temporarily, but, perhaps, for an appreciable period, by deferring repairs, or by temporary patching up. Also, such machinery is frequently employed in departments where the work is so organized that increases in output can be met by working overtime, so that there may be an appreciable but more or less hidden reserve of capacity.

Another factor reducing the effective limitation imposed by a given investment in machinery of this kind is that extra machines may well be fairly easily obtainable without much delay in normal times. Such equipment will tend to become relatively standardized in the industry in which it is used. It will thus be available as a ready product from machinery-making firms, quite apart from any second-hand market that may have developed. Again, in contrast to the heavier equipment, its installation will not be so great a problem. It will be more easy to make an effective allowance for extensions of this kind when the factory is being designed. When it comes to the actual installation, not only is there less physical work and trouble involved but major readjustments in lay-out may not be needed; a group of such machines may not take up much space and may efficiently be put almost anywhere, the flow of goods in process accommodating itself to them.

Leaving the equipment and turning to premises and land, it must be expected that here also some reserve capacity must be planned to take care of growth. This will not weigh so heavily with the really small business, in industries where such businesses can start up with any prospects. Provided that the planned location is in a general industrial area, they may be able to reckon on being able, normally, to find larger premises into which they can move if they wish to expand, and may be attracted by the relative cheapness of genuinely small scale accommodation in such areas. Such firms may, therefore, allow very little for expansion in their original premises,[1] preferring to fill the factory which they occupy — in fact, they will frequently have to do so, if they are to scrape along at their small size. The larger factory, which will not find it so feasible to plan on a hermit crab basis, will certainly need to have at least land available for extensions, and will generally have some reserve capacity in its premises also. It will need to have room to accommodate extra process machinery, in so far as it may have planned only a small reserve in its initial complement of this. Generally it will also desire to leave some room to turn around, especially if it is in an industry where developments in technique or changes in the specification of the product are liable to call for rearrangements of the space allocated to particular processes.[2]

Of course, the reserve capacity in land and premises may not show itself in the costs as reckoned in the accounts. Land, as such, will not give rise to current costs, since it will

---

[1] Even here it is often the case that labour shows great local immobility. See p. 223.

[2] In the multi-product business, it will have to be able to accommodate changes in the balance of its output, in so far as the different 'products' — which may be different items in a range of nominally the same product — will differ in their relative use of the services of different departments.

H

not be thought of as depreciating simply by its being occupied by the business. It is also quite usual not to depreciate factory premises by way of cost-charges but to write them down out of reserves provided from profits as shown in the accounts. However, since these factors of production have to be provided at the cost of an initial investment, the business man will require the prospect of a satisfactory return on such investment, and, in this way, it gives rise to notional planning costs at all events.

Where any of these factors are rented, as has been seen already, the accounts will show current cost charges covering the rents that have to be paid. Otherwise, the only cost charges which must appear will be the costs of repairs, but in quite a number of cases business men enter the schedule A (income-tax) assessment on their premises as a rent charge in their profit and loss account, crediting it back as a sort of notional income on investments in the appropriation account. Except for repairs and for the rents which have actually to be paid out for such rented factors, the costs which will appear in the accounts for the indirect factors of production which we have been discussing so far will be purely accounting charges, in so far as they will not necessarily involve any current money expenditure. The business man will have committed himself to such factors of production, his investment will be bygone expenditure, and the business will be able to make use of them, whatever their current earnings may be.

The case is different with the factors of production which make up the remaining part of the overhead organization of the business. These consist of the indirect labour and office and management personnel, and the whole of their current costs will involve paying out money. They make up an important part of what were called paying-out overheads in the accounts chapter, and, in so far as current earnings do not bring in enough to cover them after meeting the other paying-out costs of production, their use will involve a drain on the cash resources of the business.

The business will not be so deeply committed to its employment of these factors of production as it is with its capital investment, but it will not lightly wish to cut down on such organization. For, in a very real sense, these factors determine the personality of a manufacturing business. The personnel employed will be much more valuable to the business, in so far as they acquire an increasing familiarity with its methods of production, with its particular product, and with its particular market. To let them go means parting with trained and experienced personnel who will, perhaps, not be available if subsequently the business wishes to re-expand, thus leading not only to the strict costs of training newcomers but also to the inconvenience and bother which necessarily arise with the introduction of new personalities into the organization of a business, which, at its best, has to function as a team of people who know one another.

For this reason, a business man starting up may be very cautious when planning the personal part of his organization and plan to rather finer limits, preferring to extend gradually so that the organization settles down. He may plan to finer limits in the matter of reserves just because people are much more flexible than machines in the amount of work that they can do, so that for short periods there may be a hidden reserve in the establishment not merely because it will be possible to work overtime but also because, for limited periods, human beings can extend themselves and take on responsibilities which would overwork them in the longer run.

Some reserves, however, implicit or explicit, there must be, and it will be necessary that the organization of the business will be able to take care of it at the peak level of activity which is anticipated when the initial plans are made. Further, businesses normally can expect not a steady output but one which fluctuates with the trade cycle and with the seasons. It will be the persons involved in the overhead organization who will particularly have to cope with the uncertainties of business life and with the changes in policy and direction that result. The type of personal organization which will be set up will reflect this, and is thus affected by the need for the flexibility, in the same way as the impersonal side (ref. p. 88).

A business man is notoriously interested in flexible minds, among the management staff at all events. Not only in management proper, but also in the drawing office and among the maintenance and repair staff, he will generally want men who can turn around with changing needs, rather than those who will be most efficient so long as there is no variation in the job that they have to do. The latter will often appear as extremely inefficient in the ordinary business.

An instance which comes to mind is that of a works manager who had been a notable failure in at least one business, but who then managed to get appointed to a factory where his task became a routine for reasons peculiar to its market. In that factory, his rather inflexible mind became an asset, and his habit of ' getting his neck into a knot ' when the unexpected happened could not show itself to upset the workers whom he controlled or his colleagues in management, and his factory became a byword for its efficiency. In personnel, then, as in capital investment, it will not necessarily pay the business man to set up the sort of organization which would really minimize his current costs for the production of a given output; he has also to reckon with the costs involved in meeting the changes which his business can expect.[1]

It is possible to draw a similar distinction between the persons making up the personnel of the business to that which has been drawn in the case of capital equipment. They also may be imagined to have differing ' capacities '. At one extreme will be the lower ranks of supervisors, one of whom will be required for every so many direct labourers, or the

---

[1] This factor also will be specially important for the multi-product business, as distinct from the rigidly single-product business which is imagined in this chapter.

wages clerk who will be able to make only so many entries per day, and who will have to be duplicated when the entries increase beyond this. At the other extreme will be *the* business man, in the sense of the person referred to in Chapter I as having the planning function centralized in him, so that he at least says yes or no, and thus takes the final decisions — he will have to cope with whatever size the business grows to. At the lowest level, the numbers of such indirect personnel will vary with output very much as the number of process machines will have to do. Accordingly, for the sake of brevity, any future reference to increases in process machinery may be thought to apply to them.

In the analysis of costs, it is necessary to draw a sharp distinction between the fundamental features of a business's organization and others. It is suggested that it is the investment in the largest capacity (least ' divisible '), indirect factors which really characterizes the business; when it changes this it will have to make fundamental changes in its organization, and these need a quite separate discussion. It is, therefore, convenient to discuss first the behaviour of costs in a business with a given organization in this sense. This corresponds very nearly to what is normally called the short period in traditional economic analysis, and we shall use that term for brevity's sake. Changes in the organization of the business are the essential features of what is usually called long-period change, and the effects of changes of the latter sort will be analysed in the next chapter.

(3) THE BEHAVIOUR OF INDIRECT COSTS

So long as the business does not vary its complement of indirect factors at all, they may be regarded as causing a constant charge per production period to be entered in the accounts, and the average indirect cost per unit of product will, consequently, be the result of dividing this total cost by the size of the output that is being produced. The average indirect cost, therefore, falls with increasing output and rises as output falls, the fall getting proportionately less steep if output continues to increase, but rising more steeply proportionately if output continues to fall.

Apart from the direct factors of production, which will be discussed separately later on, the business will be able to increase its output until it runs up against the tightest of its planning limits. For short periods these will generally be in its machinery, for human beings will be able to take extra responsibility, as a temporary measure at all events — it may be necessary for them to work overtime, in which case the total indirect costs will rise by the amount of the overtime charges per production period. Similarly, overtime which will affect indirect labour as well as direct labour, may be used to get an increased output from the most limited equipment.

If, then, the business does not increase its machinery, it will be able to increase its output without any rise in its indirect costs up to the limit of that machinery when worked under normal conditions, and, up to that limit, its average indirect costs will continue to fall along the same curve. Beyond that limit, extra output will be obtained, but at some extra cost. Either the business may work that machinery overtime, when the main increase in costs will come from the associated direct labour — for simplification we may ignore any rise in indirect labour costs — or it may install extra units of the machinery which is limiting its output, in which case the total indirect costs will rise by the amount of the cost-charges on the extra investment, and the curve of average indirect costs will rise abruptly to a new level, after which it will continue to fall in the same manner as before. If output goes on increasing there will be a limit to that increase without the business making extra investment in the largest capacity machinery, etc. Such a change is better regarded as involving long-run reorganization of the business and will not be discussed further now.

If output falls, as we have seen, average indirect costs per unit will rise with increasing steepness. A continuous decrease in output will, sooner or later, mean that units of the smallest capacity equipment become idle. If the business

DIAGRAM I

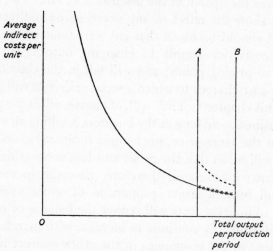

NOTES

A. Limit to output from process machinery. (Limit to output from direct labour-force working normal time may be less than this.)

B. Limit to output from largest-capacity equipment — absolute limit to output without increase of scale.

— average indirect costs per unit of output with unchanged equipment.

*** the same, if direct labour can be available to work sufficient overtime.

---- average indirect costs per unit of output after new process machinery has been installed.

man is convinced that the reduction in his output has come to stay, he might, of course, dismiss some of these low-capacity factors or sell off some of the low-capacity machinery, in which case his total indirect costs will fall, and the curve of average indirect costs will fall to a new level, after which it will continue rising with decreasing output, as before. Further

reductions will uncover some of the equipment with the largest
capacity, but, once again, any change in that is better regarded as a fundamental long-run change in the organization
of the business.

Diagram I draws the curve of average indirect costs, and
summarizes the upshot of the discussion so far. The diagram
does not show the effect of any overtime on indirect labour
costs. It should be noted that any variations in the average
indirect costs due simply to changing output will not be
relevant to pricing policy, and will fall in the class of extraordinary cost charges to which special reference will be made
later in this chapter.[1] They will, of course, affect the fortunes
of the business. So long as the business is selling an increased
output at the same price, unchanged indirect factors of production will mean that the profit and loss account debits will
remain unchanged, and, therefore, that the increased net
profit will form a larger proportion of gross profit; any
addition to indirect costs will reduce the balance of net profit
but it will probably continue to increase with increasing output because of the economies in the other indirect factors of
production. Similarly, reductions in output, prices remaining
unchanged, will cause the net profit to fall both absolutely
and proportionately to gross profit. Any reductions in the
investment in indirect factors of production which accompany a decline in output will reduce the fall in the net profit
through the saving in profit and loss account expenses, but
it will then continue to decline disproportionately because
of the incidence of those indirect costs which cannot be
reduced.

(4) THE BEHAVIOUR OF DIRECT COSTS

The behaviour of direct costs of production can be very
simply described. In general, average direct costs per unit

[1] See p. 109.

of product will be expected to remain constant over large ranges of output, so long as the business continues to employ the same methods of production, and the total of such costs will vary proportionately with total output. The specification of the product will call for so much of each material to be embodied in the finished product, and the quantity of the materials so used must necessarily be constant per unit of product. The balance of such materials used in production will consist of any amounts which are ' cut to waste ' and the losses in process or elsewhere. This wastage will normally vary more or less in proportion to the usage of materials. Very high outputs may cause some extra wastage, because abnormal inputs of materials cannot be handled so efficiently for technical reasons — this sort of waste may be avoided if the business does expand its process machinery and equipment. Also, when a business is fully extended, the management may not be able to control the usage of materials so effectively, so that wastes increase. Equally, on some processes it is true that higher through-puts always lead to better technical usage of materials. At very low outputs two opposing tendencies may be met : the costs of direct materials wasted may decrease because it is easier to control them, and the management has more time and incentive to do so ; on the other hand, in some processes it may be technically impossible to utilize materials so efficiently when the through-put falls to a certain level (this again will be removed if units of process machinery are put completely out of use). For simplicity's sake, we shall ignore these extreme possibilities of variation in the usage and cost of materials. They will not be very important in relation to the average usage of materials, and, in any case, will not be relevant to the determination of prices, since they should be classified as extraordinary costs.

It is easy to generalize about the costs of direct labour when it is paid piece-rates — so much per unit of product or per operation performed — for then the average direct labour cost must remain constant whatever the output, so long as the specification of the product remains unchanged. If the workmen are employed overtime, then, of course, the average direct labour costs of the output produced during the period of overtime [1] will rise to the overtime level. However, the effects of overtime will be considered separately, after we have considered what happens when labour is not paid on a piece-rate basis.

In many cases direct labour will be employed upon a time-rate basis, its wage being reckoned as so much an hour. The average cost per unit of product of such labour will then depend upon the productivity of the workmen, in the sense of their average output per unit of time. The conclusion will remain that the average costs of such direct labour will tend to be constant whatever the output, subject to any qualifications about the effect of overtime, but it will be necessary to take a little space for the analysis, since we have to distinguish two possible ways in which the output may be varied with time labour: the existing labour-force may remain unchanged but work for different hours, or the number of workpeople may be varied, some of the workpeople being stood off when output falls, and additional workmen being engaged when it is desired to increase output. It will be convenient to commence with the latter case, for which we must consider what will happen to average productivity when the numbers employed are varied.

There are, of course, great differences in the skill and energy of individual workmen, but these are *potential* differences and the question is, how far will they come out in actual performances ? Even if they do, so long as only small changes in the total employment are involved in the change

---

[1] Similarly, if there is a guaranteed minimum wage which becomes effective when output falls so low that piece-rate earnings do not reach this minimum. If output continues to fall below such a level, then the average direct labour cost will rise progressively. This latter situation can, of course, be met by the dismissal of sufficient redundant workmen, and we may assume that it will be if low output continues ; accordingly, this sort of rise in the average direct labour cost can be ignored in order to simplify the theory.

of output, it is unlikely that the output of those stood off or taken on will be sufficiently different from the average of all workers for that average to be markedly affected. Average direct labour costs can, therefore, certainly be treated as constant for relatively small changes in output, whatever the differences between individual employees, so long as the total numbers employed are relatively large. If, however, the business pays a *flat* time-rate to all workers of a given class, the differences in the actual performances of individual work-people will not be anything like so large as the differences in their potentialities, and, in fact, are not likely to be very marked where numbers of men are employed in the same occupation. The case may, of course, be quite different where differences in the output of workers are recognized in the wages paid, so that the time-rates come to approximate, as it were, to compounded piece-rates.

Flat time-rates reduce the incentives for workmen to show any marked differences in capacity and leave more scope for the tendency for a regular pace of work to show itself.[1] That tendency will always be present when men work in groups; it does not arise only from deliberate ca' canny, but, to some extent, no doubt, arises from an inclination among a group to establish a general rhythm, which can usually be overcome only by a strong enough incentive to individuals to break away.[2] When a reduced output leads to

[1] This does not, in itself, condemn the use of flat-rate wages where high output is required. There are, in some industries, good reasons for preferring the simplicity of flat-rate payment, quite apart from any preferences for this system that may be held by the workers or the representatives of their trade union. In such cases, a rather high flat-rate may be accompanied by a high general level of output, for it will act as an inducement to labour to seek to enter the business, subsequent selection of candidates for employment keeping the output per man up to a correspondingly high level.

[2] This tendency is often condemned, but it is perhaps not sufficiently recognized that the quality of man as a social animal will naturally show itself most in the smaller societies in which he is most in contact. Even the tendency to think in terms of sharing out work is not, in itself, to be condemned ; it is certainly only to be overcome by removing any conditions of fear and uncertainty which give rise to it. The other motive which is often recognized, the feeling that for a given wage it is sufficient to give what is recognized as a fair

workers being dismissed, it may, of course, occur that the least efficient men are dismissed first, but, for the reasons indicated, we should not expect the average output to be much affected. Further, a business is frequently not free to dismiss on an efficiency basis; the sentiment of the workshops will be in favour of shortness of service, family obligations and other such factors being taken into account, and these have no necessary connexion with efficiency. It may occur that a reduction in employment will make those who are left work harder, but this is unlikely to occur,[1] and there will probably be a counter-tendency for the workmen to go more cautiously, in view of the general preference for sharing out work, when that is obviously falling.

When output is being increased by the taking on of additional workers, if any large numbers are involved, we should expect that, during the period in which they settle down, their productivity will be rather lower than will be usual in the business concerned. Apart from that training period, however, we should not expect average productivity to be greatly affected. Granted that wages are on a time basis, the newcomer who is much more efficient than the average will generally settle down to the pace of work which prevails in the factory. Quite normal forces will restrain any tendency on his part to show excessive zeal which might jeopardize the established position — which may be justified when seen as

amount of work, is also not to be condemned in itself, and may properly be overcome by giving an adequate reward for extra output where that is required. The workman has some justice on his side in maintaining that the fairness to his employer of what he produces is to be measured by his product rather than by his effort, taking some ' rent of ability' for himself. It might be added that, in practice, it appears that the spare energies of the better man are often employed in helping his weaker brother along, so that total output is often not so much set back as might appear. However, these observations are perhaps out of place in what purports to be an objective work on business theory. They are made in order to remove any feeling in the reader's mind that this tendency is reported only as part of a ' reactionary' condemnation of the general attitude of the worker as it seems to be reflected in his practice, and the fact itself must be recognized whatever we think of that practice.

[1] Assumption 6 has ruled out any *general* changes in industrial output and employment, when this result is most likely to occur, see Chapter VI, page 205.

the working pace which workmen are to keep up day in and day out at the given rate of wages. If, on the other hand, the newcomer is markedly less efficient than the average he will, in normal times, be dismissed. If it is difficult to introduce newcomers into a particular process or factory, so that the costs of their settling down may be very high, or if the available additional workmen are markedly inefficient, this does not mean simply that the costs of additional output obtained in this way will be very high; for such circumstances will act as a restraint on the speed at which output is allowed to increase. There may, for this reason, be a limit to the output which the business man is prepared to produce over a given period. He will certainly not let output expand at so fast a rate as to disorganize his factory and lower the general standard of work which he has established.

There remains the case where output is varied by varying the hours for which a given, time-paid, labour-force works, rather than by varying the numbers employed.[1] If output continued to go solely according to the productive rhythm which appears to be established by workers working a full normal day, we should expect that *some* shortening of the working day would bring an improvement in average output per hour of the shorter day, but it is to be doubted if this will persist. It is much more likely that supervisors will content themselves with seeing that the average output per hour is maintained. If an increase in output is being secured by working overtime, it will probably be equally true that average output per hour is not seriously affected, so long as the overtime is moderate in amount or if it does not persist. When it is sought to maintain a large increase in output by heavy overtime, however, the worker will become more fatigued, and this will show itself particularly in the output at the end of the day, so that, quite apart from the effects

---

[1] It should perhaps be noted that these two cases are only distinct analytically and that, in actual fact, an increased output may be obtained both by taking on new labour *and* by increasing the working day, and a reduction in output may equally well be secured *both* by dismissals and by shorter hours.

on costs of the necessity of paying overtime rates of wages, the average direct labour costs may be expected to rise. Apart from such reduced efficiency, and if average productivity does not decline for the lengthened working day,

DIAGRAM II

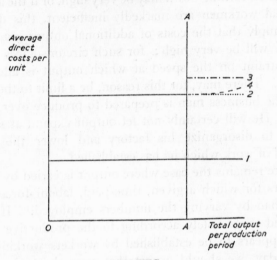

NOTES

(1) = average direct materials costs per unit.

(2) = average total direct costs per unit.
  = (1) plus average direct labour costs per unit, with no overtime.

AA = limit of output from direct labour without working overtime.

(3) = average total direct costs of *additional* output beyond OA if obtained entirely through direct labour working overtime.

(4) = average total direct costs of *whole* output beyond OA when direct labour is working overtime.

the — constant — average direct labour costs would rise by exactly the extent to which overtime increases the normal wage-rate; thus the level of average direct labour costs would rise by one-quarter, or whatever the proportion is.

The conclusion about the labour element in average direct costs is thus similar to that reached for average direct materials costs. The total of such costs may be expected to remain at a constant level over a wide range of output, and in Diagram II, therefore, the level of average total direct costs and of their constituent parts is indicated by a straight line at a constant level. Overtime will tend to raise that level *for the extra output* by a definite amount corresponding to the overtime wages, and the average costs will, therefore, rise continuously from the point where overtime is worked, being pulled up by the higher average costs of the extra output which will form a continuously increasing proportion of total output. The diagram ignores the facts that the working of exceptionally low outputs may raise costs in some processes through the wastage of raw materials, and that the working of exceptionally high output for a considerable period may lead to higher costs not only through wastage of materials but also through reduced average labour efficiency, whether arising because of overtime or because of the lower efficiency of new recruits to the labour-force. These causes of deviation from the average level of direct costs at normal outputs will generally not be very important, but if they are they will be what we have hitherto called extraordinary costs, and may be ignored from the point of view of the pricing theory, to which this study of costs is intended to lead.

(5) THE CONCEPT OF EXTRAORDINARY COSTS

This will be a convenient point in which to take up this hitherto unexplained classification of costs into normal and extraordinary. All rises in average direct costs will, of course, affect the fortunes of the business, for, at a given price, they will cause the average realized gross profit margin to fall and the total gross profit to rise less than proportionately to the total output. But all changes in these costs, due to less efficient utilization of materials or to reductions in the efficiency of labour through overwork, in so far as they are recognized to be due to the exceptional output, will tend to

be treated as extraordinary costs from the point of view of the
fixing of prices. All rises in labour costs due to paying overtime wages will certainly also be regarded as extraordinary
costs, labour being costed up at normal rates of pay. The
individual business will have to reckon with the actual or
potential competition of other businesses, and these may
have no reason to reckon in, say, overtime costs when deciding
their price policy. The existing competitors may well still
have reserves of labour or be working at normal output or
below, and newcomers will certainly plan on a normal output
basis. (Equally, any rise in the average overhead costs due
to a reduced output will also be irrelevant and for the same
reasons.) From the point of view of pricing, then, it is the
normal level of average direct costs that will be the important
thing, and this may be taken as constant, given the prices of
the factors of production.

(6) SUMMARY OF CONCLUSIONS

This concludes our analysis of the effect on the business's
costs of changes in its output, given its short-period organization, i.e. given the output for which the organization has been
set up. Stated in the simplest and strictest terms, the conclusions are that, while average direct costs may be expected
to remain constant for quite a large variation in output, rising
if extra output has to be produced by overtime, the indirect
costs will fall continuously up to the limits of the capacity
of the process machinery and equally rise continuously and
with increasing sharpness if output is reduced. It follows
that the average realized gross profit margin should, *provided
price is unchanged*, remain constant, total gross profits increasing in proportion to output. The working of overtime will
reduce the average gross profit margin, although total gross
profits will continue to increase. The average net profit per
unit of product will, therefore, tend to rise with increases in

output due to the reduced weight of the indirect costs of the overhead organization, total net profits, therefore, rising more than in proportion to total output. Similarly, the average net profit realized will tend to fall with decreases of output, and the total of net profits will tend to fall more than in proportion to the fall in total output.

It remains for us to consider what will happen to costs if total output continues to run at levels which are significantly lower, or significantly higher, than the level of output for which the organization of the business was planned, so that the business has time and incentive to make what may be called long-run changes in that organization.

I

CHAPTER IV

COSTS OF PRODUCTION: PART II
THE EFFECTS OF CHANGING ORGANIZATION

(1) INTRODUCTORY

THE previous chapter considered how a business's costs of production would vary as its output changed whilst it was, in fact, organized to produce a particular output. Assuming a given organization, in this sense, set an implicit but rigid limit to the maximum output that the business could produce — the limit imposed by the least alterable part of the business's organization. The business man will now be assumed free to set up whatever organization is necessary to produce any output, and so there will be no formal limit to the range of output with which we shall be concerned. The business will be spoken of as producing ' at a given scale of production', instead of as producing ' a given output ' ; the word ' scale ' being used to carry the idea that the business has been organized or reorganized as fully as possible to produce the ' scale-output '.

It will be necessary to distinguish the case of a completely new business from one which has been established previously. When a business is a completely new venture, with an organization set up especially to produce at a given scale, the business man will, of course, have been completely free to produce the scale-output in the most economical manner. If, however, the business has been set up previously and has already been organized to produce at a different scale, it will, at best, be a very long time before the business man can get to as favourable a position as he might have had, had he been able to start completely from scratch or suddenly wipe out all his yesterdays. It will not be very realistic to assume the lapse of so long a period as may be necessary before this complete sort of reorganization could take place, and it should be recognized that, generally speaking, his freedom will be limited by consequences of his previous decisions. The established business will usually have to do its best with an organization, or with capital investment, which the business man has modified as best he can, but which are inferior in some way to what he would prefer at the scale at which he is now running. Any disadvantage that there may be in the situation of an older business planned for a different scale of output is especially likely to appear on the technical side and, particularly, in connexion with physical equipment, since other factors of production can be dismissed or deployed with greater freedom, in theory at all events. We shall, therefore, have to make a separate treatment of these two kinds of business situations when we come to discuss the technical factors in costs of production.

(2) THE DISTINCTION BETWEEN TECHNICAL AND MANAGERIAL COSTS

A change in the nature of the problem with which we are concerned calls for a rather more complex kind of analysis than we employed in Chapter III. Until now, the nature of the management of the business and its efficiency could be taken as given, along with the other factors which make up the organization of a business. We were, therefore, almost entirely concerned with technical details of the employment of the more variable factors of production. Any substantial change in the organization of the business, however, will affect the management, which will itself have to change with the changing magnitude of its task. It will, accordingly, be

necessary to pay special attention to management, whose job
it is to run the business, to take decisions, and to supervise
the work of the other factors of production, and distinguish it
from those other non-managerial factors which are here called
' technical factors '.

It will be convenient to start with the effects on costs of
the technical factors of production, since the method of
analysis will bear some resemblance to that used in Chapter
III. We use the idea of the technical costs of production,
but these are not simply the costs of the technical factors
of production, and are defined in a special way, which may
be explained as follows. These technical, non-managerial,
factors of production may be thought of as having given
capacities when they are producing a particular product with
a given specification; their individual capacities being
defined as what they could produce per unit of time if they
were employed ' all out ' at 100 per cent efficiency. Therefore, when a particular quantity of a given product is to be
produced, it would, theoretically, be possible to state what
the non-managerial costs of production would be *if* these
factors of production were being used with the maximum
possible economy, and all of them were working at the
theoretical level of 100 per cent efficiency, allowance being
made for any necessary reserve capacity (in the sense discussed in Chapter III). We shall call this minimum level
of non-managerial costs at any scale of production the *technical
costs of production* at that scale.

This very abstract class of costs of production is introduced because it will help in answering the question how far
a business of a given scale must, *for technical reasons*, operate
at a different level of costs from that of a business working
at a different scale. The *actual* costs of the non-managerial
factors of production in a business which is producing at a
given scale of production will generally exceed their (theoretical) technical costs in so far as they will be working at less
than their maximum degree of efficiency. There is bound

to be some such discrepancy, and it is possible that no business could employ its factors of production at so high a level of efficiency; but any *changes* in these excess costs which occur with changes in the scale of a business may be thought of as the responsibility of management, as involving the efficiency of the business. It is, therefore, convenient to reckon all the excess of actual non-managerial costs of production over the technical costs of production, as we have defined them, as some sort of costs of management, in the sense that changes in these will correspond to changes in the relative efficiency of management. Adding any such excess non-managerial costs to the actual costs of the managerial factors of production — the costs of management strictly defined — we get the *managerial costs of production*, which are, therefore, equal to the whole of the difference between the actual costs of production at any given scale of output and the technical costs of that output.

This chapter will attempt to answer the following questions, in turn: (1) How will the technical costs of production vary with changes in the scale of production? and (2) What effect will such changes in the scale of production have upon managerial costs? In so far as it proves possible to combine the results of these two separate analyses, we shall make generalizations about the behaviour of costs of production as a whole.

TECHNICAL COSTS OF PRODUCTION

As already noted, it will first be assumed that the technical costs of production which are being discussed relate to a newly planned business. The business man planning to produce at a given scale of production will have to decide the quantity of the non-managerial factors of production which will be necessary. In so far as the methods of production are the same whatever the output which is planned (in the sense that each unit of a particular factor is of standard output capacity, and that units of the various factors have to be combined in the same technical manner) the business man will choose, for any particular output, what he regards as the most suitable combination of the factors. He will also, of course, plan to have a certain reserve capacity, but it will be convenient to ignore this for the moment and to discuss only the minimum technical costs which are involved by the given scale-output, apart from any reserves which may be held.

The planned output will call for a definite through-put at each stage of production, and this will be translated into a given task for each type of factor of production. The various types will, of course, have different capacities, so that some factors of production will be able to handle a larger proportion of the final output than will others. It follows that average technical costs of production must fall up to a certain scale of output, which will be the lowest scale at which all the individual factor-capacities will be effectively married one with another. The output at that scale will be the lowest common multiplier of the capacities of the various factors of production which are to be used. Until that output is reached, some of the factors — those with the largest capacities per unit — will be under-employed, and their contribution to the average cost per unit of product would be reduced by an increase in the planned output. This output may be thought of as the optimum scale of a business unit from the point of view of technical costs — on the assumption, it should be repeated, that methods of production are, in fact, not changed by changes in scale.

A business will be able always to produce at this minimum level of costs so long as it increases its scale only by steps which are equal to, or a multiple of, the output of the optimum-sized plant. For intermediate increases of output, costs will rise because the business will have to under-employ some of the larger-capacity factors of production, and the costs of this excess capacity will have to be spread over the smaller output, thus raising average costs. It should, however, be noticed that the discrepancy must become less with increases in the scale of business, because the costs of the excess capacity will be spread over the increasing output. Thus, for example, when a business is too small for the employment of even one optimum combination of technical factors, the costs of the excess capacity will be larger per unit of output than if the business were larger by exactly the output corresponding to one optimum combination.

The conclusion so far is, then, that, provided growth takes place in suitably spaced steps, the average technical costs of production will be constant, despite changes in scale, once the business has reached the minimum size. Even for intermediate growth the average costs will approximate more nearly to the minimum as the scale increases. From the point of view of pricing theory we can, in any case, ignore any excess, over their optimum level, of the average technical costs of production at intermediate stages of growth, for the business will have to reckon with the possibility that its rivals will be producing at, or may be able to grow by stages equal to, units of optimum size. In other words, such excessive costs will be extraordinary costs and will affect the profitability of the business but not the price it will normally quote.

The fact that business men will normally plan to have reserves of equipment, etc., has so far been ignored, and must now be allowed for. Its effect must be to smooth out the irregularities in average costs due to growth by less than optimum steps, raising their level by the costs of those reserves. Even if we assume that the reserves are always proportionate to output, this conclusion will be valid. For, in that case, the capacity involved in producing at intermediate levels of scale which would otherwise be excessive, will at least count towards, and may even absorb, the required reserve capacity, and so will reduce the discrepancy between costs at the different scales. In fact, of course, apart from repairs reserves, which will probably be nearly enough proportionate to total output, owing to the importance of the smaller-scale process machinery in this connexion, the strategic reserves, as they may be called, will probably diminish in proportion to scale; [1] the relative importance of indivisibilities will certainly become less. Therefore, on balance, when the effect of these reserves has been allowed for, the average technical costs of production should not merely not rise as scale increases, they should *fall* somewhat, and accordingly it should be rather cheaper to produce at increasing scales of output.

The discussion so far, however, has assumed that the methods of production remain unchanged as between the different scales. If this assumption is removed, then it will become even more likely that average technical costs will fall with increasing scale. It is, in fact, very difficult to accept the assumption, implied in the idea of *a* technical optimum, that growth will merely mean the redeployment of identical factors of production, the enlarged plant being merely a recombination of the units used at the smaller scale. One might almost accept it as an axiom that, whatever the scale of plant that may be imagined, there must always be further technical economies of production available at *some* still larger scale.

Quite apart from the existence of completely new methods of production, which would lower costs for a sufficiently large scale, but which are not yet known (and the existence of these cannot be presumed, however reasonable it may be to accept them), it does seem probable that there will always be some normal economies to be expected in the operation of at least some of the main processes. For one thing, the larger the output (of the presumed standardized product) going through the works, the more likely it will be that some process could be further mechanized, and that the extra capital invest-

---

[1] An exception may be caused by marketing conditions, with which we are not concerned now, in so far as a large market leader may insist on extra reserves so that it does not lose its leadership.

ment will justify itself in lower average costs for that process at a sufficiently large scale of output.

Further, the introduction and elaboration of mechanical methods, or of increased standardization, in ancillary operations such as internal transport or the design and manufacture of jigs and tools, will usually be possible for some increase in scale. Economies in maintenance and repair are also likely to be available to some extent with an increase in scale. For, whatever the scale of plant, maintenance and repair operations will necessarily be carried out on a comparatively small scale, and a large part will still be in the handicraft stage. Increasing scale, by increasing the runs of repair jobs of particular kinds, will enable some further economies to be made. There seems no reason to suggest that costs of maintenance do anything but fall continuously (although probably not sharply) with increasing scale.

There is a final point tending in the same direction: the business has been assumed to be single-product, but that assumption relates to the end-product, and the business may well make for itself some of the materials or equipment which it needs instead of buying them from other businesses. Continued growth must surely mean that, at some scale, it will become more attractive to do so, when any economies of scale in this new line will be added to those already open to it.[1]

When these factors are taken into account, and the possibility is recognized of the methods of production being changed as the scale increases, the general conclusion must be that technical costs will tend to fall continuously with increases in the scale upon which the business is planned.

---

[1] Of the same kind, perhaps, are the gains from the business undertaking its own research, both that which is devoted to the more effective control of its processes and the more fundamental kinds of research which are as likely to throw up completely new products as to reduce costs. Economies of scale are always expected to be in this field, although the economies of the more fundamental research are, perhaps, not strictly relevant to the single-product business that we have assumed. In terms of our previous assumptions, such gains should, of course, be thought of as causing discontinuity in the *level* of the cost-curve from the point at which they operate, rather than causing it to fall.

The analysis so far does not, however, afford any guide to the rate at which average technical costs are expected to fall. The chief question is whether they will be expected to fall more steeply as the scale is enlarged, or whether they will fall less steeply with increasing scale.

No categorical rule may be laid down, but, except perhaps in industries where the gains from fundamental research appear to be very important (and these can only apply at a very big scale), it would appear to be very probable that the larger the scale from which we start the comparison of costs the less important *relatively* will be the incidence of further technical economies for any further increase in scale, as compared with those that have become available up to the scale in question. The fundamental redesign of equipment, or changes in lay-out and methods of production, which are available at relatively small scales, will give way to the relatively less important development of ' refinements ' such as the mechanization of parts of the individual processes. The more spectacular economies of increased scale will tend to be exhausted first, and the technical economies of still larger scales frequently consist of the further development of what has been done already. In this way, the reduction in the relative strength of technical economies as the plant-scale grows must mean that, at a relatively larger scale, the further economies available will be of greatly diminished significance, and, accordingly, we should expect that, although average costs will fall with increasing scale, they will fall relatively less steeply as the scale increases. The way in which technical economies come about thus seems to rule out decreasing costs of the spectacular kind which the layman often imagines.

It remains to consider the effect on costs of the growth or decline of an ' actual ' business previously in existence at a different scale, as distinct from the costs which would be realized in new businesses planned to operate at various sizes. Up to now the argument has been entirely in terms of the effects of increases in scale of production. It has not been necessary to make a special analysis of what happens if the scale of planning decreases, for the business man could be assumed to be equally free to plan for a smaller as for a larger scale. The conclusions that have so far been reached are, thus, logically reversible : for decreases in scale of planned output we should expect that average technical costs would rise, and that they would rise more steeply the smaller the scale of output that is postulated. When an actual business changes its scale of output, however, the process of decline is not the simple antithesis of the process of growth.

To take the case of growth first, the chief difference from the case of an expansion in the scale of planning for a new business is that the business will now have already invested in some factors of production, particularly in its capital equipment, and will already have taken some decisions about its organization to fit it to a smaller scale. It will not be able to undo all these. In so far as its equipment will have been organized to produce the smaller output, it will have organized the less divisible factors of production in a certain way, so that it has so many units of given capacities. At the new scale it might, if it were completely free, find it more economical to produce with larger-scale units, but, granted that it has already invested in this equipment, it will not pay it to make the change-over, so long as the *paying-out* costs of the old equipment are less than the *average of all* costs associated with the completely new and more suitable equipment. If the equipment in question has a relatively long life, so long will it continue with costs which are higher than the costs which are theoretically open to a business at its new scale of production.

It will similarly tend to have become committed even on the personal side of its organization. This is more susceptible to reorganization, and the fact that all the costs involved have currently to be paid out in actual cash will give an incentive for redeployment which will be stronger than in the case of equipment, so much of whose costs will be 'bygones' and not relevant to current strategy. But it may still have taken on the persons in question for more or less long contracts, and, in any case, it will not always be easy to get rid of persons who served the business well at the smaller scale but who could be dispensed with at a larger scale for which they are less suitable.

However, although the costs will, therefore, tend always to be higher than those which are theoretically applicable for a business freshly planned for the given — larger — scale, it would still not be expected that they would *rise* for increases in scale, provided that those increases take place in appropriate steps, and, in fact, they will probably fall, not only because the reasons put forward when the earlier case was being considered will still apply, but also because of the supposed economies peculiar to this case. The business in question has been *assumed* to have available some technical economies which would be exploited by a business of its own scale which had started from scratch, and it must be able to take advantage of these at some larger scale.[1]

Where a business is reorganized to produce on a *decreased* scale, it is quite certain that its average technical costs will be higher than they would have been if it had come into being in order to produce at that smaller scale, until its equipment has worn out, and, unless it sells off equipment, it will

---

[1] The argument of this chapter is not concerned with the effects of changes in general technical knowledge. These will tend to worsen the position of a business which has already developed at a certain scale, as compared with one coming into existence at that scale. In an industry where technical improvement is continuous, an old-established business will never be so efficient as it might have been in the light of the latest technical knowledge. A larger-scale business will tend to have some advantage over its smaller rivals, and will, therefore, be favoured by technical change. All businesses may be able to introduce changes affecting the details of individual processes, which may be important but which are often minor in their effect, but the smaller business may never be in a position to take advantage of any fundamental changes which call for a complete change of plant or even of lay-out, because it cannot bear the disruption of current production and because such a change will be relatively a big venture. The larger business may be able to do so much more easily, first in what is relatively a piecemeal fashion by the redeployment of a single factory if it is already multi-factory and, otherwise, by reason of its share in any secular increase in demand enabling it to put up a completely new and up-to-date factory, whereas the same proportionate rate of growth will bring no such advantage to the smaller business.

be left with the equipment which it planned to have for a larger size, and it will, therefore, have excess capacity in all departments. Until the original costs of that equipment have been entirely written off by way of cost-charges, its average technical costs must, therefore, lie above the costs of a business designed to operate at the given scale of output, and, even if it does sell off some equipment, it will not be free to get rid of the large-capacity factors of production unless output falls to a sufficient extent to free at least one unit of them. Further, the odds are that the money which it gets from the sale of any second-hand equipment will not be equal to the value at which it stands in the books, so that a loss on capital account may remain to inflate the current cost charges.

Similarly, although the business will be able fairly easily to dismiss direct labour, it may take some time really to cut down its complement of such labour, perhaps at first working relatively inefficiently on short time (because that will not enable it to close down so much plant as it could if it employed fewer people on a more nearly full-time basis). It will be less easy for the business to make a fresh start with the indirect personnel, who will have been engaged for a larger-scale system of organization, and their costs will tend for some time at least to remain at what will be an abnormal high level for the scale at which the business is working.

Since average technical costs are, even for the new business, expected to rise more than proportionately with decreases in scale, the conclusion is, then, that they will tend to rise more steeply for an existing business, even when that has made such readjustments as it can. It should, however, be said once again that such rises in costs are extraordinary costs from the point of view of pricing policy, and will not affect prices so long as the business's market is at all open to competition. The business will simply have to accept the reduced net profit, or increased net loss, which will result from such abnormal costs.

(3) MANAGERIAL COSTS OF PRODUCTION

The Basic Hypothesis

The technical costs of production have been used to sum up the effect of the technical limitations facing the business man varying the scale of his business, whatever the level of his personal efficiency. If he is as efficient as he could possibly be, and if all the factors which he employs in production are working at their maximum efficiency, then he will achieve the technical cost level so far as the non-managerial factors of production are concerned. It is considered that growth would bring his business the advantage of falling costs so far as those factors are concerned, even though the rate at which costs fall will slacken with increasing growth. Technical factors as such, then, offer no obstacles to growth but must, to some extent, encourage it.

The difference between his actual costs of production at any scale and the theoretical technical costs of that scale was defined on page 115 as the managerial costs of producing at that scale. It was shown to consist of two parts : (1) the costs of management proper, in the strict sense of the costs attributable to the function of management, namely, the salaries and expenses of the persons who are engaged in the actual business of management (or such part of these as may fairly be attributed to the time that they spend on management in cases where they perform other duties as well) ; and (2) the excess, over their technical costs, of the actual costs of the non-managerial factors of production (including any allowance for that part of the costs of the ' managers ' which is attributable to the non-managerial functions which they carry out). We, therefore, wish to know in what way the growth of a business is likely to affect the level of these managerial costs.

We can disregard for this purpose the fact that the actual level of these costs will be affected by many different factors, many almost of an accidental nature or quite outside the control of the business man. These factors can be taken for granted, as can any peculiarity about the business man who is running a particular business, and the way in which the level of the managerial costs changes as the business changes its scale may be thought to be affected by the extent to which the fact of growth, in itself, makes the ease of management change for a business man of given personal efficiency.

If managerial efficiency changes, its effect may be shown in either or both of the two elements of managerial costs. Thus, for example, a reduction in the efficiency of a business (defined as a rise in the managerial costs of production, when it organizes itself to produce at a larger scale) may show itself in failure to keep the non-managerial costs down so near to the technical level as was possible at a smaller scale; alternatively, in order to get or keep those costs down, it may be necessary to increase the costs of management proper beyond the level that might otherwise be maintained,[1] or both costs of management and the costs of the non-managerial factors may rise. These two separate types of effect will be distinguished where possible in the following analysis, but the conclusions will be brought together in a single generalization, for the purpose of reaching some conclusions about the behaviour of costs as a whole, including technical costs.

In this analysis we are up against a serious difficulty as compared with the discussion of technical costs. It is not possible for us to state a clear principle, such as was maintained in the analysis of technical costs. The basic factors here involve human nature and its potentialities, and it is not possible to lay down a simple law which can be taken

---

[1] E.g. it may be the case that a certain size of the business turns out to be too large to supervise direct labour as adequately as was possible at a smaller scale, or to encourage it to maintain the same level of productivity. If this is the case, the costs of direct labour may diverge farther from the level which is technically possible ; as an alternative, however, *more* management may make it possible to keep the same level of labour efficiency, but at the cost of a disproportionate rise in the costs of supervision.

as uniformly applicable to the factor of management. Practical researches do lead to some conclusions, but they are about practical details and, at the existing state of knowledge, do not seem to lead to the required postulate for the abstract theory of the growth of a business. We, therefore, plan to proceed on the basis of a hypothesis which we take over from that amorphous repository of practical wisdom — general opinion, as we find it in every-day discussion — but modifying that hypothesis. Even if the hypothesis is not completely valid this will be a useful procedure. For, on the argument of this book, it can be only in the managerial sphere that a business's costs of production will offer an obstacle to growth, and the adoption of this hypothesis will enable us to give full recognition to the effect of any such obstacle. Any conclusions that we come to will then have been given the maximum weight in the direction of pessimism. Some tentative reconsideration of the hypothesis itself will be made in the appendix to this chapter, but it will be most convenient not to let it affect the main analysis.

General opinion seems to be agreed that there is a tendency for the efficiency of management to increase up to a certain size, but that beyond that — usually not very large — scale it will fall, and continue to fall with increasing scale.[1] As has

---

[1] The view is quite common among business men, but as a rule it is generally taken as especially applicable to *other* businesses. Cases may be found of businesses which are unquestionably efficient, where the business man is certainly not at all lazy, and which would appear to be able to grow if the business man wanted that to happen, but where it is said that the size is being kept down to one which is the limit of managerial efficiency. Such cases do, however, appear to be in a minority, and it is rarely that the business man, while asserting the rule, will admit that he has yet reached the dangerous point, provided that it is understood that the further growth of his business does not take place too fast. It is usually thought that the danger would lie some distance ahead beyond the planning horizon of the business man. It must, however, be remembered that managerial costs are not the only elements and that further growth may be justified for technical reasons despite any management difficulties that may be involved. For completeness, it should be recorded that cases appear to be rather more numerous where the business man has deliberately kept his business smaller than it could be, because his business is his way of life, and he likes it that way, with all the fun of really managing it and enjoying his relations with his workpeople.

already been said, in default of sufficient contradictory data (and the efficiency of management as a whole is a very difficult subject on which to reach really firm conclusions) this generally accepted opinion will be taken as the basis for our working hypothesis. But it will be necessary to spend a little time on the question of the exact interpretation of the hypothesis.

The general view of the effect of size on managerial efficiency appears to be compatible with two propositions which do not come to the same thing, and either or both may be involved in any single statement of that view. The first is simply the assertion that, in fact, the larger businesses of the real world *are* inefficient as compared with smaller scale businesses. The statements of this view vary from general statements about the position of labour or of subordinate management to the shrewd comment of one business man, with a medium-sized business, that some of the veritable giants who were producing the same type of good must be surprisingly inefficient when one compared the pitifully small profits which they appeared to make in relation to their comparatively mammoth turnover with the results that his business achieved. This proposition is conveniently dealt with in the appendix, since it is not necessarily in conflict with any proposition denying that such scales of business *need* be, or become, less efficient on the assumptions which are the basis for the present discussion (that the business is single product, and that it operates a single factory, are the most important of these assumptions).

The second proposition which may be thought to underlie popular opinion is that there is a general tendency for the management of a business to become less efficient as the business grows. A reservation is usually made that this occurs at a critical scale that varies with the business man's ability and with the type of product which his business is making. It is this form which is relevant to the analysis of managerial costs as we have defined them, and it will accordingly be

K

taken as the basic hypothesis for our present argument.

This general hypothesis should be carefully distinguished from the proposition that most economic text-books accept — that management becomes increasingly inefficient with the continued growth of a business. Economists have found that the application to the real world of the abstract theory of pure competition requires that long-run costs should rise with increased scale. This has made it easy for the supposition to be accepted in economics that long-run costs do, in fact, rise, and, in the absence of any other plausible explanation as to why they should rise, economists have tended to call in increasing managerial inefficiency as a fairly plausible hypothesis which could not very easily be refuted and which could be justified by assimilating the position of the business man to that of a natural factor of production with a given ' capacity '.[1] This hypothesis of increasing managerial inefficiency was then taken over without much question into the modern analysis of monopolistic competition. The question whether increasing managerial inefficiency is, in fact, a good hypothesis requires some discussion in view of its general acceptance.

The essence of the function of management is decision-taking and the responsibility for seeing that those decisions are observed in practice. The business man may do many other things as well, but they will be such as could theoretically be done by someone else acting under instructions. As a business grows, the field of responsibility of the business man grows with it and he meets that situation by delegating more and more of the tasks which he used to combine with his real job as central decision-taker for the business. At first he will probably not be delegating any of the managerial decision-taking functions, but very soon and at quite a small

---

[1] It should be noted that Mr. Kaldor *has* questioned this general hypothesis as applied to a business operating under completely static conditions, and has asserted that it could be justified only in more complex dynamic conditions. The standard literature on the subject, however, does not recognize Mr. Kaldor's distinction.

stage the business man becomes so specialized that, with subsequent growth in the business, it will be desirable for him to delegate some of the functions of management. The decisions which he must retain in the last resort may be called the policy decisions — these constitute the framework within which the subordinate managers are free to take their own decisions, including the decision that they should refer to the higher management any particular problems which they are free to settle but which involve, as they turn up, matters which more strictly concern central authority.

It is in this way that the growth of a business is most limited — the extent to which decisions can be delegated. To some extent this involves the personality of the business man and is one of the chief factors in his efficiency in a dynamic world. His judgment of Man is involved; the better he is at selecting good men who can be given wide responsibility, including that of deciding when it is necessary to refer back to him, and the better he is at leaving them as free as is necessary for them to exercise that responsibility, the more efficient he will be, and the larger his business will be able to grow without imposing too great a strain upon him.

Economic theory rightly stresses this function of the business man as a decision-taker-in-the-last-resort and ultimate supervisor. This function must remain concentrated upon an individual person. For no matter how skilful he is at evolving a group of associates who 'share' the central functions of management with him, the continuous growth of his business will mean an ever-widening responsibility, which, from the nature of the case, must impinge upon the same personality. So much must be agreed at the start of any theory of management.

Where economic theory appears to go wrong is that it regards the capacity of the business man as being 'given' in the same way as the fertility of a 'given' field, when that is producing a single product with given methods of production. In such a case, increasing output will have to be obtained by increasing the ' doses ' of the other factors of production applied to the limited capacity of the field. It is then presumed as a technological law that, given the fertility of the field, there will be an optimum dosage of the factors of production, up to which point average costs will fall and beyond which they will rise. Correspondingly, there is thought to be a particular size of business up to which a given business man will be able to cope without his capacity to govern the business being overstrained, but beyond which he will be relatively overworked by further growth. Just as the limit to the fertility of a field is considered to entail disproportionate rises in costs as larger crops are wrung from it, so the limitation to the capacity of the business man is represented as causing a continuous and *progressive* rise in managerial costs, as they have been defined here.

Any theory of management must recognize the limitations imposed by the personal capacity of the business man, but the error of the theory which has been condensed into the previous paragraph is just that it treats the way in which that personality is exercised as being as ' given ' as the fertility of a field, and does not recognize that one of the things that a business man may reorganize is the business man. Business has developed techniques of management and systems of organization, and the existence of these is well recognized in practical life as facilitating the growth of a business and *extending* the capacity of the business man. To take up the analogy of the field, it is as though there were available powerful fertilizers, which were suitable for application when a certain output had been reached and which then offset for a time the inherent limitations of natural fertility, but which would be wasted if used below their appropriate output, when they would merely add to costs.

The Idea of Levels of Management

The capacity of the business man must not be considered in terms of a *point* of optimum capacity ; it is necessary to think in terms of *levels* of management, each with its appropriate kind of management technique, and each management technique should be considered as applicable to a *range* of output. The actual scale at which a higher level of management technique can, or should be, applied will vary with the type of business, and really large-scale management will be encountered at a far smaller size of business in one industry than in another, whether size be measured by value of output or by numbers of persons employed. Similarly, in an industry where technical factors make for large-scale organization, a ' small ' business may have a large turnover and need a heavy amount of capital investment, and yet the technique of management, and with it the atmosphere inside the business, may be very much what one finds in a really small business in another industry. Now, a given technique of management will not be something which operates only at a given scale of the business; it will be available over, and suitable for a range of scale.

Changes in the type of management will be called for only at discontinuous intervals, which will vary with the nature of the industry and the personality of the business man. (At any given scale of business, the business man with a greater capacity for management will be operating a relatively smaller-scale technique than a less capable business man.) It seems generally true that those intervals get farther apart with increasing scale, so that each successive change in the technique of management will tend to be suitable for a longer stretch in the growth of a business than was the technique that preceded it.

A hypothetical example may be given: in a particular industry, there may be one system of management available for a plant with, say, up to 100 workers, but not suitable for an appreciably larger business; the next system of management may be applicable to the scale from, say, 90 to 500 workers; the next from 400 to 1200 workers; and any further growth may then require the adoption of a system of management which is applicable to sizes from 1000 to 5000 workers, and so on. The overlaps given in the scales are deliberate; in practice, a system of management will usually be able to extend itself somewhat.

For the purpose of the present theory, we are ignoring the fact that an efficient business man in a growing business will usually plan ahead so as to be ready for any foreseeable necessity to enlarge the management, for it will be better that he should himself have trained the colleagues that will be needed then, making the transition more a matter of natural growth than it would otherwise be. This factor implies, of course, that the management of a business which is growing will usually contain some reserves for further growth.

The Behaviour of Managerial Costs

Within the range of scale which is covered by a given management technique, the actual costs of management in the strict sense will fall, if anything, since the central cadre of management will remain unchanged over the scale-range. The costs of the central management will thus remain relatively fixed, while the costs of the remaining subordinate managers will tend to vary roughly with the size of the business within the scale-range. Near the limit of its appropriate scale-range the management will tend to become stretched, when the managers will have to work harder or the remainder of the business will become less efficiently run. The alternative will be to take on recruits to the central cadre of management, which will then adapt itself to working at a larger scale. As at the beginning of the new scale, then, the costs of management will tend to rise because of the addition of personnel, and then, once again, it would be expected that the costs of management will decrease over the new scale-range. In this way, whatever may happen to the strict costs of management as between the ranges of scale over which management techniques will change, it will generally be the case that they will be falling, over each management scale-range considered separately, and, to this extent, will be a factor making for falling costs over that range of scale.

It should be noted, however, that, as business gets larger, the costs of the central cadre of management will tend to become much less important, measured as a proportion of total costs, than they were when the business was at a smaller scale. The large salaries given to important business executives give a wrong impression when they are not thus related to the business's total expenditure. For example, in one large group of businesses, the total costs of all the central management, including far more than what we have called the central cadre of management, amounted to no more than $2\frac{1}{2}$ per cent of the turnover, and indeed all the costs of management in the strict sense are not generally very large, when one has allowed for the non-managerial jobs done by the managers. It follows that, once a business has become very large, we can almost ignore, for further changes of scale, the question of what happens to costs of management in the strict sense.

What happens to the other element in managerial costs — the ' excess ' costs of the non-managerial factors of production — as the scale of a business changes, after discounting the effects of changes in those costs due to technical reasons ? It seems reasonable to suggest that the business will be able to carry on at much the same level of efficiency over the range of scale which is appropriate to a given level of management. The system of management will be coping with problems that it was organized to meet, and with a technique which has been evolved to deal with them. It follows that, ignoring any tendency for the strict costs of management to fall, the managerial costs may be regarded as likely to be constant *over any given management scale*. In other words, the concept of levels of management techniques has led to the rejection of the normal theoretical notion that management must become continuously less efficient, so far as concerns the separate ranges of scale over which management techniques remain unchanged.

What happens over wider changes of scale, when the growth of the business necessitates changes in the technique of management ? Here we make use of the basic hypothesis that the efficiency of management will rise at first, and then fall when management is too large ; and managerial costs, the concept which sums up the effect of changes in that efficiency, must be thought of as changing correspondingly, falling, down to the size of business which is most easily managed, and then rising. If we write into this hypothesis our concept of levels of managerial technique, with the consequent stability of business efficiency over corresponding ranges of the scale of a business, then managerial costs must be considered to change in a series of plateaux, falling at first and then rising after a point, beyond which each will be higher than its predecessor. The length of the ' plateaux ' will, of course, increase as the scale of business increases, managerial costs being considered to be constant, therefore, over ever-widening ranges of scale.

Even now, one part of the generalization has been left obscure. Granted that it is assumed that managerial costs will rise as between ranges of scale appropriate to higher orders of management technique, once the business has passed a certain size, there is still the question whether that rise will be progressive. Will management continue to get progressively less efficient so that, at the given points of growth, managerial costs will rise more than in proportion to the growth of the business ? Theoretical discussion of this question seems normally to assume that this will be so,[1] as in the analogy of the costs of production from a given field which was stated earlier. This proposition would, however, seem very doubtful. There *may* be a steep rise, once the business gets too large for its personal management by a

---

[1] The long-run cost curves drawn in the modern text-books certainly presume it.

single manager (a point which will vary with the particular industry as well as with the capability of the individual business man), but apart from that it seems most reasonable to suggest that the rate of decrease in efficiency will tend to slow down with successive levels of management, even if the business does continue to get less efficient at each level.

Surely, if, as is assumed in this chapter, the business is producing a single product, the business must have become so organized already at some scale that the adoption of the larger scale will be merely a matter of routine. The management would then be able to carry on with something reasonably near to its previous level of efficiency. The business may lose something in comparison with smaller business in that its government becomes so much a matter of routine that it suffers in not being able to adapt itself quickly to the vagaries of everyday life, but that very routine should carry it along, provided that it is continuing to produce the same product — which is the assumption of this chapter, as well as the normal assumption of the economic theory which appears to reach a different conclusion.

We may summarize the conclusions that have been reached on the hypothesis of decreasing efficiency of large-scale management, to the extent that it has been accepted, as follows: The plateaux of managerial costs, corresponding to the levels of management techniques, will first fall to the level corresponding to the notional optimum size from the point of view of management and then rise, but the rises are thought probably to get proportionately smaller. The reader is asked to remember, when we come to generalize about the behaviour of average costs of production as a whole, that this generalization here incorporates an opinion which, although it does not appear to be at variance with practical experience, remains an opinion. Something will be said about its practical justification in the appendix.

(4) SUMMARY OF CONCLUSIONS

It remains now to summarize the effect of the analysis of this chapter with reference to the average costs of production as a whole, whether affected by technical or managerial considerations. The technical costs were thought to fall continuously with increases in scale, although the fall probably gets less steep as the scale increases. The managerial costs have been thought likely to fall for part of the increase in scale, to rise thereafter, but with diminishing strength. For the present purpose we have to imagine these two sorts of costs being added to get the actual costs of production arising from all factors. Two very broad conclusions seem to follow: (1) that, at a very large scale of output, the costs of production may be thought of as approximately constant whatever the scale. For, once management gets to the size where it really does become a routine, its efficiency will not decrease very much, and, equally, technical costs, although falling, will not fall very much. Even so, if we had not accepted the hypothesis that management does become less efficient continuously with increasing scale, the weight of the technical costs would make for falling average costs, however slight the fall; (2) that, over any scale of management, the weight of the technical factors will make for falling average costs as a whole, so that, with a given technique of management in successful operation, average costs should fall.

So far as concerns price theory, the important thing is the expectation of the business man. In so far as he will not expect to become less efficient just because his business grows — and he will be justified because an expansion does not generally come suddenly and violently, so that he can meet it with some degree of planning — he will be influenced only by the technical costs of production and will expect average costs to fall. The business man will expect an expansion of production to result in lower costs of production and hence, so long as price is not changed, in higher net profits in the long run. This will be an inducement for him to continue to quote any price which he has found justified for a smaller output — i.e. if the price is profitable now it will not be less profitable according to his expectations when once he has fully readjusted himself to produce an increased output. He may, therefore, accept any short-run rise of costs necessary to hold the expansion of his market until he can readjust.

APPENDIX TO CHAPTER IV

SOME NOTES ON MANAGERIAL EFFICIENCY

In Chapter IV the common opinion that business management tends to get less efficient with increasing size was taken as the basis of our working hypothesis — that managerial costs would fall over the early stages of the growth of a business, but that beyond this optimum scale, from the point of view of management, managerial costs would rise continuously, as between successive levels of management. This Appendix will consider the extent to which this general hypothesis is acceptable in the light of empirical research.

The first part — that managerial costs fall over the early stages of business growth — appears to have great validity. It seems that in any industry, in practice, some sizes of business are too small for efficient management, the managers being too little specialized. For example, at very small scales, even the central cadre of management will be too much engaged on process work and other non-managerial duties. Apart from this almost technical matter of the scale at which managers can give specialized attention to their duties, the small business has a positive advantage in its labour relations, and the efficiency of labour tends to be higher and more consistently maintained in a business which is small enough for them to know their ' boss ' and for him to know them as individuals or to be readily accessible to them.

The absence of this is the chief cause of the change in the ' atmosphere ' that one notices in moving from a business which is at most medium-sized to one which is really large-scale, employing large-scale methods of management. In the very large business the subdivision of the functions of management tend to make the central management rather remote from the individual workers. This problem is, of course, especially important in multi-factory businesses, and the large single factory does not appear to suffer to the same extent.

The great importance of the problem of labour relations in the large business at present has, of course, been connected with the collapse of the money incentive as a sure key to the efficiency of labour, and with the weakening of the fear of dismissal in a period of fairly full employment. It should, however, be noted that large businesses have become very much aware of the problem and many of them are making interesting experiments. It is certainly not beyond hope that newer techniques of management may produce a very great reduction in the disadvantage of the large business in its relations with its workers, especially when we reckon in the newer spirit in management during our generation, which has both produced these experiments and been fostered by them.

It seems generally true also that the efficiency of management tends to be lower beyond a medium scale as compared with smaller businesses, because large-scale management is not so easy or so immediate in its connexions with the details of the business, quite apart from any difficulties affecting the organization of labour. The stage where this happens will vary greatly between industries; in some it will occur at a much smaller scale than in others where the problem of management is much less complex. It is difficult in practice to separate out the effect of marketing factors from others arising more strictly on the production side, so it will be necessary to leave until later a discussion of the various reasons why large businesses are or seem to be relatively inefficient in practice, whether or not that inefficiency is a consequence either of size or of growth. Meanwhile, granted this postulated tendency for the efficiency of management to fall beyond a certain size, the question which is raised by the hypothesis used in the main part of this chapter is whether the position *necessarily* gets worse as management proceeds to still larger scales. No final judgment can be given in the present state of knowledge, but the kinds of inefficiency that one meets in practice, however inevitable they may seem, are often not caused by the simple facts of growth or size as such.

One way in which managerial costs may rise is more associated with the growth of business, but is outside the assumptions that have been made so far, in that the capacity and interest of the business man have been presumed to remain unchanged throughout the changes of scale. This will be likely enough for an

established business making growth at a normal rate, but it does
not apply in the case of the more spectacular development of a
business under what may be called the founder personality —
whether he be revivifying an old or founding a virtually new
business. Like any other man he will grow older, and his
efficiency in his business is likely to be affected, quite apart from
any decrease in vigour due to age, which is often unimportant for
the type of personality which is being imagined.

A young man may, at first, be completely absorbed in the
business which is his child, but gradually, as he acquires family
and other responsibilities, he will have to give some attention to
them. The best of wives will not unnaturally expect that one
consequence of business success will be that the business man
does not put in quite such long hours at the factory, when some
of his work could be lightened by taking on extra managerial
personnel. In this way the costs of management will rise, even
if the efficiency of the business does not otherwise suffer from the
devolution of responsibility. Secondly, a mature business man
who is good enough to have been really successful soon finds that
he is expected to play his part in the society he lives in. The best
type is quite ordinarily fairly heavily engaged in work for or in
the community in which he lives. The work for local hospitals,
for church or chapel, for political parties, and for other local or
national organizations, done by leading business men is negligible
neither in its amount nor in its value to the community, but has
not been sufficiently recognized perhaps, surprisingly obvious
though it may be to an independent observer moving around
industrial areas. In this way the successful business man who can
afford such social service will find himself called upon to use his
talents outside his factory, will not normally wish to refuse to do
so, and the consequence must be some devolution of management
and some diminution in the work which he puts directly into his
business, even though his actual supervision may be as live as
ever.

It should perhaps be said that the efficiency of a business
which has shown vigorous growth is usually high enough to bear
with the increasing costs of management which may arise in the
ways indicated in the previous paragraph, and such businesses
do not usually become inefficient as compared with their rivals,
even though their costs may be higher than what they would have
been if the business man had continued to drive himself in their

exclusive service with all his old vigour. When the business loses the ' founder personality ' there may be a more serious fall in efficiency. This is a more general problem.

A person managing a business of a given size has usually a good idea of how to run it (as efficiently, in his expectation) at a relatively larger size. One does not usually hear many complaints about changes in the efficiency of a business which is growing — even growing at a rapid rate — while the same person is effectively in charge of it. He will have evolved a system of management which is personal to himself and will extend that quite naturally to suit himself. Quite frequently, however, when this key person goes, it is very difficult for his successor to maintain the same system. He will not know the subordinate personalities in the same way; the limits of their freedom of action will not be a matter of working convenience which has grown up with him. It is often the easier way out for him to adopt a technique which would otherwise have been appropriate only for a definitely larger scale of the business (perhaps settling some of the personal jealousies involved in the succession by the consequently greater importance of the subordinate managers), thus making management more of a formal routine than it was under his predecessor. The costs of management may, therefore, rise as the easiest way for the new personality to control the business, and managerial costs as a whole may rise because the greater complexity of management is not effectively matched by genuinely needed specialist managers having to extend themselves in their job.

These examples emphasize the limitation of static economic theory. The actual growth of a business is not a timeless affair, but takes place in time — the lifetime of a business man. Within the strict assumptions of normal theory, and imagining the costs of businesses of different scales, it is difficult to accept as absolutely certain the assumption that business must grow continuously less efficient. We refused to accept the assumption that it must get progressively less efficient. The general argument in the main body of the chapter has been that, even if the everyday belief that businesses get less efficient as they grow is accepted, this will not be true for whole stretches of growth, but only as that growth causes the business to pass from one management technique to another (and we have also argued that any inefficiencies of management will always be offset to some extent by technical economies of scale, which may be large in some industries even if they are not important everywhere). Discussing this conclusion on other occasions, it has been found that there is frequently some reluctance to accept it. One reason appears to be a relative dislike of big business and a preference for small units as such, which many share. The conclusion, therefore, appears unacceptable, because it offers no resistance to the-bigger-the-better school, and seems consistent with political changes making for ' regimentation ' on an increasingly large scale, with the narrowing of the opportunity for individual enterprise which seems important in the politics of a democracy, however inefficient it may be alleged to be as a matter of economics.

Here it can be argued only that this aspect of the matter concerns political rather than economic analysis, and our argument merely implies that the growth of a business producing a single commodity in a single place *need* not involve higher costs (ruling out any changes in the prices of factors of production) once it has reached a moderately large size ; practical conclusions for economic policy must rest upon the practical details of every case, and are not susceptible to theoretical examination in the large.

To some extent, however, the resistance to the conclusions outlined here is, or is believed to be, grounded on fact — that big businesses are believed to be markedly less efficient than smaller businesses. Now, the argument given in this chapter was conducted upon rigid assumptions — e.g. that a business is single product, and that it is producing that product in a single place ; those assumptions have been made, and the conclusions are required, not for their own sake as settling or pretending to settle the practical question of the pros and cons of large business as we actually find it, but because those are the assumptions which most appropriately uncover the factors which are important in the theory of the determination of prices. They are also useful for the analysis of the consequences of the expansions or contractions in a business's market for a single product considered by itself. The big practical question whether big business, *as we find it*, is necessarily inefficient as compared with smaller organizations cannot be settled merely by the theoretical analysis of the few simple factors whose understanding may be sufficient for the narrower theoretical purposes of this book. It needs a more complex theory, which will have to be grounded upon the details of empirical research — and considerably more empirical data will need to be available than we have so far had.

At the same time, it is a fact that, in any industry, it is generally possible to find a smaller business apparently competing quite successfully with a larger rival. Even in industries where the technical economies of scale are known to be important, cases may be found of businesses which ought to be much too small yet surviving profitably alongside bigger businesses, which do not seem to be taking anything that could be called monopoly profits. In these cases, the quick judgment is that the large-scale business has not justified itself in view of its opportunities, and that its inefficiency can be attributed to the weakness of large-scale management.

The discussion of this question, however, is better left over till a later stage, since it involves not only management but marketing strategy, which is properly the concern of the next chapter. Management factors are so mixed up with marketing factors that the matter cannot be written off as simply as might be suggested by the apparent facts of higher costs, or costs which are not so low as they should be. In Chapter VII we return to the theory of growth and scale, and a discussion of the factors affecting the survival of different-sized firms will be found there (p. 266). There our argument will be that economies of scale are not so sensational as might appear; that the bigger firm, as compared with the smaller, has to be less specialized, to be multi-factory, to have higher quality standards, a more stringent policy as regards depreciation and obsolescence, and to spend more on research, besides any question of lethargy, red tape or extravagance arising from inefficiency in management.

Practical research shows that there are diseconomies of large-scale management, but often they turn out to be illusory. A relatively medium-sized business has advantages from the management point of view, and it must be conceded that in some industries the disadvantages of exceeding some moderate scale are very great. What remains in doubt is the extent to which further growth necessarily penalizes an already large business. Even if it should be thought that this must occur, it does not follow that inefficiency goes unchecked (recognizing that technical advantages of large size may in this respect compensate for managerial disadvantages, since it is the efficiency of the business as a whole that is relevant). The general argument of this book, and especially of the next chapter, is that normal economic forces impose some limit on the extent to which a business can wander in the

L

direction of inefficiency, and that forces which are external to the business will tend to eliminate the inefficient business man if he does not mend his ways. Those forces can be increased by social action strengthening the power of the smaller business to grow and to compete with the larger, old-established business.

CHAPTER V

MARKETS AND PRICES: PART I
THE SALES-MARKET

(1) INTRODUCTORY: THE IDEA OF A MARKET

BUSINESS activity begins and ends in markets, hiring or buying the goods and services it uses, and, at what is logically a later stage, selling its product to its customers. Between these two marketing activities comes that of manufacture or processing, which is mainly a matter of the internal organization of the business. Its marketing activities more directly involve its environment. This chapter will consider the sales-market — the market for the product — and the theory here falls naturally into two parts, the first dealing with the determination of normal prices, the second discussing the situations when normal price policy will not apply.

The sales-market of an individual business consists of all the people who are sufficiently aware of its product to consider buying it. It is necessary to disregard one type of market, the study of which has, perhaps, too much coloured the associations of the word 'market' — that of the great commodity markets of the world, where undifferentiated natural products are sold at uniform prices reached through the 'higgling' of buyers and sellers. There it is a matter of chance whether the product of any particular individual producer is sold to any particular buyer, and any such producer may be described as selling to the market as a whole, which he shares with all other producers of his type of good.

When studying manufacturing business, it is most useful to recall the more primitive association of the word — the market-place. Thinking of that leads to a mental picture of a gathering of people for the purpose of buying and selling, with a definite group of people turning over the wares, comparing prices and considering whether or not to purchase a particular product from a particular stall at a particular price, and with an equally definite group of people who sell in such a market, placing their goods where they will be considered by the possible buyers who are on the market. Such markets still exist, of course, but their importance has dwindled as the growth in the scale of business and its more intense localization have increased the physical distances between factories and their customers. Even if this older type of market is no longer typical, however, it does give the chief characteristics of the market for a manufacturing business.

At any given time, the market will consist of a fairly definite group of people. Indeed, at the very start of a business, the business man has to make up his mind what classes of customer he will try to reach, and his decisions will result in his getting into touch with particular individuals. Once his business has been established, the people who will at all regularly consider the purchase of the product will be a quite definite group, so much so that in many cases it would be possible to list by name nearly all the buyers or potential buyers, and these will usually be a smaller group than all the buyers of that particular kind of product.

Any given buyer at any one time will normally look first at the product of those manufacturers from whom he has been in the *habit* of buying. Such habits are to an important extent rational. The product of a particular manufacturer will be bought either on the basis of a sample or on that of a written specification, but what that means in practice can be determined only by experience of the particular business concerned. Even given the actual product as it is purchased, the service which is, so to speak, built into it is not obvious, even to the most discerning eye. Therefore, experience which brings satisfaction will also bring the habit of purchase, and relative unwillingness to look elsewhere. To such obviously rational preferences, of course, must also be added preferences which are, perhaps, less rational, of the kind which arise whenever men have continued social relations with one another — an important factor being the sheer liking to continue to do business with the same set of people.

At this point, the reader with a knowledge of modern economic theory may well be asking where all this is tending, and if it is not true that buyers' preferences are well recognized in established doctrine, with its recognition of business as a world of monopolies, in place of the older notion of a market in common for all the producers in a competitive industry. The separability of the individual market *is* a fact, but it will be argued that the markets are separable for most businesses in a different way from that described in modern theory.

Normally, the differentiation of markets on the basis of consumers' preferences is seen as involving the following pattern of demand behaviour: (1) at any given price of a product, the fact of consumers' preferences will cause the market of its producer to be differentiated from those of the other producers against whom he is selling his goods; (2) at that price, he can extend his market, given the prices quoted by other producers, only if he incurs selling outlays, of which the genus type is usually taken to be advertising; (3) if the producer raises his price while other producers' prices are unchanged, he will lose some of his demand but will retain the custom of those who prefer his product even at the higher price; similarly, if he lowers his price, he will attract some custom away from his rivals, but he will not take all their customers away from them, unless his price reduction is so substantial as entirely to counterbalance the preferences of all their customers (all this presumes the applicability to such a market of a demand curve, in technical language, of less than infinite elasticity).

This argument may be formally correct in terms of the

short-run situation, in the consumers' market proper, to which it really relates; it yet gives a wrong impression of the long-run situation, which is what matters to the producer who has set up a business, and is not, ' spiv '-like, concerned only with the short-run advantage of casual dealings. For, in the end, even consumers' preferences are not so irrational that a lower price will not progressively attract custom, unless the higher-price seller is offering such an additional service that the customer considers it worth while paying the extra. The question of selling costs, and, in particular, advertising, will be dealt with at the end of this chapter. The chief examples of demand built up entirely upon irrational preferences secured by heavy advertising are largely in the quasi-medical field, where people's fears and superstitions make them a prey to suggestive advertising; but this type of commodity, on which so heavy a part of the total weight of present-day advertising is concentrated, is responsible for but a small part of total output.[1] On reflexion, one is not so impressed with the applicability of this sort of case to the majority of consumers' goods as sold to the final user. There are, too, as we shall see, other reasons for thinking that the usual analysis gives a misleading impression, even in the consumers' market, of the sort of buyers' preferences to which the admitted fact of consumers' preference tends, and that long-run demand is sensitive to price.

(2) THE MARKET FOR THE TYPICAL MANUFACTURING BUSINESS

The picture of this kind of differentiation gives a totally wrong impression of the nature of the market for a typical

---

[1] It may be observed that the uncertainties of the position from the point of view of the producer of such goods has, no doubt, been responsible for the growth of amalgamations and hence to a measure of rationalization, which, although it may leave the preferences of the consumer as insubstantially based as they are alleged to be, will yet limit the total amount of resources squandered in competitive advertising.

manufacturing business, by applying to the behaviour of a manufacturer's customers generalizations which were constructed to describe the behaviour of private consumers spending their income in the purchase of consumers' goods. The typical customer of a manufacturing business is another business, not a consumer of the conventional kind. This will obviously be true for the goods which cannot by their nature be sold to private consumers, e.g. the maker of flour-milling machinery, or of semi-manufactured goods such as tanned hides, and the sales of such goods are not a negligible part of the total output of business. Even in consumers' goods proper, it is *not* typical for the manufacturer to sell to the final consumer. He will deal with the latter directly only if he is making bespoke articles (e.g. the hand-tailor of garments). The consumer is normally reached through the medium of the retail shop, but, before that stage is reached, the good may be sold to the wholesaler. In the typical case, the next stage in the distribution of the product after it has left the factory is a separate business, making its living on its own feet by reselling in competition with other outlets the goods that it has bought.

In some commodities it has become common for the manufacturer to have his own retail shops. But even where this happens, it is often true that such retail outlets do not sell only the product of their own factory, and genuinely buy on a competitive basis, in so far as the retail side will be free to substitute orders to other suppliers, if it finds that it can get similar goods more cheaply than from its own factory. That factory, of course, may have a genuine advantage, in so far as it may be able to run at an unusually high and steady level of output and thus keep at lower costs than any competing suppliers, but this is essentially an advantage which will hold only at lower prices.

Even where the retail organization sells only the product of its own factory, it must not be forgotten how important a say in the policy of any business is given to the sales side.

The salesmen will realize only too well that *they* are selling against other businesses, however much the factory management may feel in a sheltered position. They will have a vigorous say in the price policy of the business and will soon make themselves felt if they find that they are being handicapped [1] by factory costs which must be out of line with the prices at which their competing retailers can buy. This is not to deny that businesses have been known to become complacent in such positions, and there are correspondingly many instances of their reaping the natural reward of shrinking business and losses until the position at the factory end has been cleaned up in one way or another, the financial consequences for the business giving the necessary stimulus to action in the end.

Where the customer is a genuinely independent business, which is the case for the greater part of manufacturing turnover, it has been admitted that irrational preferences *will* exist, in that, besides the rational preferences referred to earlier, human conservatism will tend to keep dealings with the accustomed sources of supply. These 'irrational preferences' should, perhaps, be referred to in a little more detail, in order to show how their consequences differ from those which are generally assumed.

It will certainly be true that a newcomer to business will see the established businesses as firmly entrenched in *their* markets; that is why goodwill is valuable. He will usually have great difficulty even in getting his products tried. The existing buyers will normally have a number of manufacturers with whom they have dealt in the past, will look first at their goods, and will not look at his unless he can offer a sufficiently large price reduction to make the change-over worth all the risks involved — and such substantial price reductions are rarely possible. The new business can get established

[1] In many consumers' goods those which are higher in price have often to be sold through quite different channels in smaller quantities at a time and with greater expense. It may thus be impossible to make a significant change of price without totally changing the type of distribution.

only gradually, by persistence in looking for outlets where it does not compete so directly with the established businesses, and, perhaps even more important, by taking advantage of any temporary pressure upon supplies in a trade boom to meet orders when existing businesses are having to delay deliveries. New entry is, for this reason, relatively more easy in the industries which have heavy seasonal booms. Even though it may still take time for the new business to get its share of the steady trade, it can at least get its goods tried during the rush periods, and may thus begin to build up some goodwill.

This difficulty of entry was vividly illustrated in a conversation with a manufacturer who was discussing the future of his son, going from the University into the business which the father had built up. He said : ' My son will have a much easier time than I had. When I started up on my own, I spent days in every month tramping round the country with my samples, and, although I knew and pleaded that they were good value, it was a long time before the buyers would look at them seriously. They would be quite polite, would say that they were sure that the samples were all right, but that they were satisfied with their existing suppliers, who looked to them for orders. I gradually built up my market, at first by finding one or two lines on which I could specialize, and by being willing to take any odd orders which might turn up. Then, in very busy times, I began to get orders from buyers who were waiting delivery from businesses who were held up for deliveries, and gradually they began to deal more regularly with me. So I began to get my share of the business which was going, and the quality of what I offered brought me more business. Now when my son goes round, he will find people who will know of him, and who will give him that preference which was denied to me until I had earned it.' The father went on to stress that he thought that his biggest difficulty would be to see that his son realized his good fortune, and that, in the long run, the market had to be kept as it was got, by service, so that one could not sit back and take it for granted.

These preferences for established trade connexions are thus very strong, but none of them will stand for long if the seller is quoting a price which is higher than that at which similar goods can be bought from another business. Of course, it sometimes happens that an aged buyer keeps too long to his established connexions, but buyers are mortal. There are too many business men who tell stories of how an old customer changed his custom when a new buyer was appointed, for it to be assumed that irrational favours last. A new buyer will always look around and make certain that he could not do better than his predecessor. To some extent the new broom will sweep clean just because it is new, but the strength of the representations made by displaced suppliers will usually ensure that new suppliers are not taken on *against* the advantage of the business concerned.

Even where inefficiency in buying exists, it can continue only on the basis of small differences in price. If the differences are significant, the consequences of these ' irrational ' preferences will show themselves too directly in the profit and loss account to be ignored. The business-man customer, as distinct from the consumer-customer of the text-books, has, in this way, an ever present check on the cost of any preferences that he may have, and one which will be much more sensitive than anything that can be assumed for the final consumer. He will not usually be ignorant of the opportunities which he has for buying elsewhere. Frequently he will not have all his eggs in one basket, but will be buying some goods — even if only specialities — from other businesses who could make the particular product that he is already buying from any one business. In any case, he will know of the existence of other businesses which are already established, whether he trades with them or not, will know a good deal about their reputation, and will generally have an idea of the prices that they are quoting.

The reader whose economic experience is coloured by the ' sellers' ' markets of war-time and post-war shortages will probably have realized that such circumstances are regarded as abnormal. When a buyer cannot get enough materials to satisfy his business, which in turn has queues of customers who will take the product at a price giving normal margins on abnormal costs, he will not lightly give up any source of supply. He will have difficulty in getting supplies from those with whom he has not ordinarily dealt. In these times trade tends to continue to run through the ' ordinary channels ', and existing business men may get an illusion of their being embedded in their markets, instead of their having customers who prefer to deal with them so long as there is no disadvantage in so doing. However, in established businesses the situation will be seen for what it is,[1] which is why there is so strong a reluctance to exploit the situation.

The general situation, then, is that, so long as its price is right, an established business will have a more or less clearly defined market, and will be protected from the efforts of would-be competing businesses to cut into that market. It will extend its market by offering better service at its price, thus building up a reputation. Its market will, equally, contract if the business fails to offer as good a service as competitors offer at the given price — in this way the complacency of an old and well-established business may easily lead to a decline in its position, perhaps several generations after its foundation. But the necessity that the business should quote the right price will be paramount, and the right price in the long run cannot be higher than its competitors would quote.[2]

The manufacturing business will know that it cannot long

---

[1] The older business men sometimes get worried about the attitudes of younger colleagues, or rather the possible effect on their attitudes, of the easy times of a sellers' market.

[2] It is not necessary that there should be a large number of *actual* competitors. In fact, if the business man's price policy is right, the entry of newcomers into his market will be discouraged.

continue to get a price which, quality for quality, is higher than the customer would get elsewhere. The business man will have to face competition not only from businesses who are already established and producing his type of goods; there will also be the potential competition of newcomers, to whom the possibility of being able to quote a lower price, or to secure an unusually generous margin of gross profit at the existing price, will seem to afford a guarantee that in the end they would get established and would be able to carve out a share of the market from those who are already in the industry.

In the long run, then, demand is very sensitive to differences in prices, and even a well-established market will give no protection against the competition of those who are able to quote a lower price for the same quality product with the same level of associated services. The business man thinks in terms of a right level of price, to pass which would mean that he would have the ground cut from under his feet and lose his market through the encroachment of other businesses, and that it would be only a matter of time before this happened, no matter how securely he may be established. It may, perhaps, be objected that this is no reason why he should not try how high he can put the price, cutting it at once, as it has been stated that he will, if interlopers begin to encroach on his market at their lower price. He would do this, of course, but he will not be anxious that this situation should arise. Markets, once lost, may very well not come back for some considerable time, even if the price is lowered again.

To get the right picture of this sensitiveness of the market, it must be realized that the business-man buyer may have preferences but that he is not ordinarily ignorant, or, if he is, it is not for the want of trying to get any information that will bear on his business conditions. Generally speaking, the buyer will not give his favour exclusively to a single business without at least knowing what prices are like from other businesses, whose salesmen will be approaching him anyway (and with especial eagerness if they have reason to think that they can undercut his usual sources of supply). The business-man buyer will be well aware that faulty buying will in the end endanger his business, and its effects on his market will usually give him danger signals.

A business man will, all the time, be forming impressions of what is happening to the market — or, strictly, group of markets — for the kind of product that he sells, and he has many sources of information, ranging from what his salesmen pick up in the places where they meet others, and from what buyers tell him, to the impressions that he gets from other business men in his industry, and such wider sources of information as the trade papers. He will argue that, unless there is something wrong, his share of the total trade should expand at least at the same rate as the total, and he will hope and 'drive' to do better. In the same way, he will not expect his market to contract at a sharper rate than the total trade in his type of goods. There will, besides, always be particular businesses with whom he will expect to keep abreast, and about them he will usually be well informed.[1]

Any impression that he is losing ground will soon cause the business man to ask why, and he will quickly discover if the reason is some unavoidable peculiarity of his particular market, such as the geographical location of his customers — e.g. a business man selling consumers' goods mainly to the industrial North would expect his total sales in the trade cycle to fluctuate more than the sales for Great Britain as a whole. He will probably have rules of thumb, or at least hunches based upon experience, which allow roughly for such peculiarities. If he finds reason to suspect that he is meeting finer prices, he will have ways of checking up on that, and his usually very fair impression of the efficiency of his rivals will soon cause him to suspect the existence of any

[1] It is worth noting here that the author has had a valuable guide in the selection of particular businesses for detailed study from what *other* business men have told him about their characteristics, and would pay tribute to the generally high standard of accuracy of the information that he was thus given.

more favourable opportunities of buying that they may have discovered.

It will not be only his immediate rivals that he will watch in this way. His natural interest in whatever he can find out about his industry and business in general will keep him fairly well informed, and he will always be interested in what is happening to other businesses, even if they are not ordinarily in competition with him, especially if they use the same sort of materials or other factors of production. For example, part of the interest of a shopkeeper's holiday appears to be looking at other shop windows, especially in the same line of trade, and noting prices as well as other features of interest, such as window displays, and so on. In such ways he gets a check upon what is happening outside his immediate horizon, and it may be noted that this sort of check upon prices, casual though it may be, causes information to pass from one apparently separate market to another, and is a real deterrent against a manufacturer quoting different prices to customers in the same broad class. For, since they will be working on very similar gross margins, their prices will tend to differ accordingly, and, sooner or later, the manufacturer can expect to feel the backwash of the less-favoured customer.

This is also one of the reasons for a manufacturer of branded consumers' goods finding it desirable to fix the reselling price and to see that it is maintained. Such goods will otherwise be tempting to the price-cutter. Selling a nationally advertised product at prices which are notably low is not only good for trade in that article; it may also be used as a magnet to attract custom to other lines, where the usual margin is maintained. Such price-cutting was a normal policy before the war in the case of some departmental stores, with their heavy overhead costs, situated in the centres of provincial towns. When times were bad, the known availability of such things as branded biscuits, sold cheaply, perhaps at cost or even less, could be used to draw regularly the week-end shoppers to the stores.   In these circumstances, the supplier of the goods which thus appear at strangely low prices, knows that, sooner or later, he will get a strong inquiry from the customer who thinks himself unjustly treated, which may be settled by the sight of the invoice, but which will leave an atmosphere not tending to encourage the stocking of the goods in question by other sellers who cannot cut prices to the same extent.   There will be a more general discussion of the question of price maintenance at a later point in this chapter, and it will be convenient to leave over any consideration of where the public interest may lie.

(3) THE DETERMINATION OF PRICE

The Normal Cost Principle

The business man's conviction that, in the possibly-not-so-long long run, his demand will be very elastic if he charges too high a price, will lead to his charging what he believes to be the right price, and then meeting the demand of his market at that price up to the limit of his production capacity.   He fixes that price by adding a definite margin to his estimates of the average direct costs of producing a particular article. We shall call this margin the costing-margin, to distinguish it from the realized gross profit margin shown in the trading account, but these two margins will have some sort of equivalence.   The costing-margin may well differ from product to product in the case of a multi-product business, but the weighted average of the costing-margins will be equal to the realized gross profit margin so long as the realized circumstances do not differ from those that were implicitly assumed in the costing-margins.   The first condition for their equivalence is that the business man actually get the prices that have been quoted on the basis of his costing-margins.   The realized average price of his actual output will be lower if there are any falls in the prices of raw materials, so that the consequent stock write-offs affect the revenue.[1]   In very seasonal trades, such write-offs may be an important cause of the manufacturer charging as costing-margin a very much higher figure than he will get, or expect to get, in his realized gross profit margin when end-of-season clearance sales have occurred.

The realized gross profit margin will also diverge if the level of average direct costs differs from that estimated in the costings.   Quite apart from the case where the prices of materials or labour may have risen or fallen while the manufacturer was still fulfilling contracts based on his earlier costings (which will be taken into account in fixing future prices), there will always be divergences of the kind that may be ascribed to chance.   There is one further reason why the average direct cost of labour may change — if the business man is working at such a level of activity that he has to employ his labour overtime.   Then, as we have seen, the average direct cost of labour will rise.[2]   Such overtime will not be allowed to affect the costing-margin in normal circumstances, for there would then be a danger of the business's price being undercut by competitors who are not working overtime, or of the larger costing-margin making entry into the market more attractive to newcomers.

The application of his costing rules and the resulting costing-margin will yield the business man what we shall call his costing price, and he will quote that price as a rule, never quoting above it in normal circumstances,[3] and going

---

[1] If the accounts are drawn up in such a way as to separate factory costs from these charges, then, of course, such falls in stock values will not affect the size of the gross margin shown as realized *before* bringing their effect into account.

[2] Similarly, it will rise with the working of short-time, if the existence of a guaranteed week prevents the standing-off of prime cost labour.

[3] I.e. ruling out abnormal situations such as war-time, when there is virtually no possibility of competitors appearing, and when all his existing competitors may, like himself, be producing all that they can produce or are allowed to produce. In many cases the intervention of governmental authorities will expressly limit his costing-margin so that the situation cannot arise anyway. Even where this does not happen, the business man will be very reluctant to depart from his normal price policy, as was shown in a good many instances during the last

below it only when the competition of others convinces him that he has made a mistake in the rightness of his costing rules. The costing-margin, and with it the business man's price, will thus be arrived at by competition or, in the case of a business man producing what he believes to be a unique product, by his idea of the margin at which he would, in the long run, have to face competition. It may formally be reached by quite elaborate calculations on the basis of existing costs, or it may be given by rule of thumb, but the consequences will be the same, in so far as, in either case, the level of the business-man's average direct costs will determine his quoted price, which will lie a definite distance above those costs for an individual article produced by a particular individual business.

The costing rules may very well differ for different products within the same business or for the same sort of product between different businesses (which does not mean that such businesses will quote different prices, see p. 169) but will tend to remain unchanged in any particular case. Even in the case of the most detailed costing rules, there will be at least some element of rule of thumb, even if it is only in the allowance for net profit. In some cases the costing-margin itself may be simply determined as a proportion of direct costs, by some sort of rule of thumb which has been evolved on the basis of experience, and which will be revised only if circumstances change so as to make it obviously wrong. Such simple proportionate rules will be used in the case of very small, rather multi-product, businesses, e.g. jobbing plumbers, and in other cases where the precise imputation of overhead costs would be impossible and any attempt be merely another convention in disguise. They

---

war. Inflationary conditions sometimes made it very difficult for the business man to stand out, in so far as his retail customers, whose quantity turnover was restricted by rationing, might desire to sell higher-priced goods in order to sustain their money turnover. One reason why business men on the whole co-operated so well with the war-time controls was because these fitted in with their instinct for the right normal policy.

will also be used in the business man's first rough calculations, whether or not it is worth producing a particular article at a given price, or what price he might quote for a particular product.

Even the most elaborate methods of calculating the normal cost price will be misleading, if we think that the business man is thereby assuring that he will cover his costs at every particular moment, ' plus an allowance for net profit generally of the order of 10 per cent ' as undergraduates sometimes say (completely misreading the effect of the summary which they quote from the article by Hall and Hitch [1] — the first reference in economic literature to this pricing practice of businesses). We must distinguish two kinds of cost calculations. Cost accounting proper, which is a comparatively recent development, makes a careful allocation of all the costs of operation so that a business man can use his accounting records as a valuable guide to his control of his business.

Cost accounting has become a most valuable weapon in the case of the modern large multi-product business, especially where the directors are rather remote from the day-to-day operations ; such accounting then gives them figures on which they can keep a careful eye, ask questions and take active steps, without waiting for the end of the financial period when quite a lot of milk may have been irretrievably spilt. Cost accounts will also help in the explanation of the financial results of the final accounts, showing, on the basis of the assumptions which they make about the way in which the overhead costs should be imputed to particular products,[2] how the net profit which the business has earned has emerged from the production and sale of what is perhaps a large number of products with differing specifications.

Where such cost accounting exists, it will, of course, tend to be used by the business man as a basis from which to

---

[1] *Oxford Economic Papers*, No. 2, May 1939, Hall and Hitch, ' Price Theory and Business Behaviour '.

[2] Note that this *is* a matter of assumptions, and not the precise and ultimate truth which it is sometimes naïvely thought to be.

reach his costing-margin and his normal cost price, but this is a quite distinct matter, which has been indicated by the use in this chapter so far of the word 'costing' to denote the operating of 'costing up' which is involved in the calculation of the normal price. It is an estimate referring to the future, whereas the other is a backward-looking assessment.

THE SPECIAL CASE OF CONVENTIONAL AND FIXED PRICES

It is very convenient to discuss the theory of the sales market, as has been done so far, in terms of a business man fixing his price for a product with a given specification. The business man will, however, see his problem in different terms in the case of many consumers' goods, for he will often be working to a fixed selling price, and will then have to decide the specification of the article that he will produce at that price.

Perhaps the most important cases where this happens are where the market has come to deal in prices which are fixed by convention rather than by deliberate policy. Before the inflationary conditions of war made the system unworkable, many consumers' goods which were in sufficiently general consumption as to be likely to be sold by a number of retailers in any given area, but which were purchased only intermittently by any individual consumer, had come to be sold at conventional prices. In any one area such things as towels or boots and shoes would be sold at generally recognized prices. Thus, for example, one would find men's shoes being sold at the following 'price tickets' (the precise prices were subject to local variation, and any one shop might not sell at the whole range), 5s. 11d., 8s. 6d., 10s. 6d., 12s. 11d., 14s. 11d., 16s. 11d., etc.

This practice was a natural development once the spread of specialized retailing had led to the practice of marking goods with their sale prices. Consumers with different income levels and tastes would tend to shop with an idea of the price which they could afford for, say, a pair of shoes. Instead of the shop offering an infinite range of prices with correspondingly bewildering range of qualities, each minutely differentiated one from another, it was convenient to settle on a definite range of prices, corresponding to fairly clearly differentiated qualities. The consumer wishing to buy such goods naturally tended to ' shop around ' a little before settling on his purchase, and it was a natural consequence that the various shops should find it convenient to settle on approximately the same ranges of prices. This reduced the shopping worries of the consumer who could now start his inquiries by comparing what the shop windows offered at given prices. He could then narrow down the range of shops which he actually entered, and, once inside, his problem was simplified into making a judgment of the quality which he was offered at the same price between different shops, and, in any one shop, into making up his mind whether the increase of quality which corresponded to a step up in the price ticket was worth the extra money to him.

The convenience of this system of conventional prices will no doubt cause it to be re-established when the price-levels have again settled down. Fixed retail prices have also come about as a deliberate result of policy on the part of manufacturers branding their goods and then fixing their re-sale price. Similarly, the development of the fixed-price chain stores has led to their having a maximum retail price, and to a wide range of goods having to conform to this if they are to be sold in those shops.

Such fixed retail prices, when the customary retail margins have been deducted, are readily translated into corresponding prices for the manufacturer, ex works. As has already been said, his problem is now to determine the specification of the product which is to be sold at that price. This is, however, only the problem of determining the gross margin which he will charge, and this has already been discussed. Given the gross margin, he will know the limits that he can offer in the specification of the good; the difference between the fixed price and the gross margin will be the amount which can be spent on direct costs, and these control the specification. Competition will ensure that this quality is at least as good as any rival would offer, and thus in the end will determine the gross margin itself.[1] Accordingly, it is not necessary to present any special theory for the cases of prices fixed by convention or otherwise.

There is, however, a special consequence of such fixed prices to which it is interesting to call attention. The quality which is offered at any given price will naturally depend upon the costs of the factors of production making the product, and so will vary with the prices of materials and with the wages of labour. The quality of such goods, therefore, tends to increase in a trade depression and to decrease in a boom. The manufacturer of towels of a kind generally purchased through the ordinary retailers will, therefore, be able to make them longer, or heavier in substance, in the depression than he can in the boom, and competition will force him to do so. It is surprising that statisticians searching for subtle indices of the trade cycle have overlooked this type of valuable material![2]

The Costing Margin and the Effect of Competition

As was seen in Chapter III, the actual costs per unit of output realized in any accounting period will depend upon the output that has been produced, since the indirect or overhead costs will be relatively fixed in total amount.[3] The

---

[1] Given this, the ordinary consumer is not so silly as he, or she, is sometimes made out to be in refusing to look at an article which seems to be 'too cheap'.

[2] By way of another illustration, it may be mentioned that the present author, as an undergraduate, was interested, during the depression of the 1930's, to notice the increasing quality and size of the ties offered by Messrs. Woolworth for their fixed price of sixpence.

[3] In actual cases, it is necessary to make the distinction, which could be ignored for the simplified theory of costs which has been given in this book, between fixed and variable overheads. For, in the typical multi-product

business man will have to quote his price in advance of his securing an order, and his allowance for overheads must, to that extent at least, be independent of the realized costs. Where, therefore, he builds up his normal cost price in a detailed fashion, by adding, to his estimates of average direct costs, an allowance for average indirect costs (adding to that an allowance for average net profit per unit of output), he will, even if only implicitly, have to assume a figure for the total output (usually called the budgeted output).

So long as output is not falling (and, generally, in a business whose product has never fallen, or always continued to expand), he may well allow the figure at which average indirect costs stood in his last financial accounts, or, where cost accounts exist, he may use the average indirect costs which they impute to the particular product. To the extent to which his actual output exceeds the budgeted output, he will, of course, work to lower average costs [1] than was assumed in his costing calculations. If output falls, the business man will not revise his prices so as to charge a higher allowance for average overheads — that would be absurd, as causing the charging of a higher price in a falling market. It would bring the danger of his market going to competitors. In such cases, then, he will continue to make the same costing allowance for average overheads, and will get a price which would have come out right only if he, in fact, had got his budgeted output. In the circumstances, he will make less than the average net profit which he allowed in his normal cost price, even making a loss, of course, if output has fallen sufficiently.

In industries where the output is known to have regular

business, some of the costs, which for reasons of convenience are charged in the profit and loss account, will be direct expenses for the production and sale of a particular product — the direct selling expenses must be charged there and not among the prime costs of the trading account — and others will vary more or less directly with total turnover, although not affected by individual products in so directly determinable a manner.

[1] Apart, of course, from the effect of the extra costs of working any overtime.

and marked fluctuations over the trade cycle, this fact will be allowed for in the price determination. Here, the budgeted output will frequently be a notional one which can be described as covering that proportion of capacity, or a little less, which the business man can hope to achieve on the average, taking the good years with the bad. In bad years the realized profit will fall and may eventually become a loss; it will rise in good years because of the difference between the costing figures for average overheads and those actually realized on the larger output.

In an industry where there has been a history of decline for some years, as in some of the older British industries before the war, the business man may report his costing rules in a different way. He may say that he averages his over-heads on the basis of full normal output — which will prob-ably be the figure for the last output achieved in relatively prosperous conditions, or the budgeted output then assumed, but will certainly be larger than the output which he currently produces. In such an industry and in such conditions, then, it will be normal for the businesses to be running with an actual rate of net profit which will be less than allowed for in their costings, possibly even at a net loss. It should be noted that the fact of the costing rules will set some limit to the fall of price, in so far as there will be some resistance to quoting still lower prices. If price-cutting does appear, however, the business man will revise his costing rules and price on an even finer margin; it will be necessary for him to do so, so long as he wishes to remain in business.

How will the allowance for net profit be arrived at ? For most established businesses it will be a matter of experience, so long as they are producing a product of a familiar kind; it will be the net margin which they expect to get on the average. In the case of a new product, it will express the producer's judgment of the margin which it is safe for him to take into account in his costings. This margin will vary between different businesses, as also, of course, will the charge on account of overheads. But, although from the business man's point of view there are two factors which are thus involved in his costing-margin — the allowance which he makes for overhead costs and that which he makes for net profit — the distinction is not very useful for economic analysis, when we are considering the determination of the market price for any particular kind of product. The quantity through which economic forces work is the costing-margin which is the total of these two, just as, in the accounts of a business, the quantity which shows the effect of the business's environment is the realized gross profit margin.

It is easy to see how this comes about, if we suppose a man to be contemplating setting up a business to produce a product of a kind which is already being marketed. He will be able to estimate the price at which it is now being sold. The other quantity which he will be able to estimate is his average direct costs per unit. He will, perhaps optimistically, estimate what he can hope to sell, and, if the gross profit margin looks as if it will yield him a fair return, then he will try to create a market for that product. In the same way, an established business which is already working at a given gross profit margin and considering the possibility of producing a new product, will first estimate the gross profit margin which that product is likely to carry with it, and, if it looks favourable in relation to other opportunities for expansion, once again the new market will be entered.

The size of the gross margin which will in these ways attract new enterprise will depend upon the type of article. Articles which carry high sales and service costs, or which require very heavy overhead organization, such as those classes of mass-produced goods where a lot of the costs are in the drawing-office, tool-room, etc., and those consumers' goods which are the subject of fashion or are produced for the more particular tastes of individuals rather than the common needs of the mass market — all these will alike tend to carry a heavy costing-margin if they are to justify their production. In the long run they will yield a proportionately heavy margin of gross profit in the price.

However distinct the market of an individual business may be at a given moment, its product will frequently resemble the product of other businesses, in so far as it is produced on the same type of machinery and with roughly the same sort of overhead organization. For example, one can classify businesses in the boot and shoe industry by the grade of product which they produce, or businesses in the engineering industry by the kinds of machinery involved (even though in this case the product turned out by one business may be a very different article from that produced by another, so that the markets are even more clearly separate in the latter case than in the former). Now, as we have stated previously, it is nearer the truth to regard any individual business as having a unique market at any time rather than a market which it will share with others, so long as their respective prices do not change — the typical case being that relatively few businesses are recognized by particular groups of customers as capable of offering the same type of good. If, however, the gross profit margin on any particular market is thought to be unduly generous, it is a comparatively easy matter for other businesses, which have the right equipment and organization already, to ' try their arm ' in that particular market.

Sometimes, of course, mistakes will be made. For example, to quote one case for which several instances can be found, one sort of clothing may be technically producible by a large number of businesses. It may be at first the product of a section of the industry. The gross profit margin may seem attractive to businesses at present producing other articles which do not carry so large a margin. They, therefore, go out for the new market, and, at first, seem to be justified. They get the larger margin, and, at first, find that they can carry the articles alongside their existing products with much the same organization. As the trade in the new line develops, however, it is frequently found that the position is not so simple. A relatively small proportion of the new article was interesting as an addition, and the management could easily take on the special work that was involved. A growth in the proportion, however, will ultimately mean a change in the organization, and average overheads will have to rise in order to accommodate the extra trouble that the new article really involves, and the realized net margin will not be so good as was thought available at first. In so far as this may be a gradual change, it quite frequently takes some time to realize what is happening, and the business may end by handicapping itself for the more mass-production market where it was originally.

That mistake is only a particular example, mentioned because of its general interest. It must not be thought that such enterprise and any consequent success or mistakes are rare. A progressive business will always be looking round for ways in which to grow and new products will be attractive, granted the difficulties that may exist in the way of the business expanding in its original market. To the extent to which they do use common equipment and overheads, they may help to spread the burden of these costs, thus giving the business, it will be hoped, a better net profit margin. For this reason, a business man will not be afraid of trying new products which he thinks he can carry alongside his old. The gross profit margin which appears to be available at the existing level of market price will be what first attracts his attention to the possibilities.

The result is that, in industries where the products, even though sold in fairly separate markets, are produced by much the same processes, the price of an article produced for one especial market cannot in the long run yield a more attractive margin over the direct costs than would be available in the other markets. In consequence, over such industrial networks of businesses, the gross profit margins will be approximately the same. Where there are marked differences in the efficiencies of individual businesses, the consequences for the costing-margins depend upon exactly where the inefficiencies show themselves.

Our general rule is that price cannot differ for the same grade of any particular article. If a business is relatively inefficient in its usage of the direct cost factors, then it will have to take a smaller costing-margin than the more efficient firms. If its inefficiency shows itself in higher average overhead costs, either because of genuine inefficiency in its organization or because its market is not at the size where it would be normally efficient, but its direct costs are at the same level, then it will take the same costing-margin, but that margin will leave it a lower margin of net profit. This will frequently be the case with the small growing business. It is quite common to hear that, up to a certain stage, the business could not get its price, i.e. it could not get the net profit which was thought normal.

It is worth recording the strong impression that costing-margins seem to have some stability even between industries making quite different products and employing different types of techniques. A good deal of research would be necessary in order to get satisfactory statistical results, if it were possible to give the right weight to all the relevant factors. Common-sense judgment, however, appears able to make the sort of classification which suggests the existence of a regularity in the relation between the costing-margin and other factors, such as the relative importance of overhead (non-process) departments, the relative weight of capital investment, the amount of ' care and attention ' or ' headache ' that the typical product involves for the management, and so on.

After a series of detailed investigations of individual businesses, one finds it possible to compare — in rather an impressionistic fashion, it is true — a business, which is being seen for the first time, with others that have been studied, even though it might be in a clearly distinct industry.

On this basis it has, on occasion, proved possible to make what turned out to be a quite good guess at the costing-margin, i.e. at the gross profit margin that might be reasonable for such a business on the basis of previous experience. It was the realization of such regularities which led to the impression that manufacturing industry must be in some ways more competitive than is generally recognized, and, thence, to the development of the present theory.

It is, therefore, held that the characteristic of competition is that it tends to make the gross profit margins similar for businesses of similar kinds from the point of view of costs. The importance of the gross profit margin as a stimulus for potential competitors is well recognized by business men, and is the major reason why trading accounts are not published. Another business man could probably make a good guess at it, but a guess is always a different thing from certain knowledge, and will usually lag a little behind the facts.

In the course of time, and given experience in meeting the competition that arises in its market, each business will evolve its costing rules. Where the product is fairly standardized and where the direct costs do not differ much from business to business, those rules will amount to the same thing in terms of the costing-margin, even if it is formally calculated in two parts — the allowance for overheads and that for net profit. If all businesses were equally efficient, the net margins would tend to be the same for all businesses employing similar processes, but the net profit which is relevant to competition is, of course, the expected net profit of a new entrant into the market.

It is a familiar argument that, where a product requires a fairly large-scale organization, so that a new business would not have so much hope of managing on any price that would give it a chance of getting into the market, the market will be less open to new entrants than will be the market at the opposite extreme, where the amount of capital investment which is required is within the possible reach of substantial

margin will normally enable businesses to replace their capital assets and to cover their other indirect costs of production. While, therefore, the margin does not change during short-period fluctuations in output, it will usually rise if there is a permanent rise in the prices of the overhead factors of production — due, e.g., to a more or less permanent rise in the general price level affecting that of salaries and the prices of capital goods. It must, in the long run, stand at such an absolute level as will cover these costs, although, in so far as they may change in proportion to changes in the level of direct costs, the proportionate costing-margin may remain unchanged.

The way in which costing-margins both reflect and determine the competitive forces at work in industry may be seen in the history of many modern industries, where one is able to trace the facts about the industry and its constituent businesses from the beginning. The following is an abstract account of the general pattern as it is to be traced.

The product will be pioneered by a very few businesses, which will be small scale, and will have to incur relatively heavy costs in introducing it to the potential consumers. The gross margins that they will charge will reflect these facts, and, high as they may be, may well yet not be high enough to give reasonable profits in these early days. Potential competitors will be discouraged by the obvious lack of a ready-made market for the product, by the lack of a general knowledge of the technical know-how, and by the apparent modesty of the profits of the existing businesses.

As the product becomes established, the given prices will make entry seem more attractive to newcomers, who will see an expanding market developing for a product about which something is beginning to be known, and for which the established businesses are beginning to make satisfactory profits. Those businesses will find that, whilst the increasing general demand is causing their markets to expand, other businesses are beginning to set up, and to get a market for

N

themselves in the general expansion. The older businesses will naturally expand as quickly as they can so as to keep their goodwill as first-comers. If, in fact, there are no technical economies, the gross profit margin which was originally established will tend to persist, excepting in so far as the net profits which it yields induces new businesses to quote lower prices. In this sort of case, then, the profit margin will be competitively determined, and it will be the pressure from newcomers which will tend to keep it down or to reduce it.

More typically, however, the modern industry will be one where technical economies of scale are important, and in any case it will be usual for such economies to be fairly substantial, at all events, for the early stages of growth from the very small sizes of the pioneers. In this case, prices will not tend to remain at their existing level, and will be brought down by the actions of the older firms, often against the desires of the smaller businesses who would rather establish themselves at the higher price levels. The older businesses will tend to expand more quickly and also to be at larger sizes than the newcomers. Technical economies will lower prices whichever way they show themselves. If they reduce the level of direct costs, then the older businesses will tend to preserve their old margins but lower prices — which means lowering the effective margins for the smaller newer businesses. If technical economies reduce average overhead costs per unit at the new scales, then the larger businesses will find it desirable to reduce their gross margins. As explained on page 164, since these businesses will not have had any major set-backs but will have set the price for the market, this reduction in margins will tend to come about automatically. For they will usually be charging a profit margin which is equal to their latest ascertained average overhead costs — and these will, by hypothesis, be tending to fall — plus a fixed margin for net profit. In any case, this policy will pay them, since it will give them higher total profits, given their share of the expanding market. The price policy itself will tend to strengthen their position in the market at the expense of the newcomers, whose costs will be higher. In this way the older businesses set the price for the industry and keep their historic lead.

Of course, the industry may meanwhile have undergone too great an expansion, especially if the expansion of the industry coincided with a boom period when it was relatively easier for new businesses to get capital, and too many small competitors will tend to enter the industry without any real prospect of growing to a sufficient size to maintain the position, let alone improve it. There may be a subsequent period when the struggle of these businesses to keep in, and to get the expansion which they need, causes price-cutting below the normal price which the older businesses would set. But this will be met with corresponding price cuts by them, and, in the end, the number of competing businesses will tend to be reduced by the squeezing out of those smaller businesses who are in the weakest position.

In the end, these economic forces will tend to work themselves out and the industry will present a more stable pattern of relatively few businesses. The prices will be effectively set by the prices of the larger businesses with lower costs, but the other businesses will have developed their own rules about their gross margins which will reflect this. Even if they do not explicitly follow the price leadership of the larger businesses, the latter will effectively determine the gross margins which the others treat as normal. The margins will have fallen to the level at which new business is no longer attracted to the industry, and the price policy will be stable, failing any major technical developments. If these latter occur, bringing about a general fall in the level of costs, the pricing policy of the larger business will again reduce gross margins, even if these are not large enough to yield normal profits to the smaller businesses — who may in any case not be able to take advantage of the newer knowledge so quickly.

Prices will thus tend to remain at a level which not only discourages new entrants but which makes life difficult for the less efficient established businesses. Paradoxically it is price leadership of this sort which is often described as monopolistic in character. That is, however, not a true picture, for the price leaders will tend to keep prices below the level which their competitors would desire, and the absence of new entrants is rather a proof that price is being controlled by the competitive forces recognized by our theory, than any evidence that the bigger businesses are using their position to get and retain abnormal profits. In so far as they do, they will be exposed to competition not only from new entrants but also from the existing businesses whose size is too small for maximum economies and who will be only too anxious to grow, if they can do so without worsening their position.

The above example also illustrates the working of the general principle that the profit margins on which an industry works will tend to be reduced by advances in technical knowledge. Returning to more stable circumstances, it does not follow that the business man will add identical costing-margins to all his products, if his business is multi-product. It will be quite consistent with the present theory for him to charge a margin which varies for different products, either because they involve differing proportions of overhead costs, making a different call upon the overhead organization of the business, or because their markets differ in the extent to which they are liable to the competition of new entrants. It will also be consistent for him to make small shadings of price to important customers, or to perform special services for them, such as holding some lines in stock for them; such reductions will sweeten the relationship, recognizing in one way or another that a larger, more regular customer involves lower costs in the long run. The concessions will not, however, be so large as to endanger market policy.

It will be normal for lower prices to be charged to wholesalers than to retailers. The wholesaler gets a margin, which will be *his* gross profit margin, because he renders the service of holding goods in stock for his retail customers, and breaking bulk — selling in smaller quantities than he buys — or, rather, that is the origin of the wholesaler's margin, and he will only continue to get trade at that margin in the long run if his services are valued accordingly by both the other parties to his transactions. In some markets, the wholesaler has taken advantage of bad times to push some of his function back on to the manufacturer, getting him, in effect, to hold the wholesaler's stocks, through the latter ordering in small quantities more nearly as he sells to retailers, and still demanding wholesale terms, but expecting prompt delivery.

When this happens, the manufacturer will often find it profitable to take over the wholesaler's functions, establishing contact with the retail customers himself, and to retain the wholesale margin for himself, since he has already been compelled to do so much of the job.[1] The wholesaler will then be left only with that part of his market which it is cheaper for the manufacturer to leave him — the most troublesome part — the smallest retailers.

On the other hand, where the wholesaler is active and does his job properly, the manufacturer will usually find that it pays him to let him have goods at a reduction corresponding to the margin providing for the services which he renders. With the development of large retail stores and chains, each large enough to order at one time the quantities normally ordered by a wholesaler, it will be usual for them to be treated as such in the price that is quoted to them.

In modern times, however, the development of advertising, to which fuller reference will be made at the end of this chapter, has enabled manufacturers in many lines of con-

---

[1] The theory of selling costs will be considered at the end of this part of the chapter, but it should be noted that this will involve the manufacturer in extra selling costs, in so far as he will now have to make contact with the retailer directly, may well have to ' brand ' his product, and, in that case, will incur the level of advertising costs necessary to sustain the new form of his market.

sumers' goods to seek a more stable market, in the sense of one where they are not so dependent upon the decisions of the wholesaler as to where he will get his goods. In such cases, the goodwill of the final consumer cannot attach itself to the unidentified product of a particular manufacturer. Branding enables him to by-pass the wholesaler and create an individual market among the ultimate consumers, but this will be at the cost of the possibly heavy initial advertising which is necessary in order to make retailers think it useful to stock the good, and of the — not necessarily so heavy — recurrent advertising to keep the brand-name alive — especially with new consumers.

Price Warfare and the Breakdown of the Normal Cost Principle

Subject to these different margins, the manufacturer will stick to his costing rules, and maintain his price so long as his costs remain unchanged. He will not raise it when the market is temporarily strong, for other businesses may have more reserve capacity and be perfectly content to encroach on his market at a price which they think will be profitable in the long run. Even if that is not the case, the enlarged margin will give a loophole for new ventures, which may thus become established in the market. The manufacturer will not willingly cut his price, apart from the extent to which it will reflect cost changes, when markets are weak and demand is falling. That might gain him a temporary increase in sales, but it will be temporary, for his rivals will cut their price to protect their own markets when they know that he has cut his.

In the event of such a general price-cut, each will get only whatever increase may occur in his own market because of the price-cut. That increase will be small, if any, for price-cuts on a falling market will not induce the normal customer of a business man to add to his stocks, and the effect on the final price to the ultimate consumer will be decreased by the various margins that have to be added — the demand of such a consumer will not itself tend to be very price-sensitive in a depression (at least, not for the whole group of similar products, taken as a whole, as distinct from one of them being reduced independently). Price-cutting will then normally mean merely a fall in the total receipts of the whole group of competing producers, and, since their costs will not be affected, they will be worse off. The business man's prejudice against price-cutting, then, is very rational; nor is it necessarily anti-social, in so far as prices should normally cover costs.

To understand how such price-cutting comes about, we must refer back to the analysis of costs. We then distinguished the break-even level of output, the output at which the business man would cover his costs on his pricing rules. The falling of output to this level will mean that the business will not earn anything for profits, but that will not affect the business man's conduct. He will simply not pay any dividends, or will pay them out of reserves, if the business has any spare cash (the latter alternative may have important consequences in so far as it will deplete the cash reserves and leave the business in a weaker state). Nor will it have much effect for some time if depreciation is not covered. The business will show a loss in the profit and loss account equal to the debits on account of depreciation, but the real costs which correspond to these financial operations take some time to emerge and can generally be avoided for a period, especially in a depression, when there will be excess capacity in equipment anyway in view of the lower output. Even some repairs will be postponable, and this may be helped for a time by the decreased usage of equipment.

If output falls progressively, however, it may uncover the paying-out overheads, the wages and salaries of the staff, and so on. Failure to pay them would mean a reduction in the business's scale, which would be a step that a business man would be reluctant to take, since such staffs are very important and, once they are dispersed, might be very difficult to replace. If such costs are not currently being covered, the business will have to draw on its cash reserves in order to keep going.

When the cash reserves are exhausted, unless the business can borrow, which is not very likely, it will have to sell assets to keep going, or close down. In these circumstances, the weaker businesses, those that are not so well established and hence have had less profits, and the less efficient, whose costs will be higher, will suffer first, and will see their rivals still hanging on. It is then that the temptation to try the desperate remedy of the price-cut may come. The price-cutting business man will expect the benefit to be temporary, but it may give him a very big increase in trade for the moment, and that would improve his cash position. Such price-cutting is peculiarly liable to happen in industries selling products of high individual value, on contracts; in such cases a lot of the costs may be overhead, and a large proportion of these may be paying-out costs. A single large contract may be very worth while, and may form a substantial part of the total market demand. The business that gets it will be able to carry on for a while; its unsuccessful rivals will certainly be seriously damaged. That is one reason why strong price-rings tend to be built up in such industries, but similar cuts may occur in any industry, given the provocation.

There is one circumstance in which a business may wish to cut price as a regular policy — the case of a very small business in an industry where economies of scale are important. Usually in these cases a large efficient firm will have arisen as price leader. Its costs will be below its rivals' and so to its costing rules theirs will tend to conform. They will not ordinarily wish to undercut, because they will expect the leader to retaliate. If one of them is very much smaller than the others, it will be constantly wishing to expand its share of the market, and the — to it — relatively great increase in demand that will come from a price-cut may be a big temptation in a depression. This is similar to the case that we have just discussed. As its *normal* policy, however, it may wish to shade its price below the price leader, hoping to escape unnoticed because of its size while growing steadily because of the difference in its price. Such a firm may thus be an ever-present source of weakness to the pricing set-up of the whole industry, although it is usually the first to complain about another aspect of the price leader's policy — that it maintains relatively modest prices in a boom, when the small business would like to see the whole level of prices in its industry move upwards so as to increase its profits and hence improve its chance of growing.

The possibility of price-cutting of this kind is responsible for industries adopting price maintenance schemes, knowing full well that, if a depression should go on long enough, someone will try to cut prices, but hoping to delay the price-cut by reason of the agreement. Such schemes have been heavily criticized as overtly monopolistic. Quite clearly, the price-cutting which they seek to prevent is not, in itself, of social value. It leads to a fall in prices, but it also causes a fall in incomes and so increased unemployment. In so far as the group demand is inelastic, the group would have had higher receipts and have been able to go on employing its overhead staffs longer. In a depression there is no virtue in lower prices as such, and there will be some harm in having increased unemployment when there is no alternative employment for the displaced personnel. The social interest really turns on the size of the gross profit margin which the agreement will afford.

Generally speaking, such rings do not appear to set excessive margins, being too much held in check by fear of the emergence of possible competitors. Experience suggests that the profit margins that are set are usually not unreasonable, and they are maintained in boom and slump alike. If high profit margins are set, failing some stronger sanction, they will offer to a newcomer the attraction of being able to get into the market in good times, setting his price just below the ring's and growing until the price policy of the ring has to be revised in order to keep his encroachment within bounds. Rings of this kind will only succeed in maintaining high margins if there is a limitation on entry, and that can be the subject of legislative and other action. This will be more appropriate than simple prohibition of agreements which are very difficult to stop where they do most good to the businesses concerned.

(4) SUMMARY OF CONCLUSIONS

For the purpose of later analysis, the chief conclusions reached so far are: (1) that the price which a business will normally quote for a particular product will equal the estimated average direct costs of production plus a costing-margin; Chapter III has shown that average direct cost will tend to remain at a constant level, whatever the output which is being produced, given the prices of the direct-cost factors of production and ignoring any extraordinary increase in direct costs (due, e.g., to overtime wages being paid for extra output in the short period); (2) that the costing-margin will normally tend to cover the costs of the indirect factors of production and provide a normal level of net profit, looking at industry as a whole, and may reflect any general permanent changes in the prices of indirect factors of production, but will remain constant, given the organization of the individual business, whatever the level of its output; (3) that, given the prices of the direct factors of production, price will tend to remain unchanged, whatever the level of output; (4) that, at that price, the business will have a more or less clearly defined market and will sell the amount which its customers demand from it, its sales thus equalling its limited share of the market for the kind of goods which it is producing. The next chapter will complete the analysis, which is necessary for the understanding of the determination of prices, by considering the nature of the markets for the factors of production and the determination of their prices.

(5) SELLING COSTS

There remains one topic which has not been discussed so far — the selling costs, the costs of actually selling the commodity to the customer, including any expenditure incurred in order to persuade potential customers to buy it. Up to now, it has been convenient virtually to ignore any special consideration of these costs, tacitly including them in the indirect expenses of the profit and loss account which the business will have to recover from its gross profit margin. The reader may well have wondered whether these costs do not call for special treatment, and if they do not, in fact, vitiate the previous analysis. It may be agreed that, apart from this question of selling costs, an individual business will have a limited market, and that a price cut will bring only a temporary expansion of demand. It will consequently be made only when the business is more or less desperately needing short-term relief, or when it has to cut in order to keep its market against lower prices being quoted by other businesses. The question is, however, how far a business may remove the restriction on its markets, given by the otherwise fixed preferences of its customers and potential customers, by spending money in order to influence those preferences in its favour.

Apart from advertising costs of one sort or another, the rest of the selling costs consist of the expenses of the actual operations of getting the commodity to the customer and selling it to him. Once a business has chosen its product, its location, and the way in which it will sell its goods (i.e. whether through agents, through wholesalers, through retailers, or direct to the final customer) it may reasonably be argued that these costs are as given as the production costs, and as definitely entailed by sales as those are by production. The business will have to treat such expenses as necessary if it is to make its sales. It will have to maintain a sales and despatch staff which is adequate for its purpose, will have to produce the necessary catalogues and price lists, and the samples which its market requires, besides having to meet the costs of packing and transport. Leaving the case of advertising costs on one side, these other selling costs do involve some accompanying services to the customer, and are the expenses involved in those services — informing him of prices, sending him descriptions of the goods which are for sale, calling on him with samples, making any modifications in the samples to suit his needs, sending him the goods with a particular speed of delivery, and selling or delivering the goods in particular minimum quantities and at given terms of credit.

All these services can be given some sort of value by the customer, who will often have demanded them specifically. They will, therefore, not give rise to irrational preferences and should be thought of as being included in the final specification of the commodity as the customer gets it. It is, in fact, sometimes impossible to allocate some expenses either to production or to selling. The very design of the good will often be decided only after the selling department has had a very large ' say '. Selling considerations will certainly be obvious in the wrapper or container which encloses the good. Some part of such costs must be incurred if production is to take place, and certainly many of the sales department's decisions are reflected in the factory costs, where they are embedded beyond the reach of an investigator.

It is, therefore, not considered that the explicit recognition of these costs calls for any special modification of the theory that has so far been developed ; they merely change the quality of the good which is offered from that which it would otherwise possess in the form in which it was finished at the factory.

Where they can be distinguished from what are more strictly costs of production, they have, however, a peculiarity which our theory must take into account — as has been noted before, they are reckoned among the indirect expenses of the profit and loss account. Yet it is also the case that they can be divided into variable and fixed costs in a manner parallel to the division of production costs into direct and indirect costs. A large part of the expenditure upon the central sales office, together with any fixed salaries which may be paid to salesmen, will be fixed in total amount whatever the level of sales may be — the total will depend upon the circumstances of the particular business as well as upon the way in which it organizes its sales. Another part of this overhead sales expenditure will be fixed for a given range of sales, but will vary with sales in a discontinuous fashion, very much as the expenditure upon process machinery will vary; and the rest of the selling expenses such as salesmen's commissions will vary in total with the amount of sales and will tend to remain constant per unit of sales.

It would therefore be possible, when one is analysing an individual business for its own sake, to lump sales costs in with others and proceed on the basis of direct costs of all sorts, and the corresponding indirect costs, but it would be misleading from the point of view of pricing theory. The fact that business men allocate all selling expenditures to the profit and loss account, and do not include the variable part of them in direct costs in the trading account, is quite justifiable, in so far as businesses may differ in the natural and other advantages of their situation, etc., and so may incur different costs in getting to the customer what he will consider to be goods of equal value, when he has reckoned in the amenities which are included in the sale. In this way any peculiarities affecting the level of the business's selling costs will not affect the price which it can get, but will have to come out of the costing-margin which the business can add to its direct costs of production. The costing-margin tends to cover only normal selling costs.

At the same time, when the information is available — as it will be for some items of selling costs at all events — the business man will make use of the distinction between variable and other selling costs in the same way as he does the corresponding distinction between costs of production, entering an accurate estimate of the variable costs, but having to make a more or less arbitrary allowance for the average of the less variable costs.

Since they do not lead to any important modification in the theory that has been developed, it is not necessary to spend much time making any separate analysis of selling costs, of the kind that we have just been discussing. It should be stressed that these non-advertising expenses make up the bulk of the selling costs of the typical manufacturing business, and that advertising costs are often taken wrongly, therefore, as the genus type of selling costs. It is wrong to describe business as though it were everywhere dominated by advertising. Further, a good deal of the advertising which is carried on is informative in character, and not devoted primarily to customer-snatching persuasion, of the kind to which economic text-books pay so much attention (another example of the existing theory of demand being too short-run in its outlook).

(6) THE SPECIAL CASE OF ADVERTISING

In the case of businesses selling non-consumers' goods, and also the case where unbranded consumers' goods are sold through wholesalers or direct to retailers, advertising will be quite unimportant so far as creating preferences is concerned; the preferences of the business-men customers will be of the kind that have been described and based upon custom and judgment. For this reason the greater part of business advertisements have the sole function of giving information — letting potential customers know that such and such a business makes the listed products, and giving the address at which it may be found. Important businesses may think it suitable to make this announcement in an important fashion and in an attractive manner, but their announcements remain informative and so escape the wrath of the modern economist who sees advertising as the handmaiden of monopoly.

A business whose goods are purchased at all regularly by the business-men customers whom we are imagining, may have relatively heavy advertising expenses when it first starts up, in order to be sure that all potential customers know that it has entered its particular industry, but afterwards it will settle down to the more or less routine trade advertisements — in the specialist trade papers, and in appropriate trade lists and directories — reserving any more detailed information for its regular customers and others with whom it comes into contact in the course of business. The typical customer will not be influenced by the advertisements, and will keep to his established connexions, unless he becomes dissatisfied with the price or quality of what they offer. If that happens, he will make inquiries of other suppliers, and, although he will generally know other sources to which he could turn, the trade advertisements will probably be used for additional names or even just to obtain the address of a business of which he knows. In the case of this type of goods it is difficult to say that advertisement is an absolute necessity, but the relatively small costs involved may be thought worth while.

Given the business's type of product, which will determine the amount of advertising which is conventionally necessary, the expenditure on advertising will tend to be a constant amount per period and not to vary with sales, nor will the amount of advertisement have any influence upon the volume of sales. The business will make the usual amount of advertising and will get its share of the market.

Trade advertisements will be more important for businesses producing goods which the individual business buys at less regular intervals; i.e. it may be more important that the business does do the routine amount of trade advertising, which may be rather heavier for this type of product. The irregular customer will quite possibly not always be up to date in his knowledge of the state of the market, and, since such goods are frequently made under special contract, there is always the possibility of some variation in the prices which are being quoted at the same time. He may, therefore, look around a little, and the presence of a business's name in a trade advertisement may be important in so far as a large part of the sales at any given time may be made to such irregular customers, who have not developed the attachment to particular suppliers which comes where connexions are more regular. Because of the advertisement, the chance of inquiries will be increased. Even so, the advertisement will have little value in the matter of creating preferences. Even the getting of inquiries may be more influenced by the reputation of a business, and inquiries only start the process of choice, in which the potential customer will make up his mind on the basis of price and his judgment of what he is offered at that price, possibly helped by expert advice.

In what has been regarded as the typical case, then, where the manufacturing business is not selling branded consumers' goods, it may find it profitable to incur fairly heavy advertising costs, [1] to get its name known when it first starts, but irrational preferences will not follow from the mere fact of the advertisement, and an established business will merely make a relatively constant amount of informative advertising. To increase advertising in an effort to create preferences on the part of business-men customers will be otiose.[2]

---

[1] In relation to the normal level in its industry ; it may still be light as compared with the position where advertising is more important.

[2] Occasionally, business men, driven by an organization which is too large for their market, get misled by the text-books or the persuasions of advertising agents, reinforced no doubt if there seems no remedy for their position except recourse to the witch doctor, and indulge in a high-pressure advertising campaign for just the class of goods where it should not be important : but they find

The present abnormal circumstances may give a misleading impression of the significance of advertising to manufacturing businesses, even where their product is very remote from the private consumer, for we have large companies indulging in continuous campaigns to tell the ordinary man in the street about themselves. We have, however, just passed through a period when advertisements were virtually costless to the business, because of the effect of E.P.T., and even now almost half the costs of them is effectively paid for by reduced taxation, since the Inland Revenue allows such expenditure as costs for the purposes of income-tax. During recent years, there has been a much stronger incentive for such advertisements, because political tendencies have caused business, and particularly big business, to come under fire in one way or another. These advertisements thus serve political or quasi-political ends, but are socially beneficial in so far as people may come to wrong judgments through not being aware that the companies concerned *do* serve the public in this way or that, and they are, in any case, understandable, in so far as those in charge of such businesses feel that there is a political case for the sort of enterprise which they represent which might otherwise go by default.

The writers of the normal theoretical text-books might well admit the argument so far, although they have ignored the relative importance of the type of business to which it refers. The case is otherwise with the advertising, which to them is the very type of selling costs and the clue to some of

out their mistake. One can recall an interesting example of this in an old-established business whose factory and organization had been expanded by its war-time products, and which tried an aesthetically delightful advertising campaign to expand its share of the market in the producers' goods which it normally made. This may have helped at least one of its problems, in so far as it got capital from investors who thus knew its name, so that it could carry on for a little longer as it was, but to the outside observer the advertising brought suspicions that the position of the business was not good, and the later plight of the business was expected. The market of that business could grow only on the basis of the judgment of potential customers, and advertising did nothing or very little to convince them that the inherent qualities of the product would justify their turning from their usual suppliers.

O

the typical ' wastes ' of modern business. This type of theory, which easily becomes translated into political statements, sees a business as normally restricting its output so as to get the high price which its inelastic demands [1] are thought to offer it, and then extending its market on the basis of incurring selling costs, which remove it still further from the reach of competition, instead of it seeking the, perhaps more risky, course of extending its market by reducing prices and thus benefiting the consumer.

One part of this argument falls to the ground, in so far as price is determined by the long-run behaviour of demand and will be set at or below the level at which the demand will be very elastic — i.e. very sensitive to price. This will be determined by the costing-margin and the current level of direct costs. The net profit which the costing-margin allows on the average is regarded as competitively determined, and all costs, other than advertising, involve some corresponding service to the consumer. Advertising does itself, when it is purely informative, for it enables the consumer to choose more rationally between the various opportunities for expenditure which are open to him. In so far as advertising is persuasive, however, all it does is to raise his appreciation of the ' real ' services which the product gives him, and this is much more open to suspicion, since the persuasive use of advertising in itself means more economic resources going purely to increase the apparent satisfaction with a given flow of real goods and services, instead of increasing that flow.

So far as the other part of the normal economic argument is concerned — the extension of the market for the individual business purely on the basis of advertising — it appears that two questions should be answered : (1) How far will advertising extend the share of the market going to a business solely because of the persuasions of the advertisements ? and (2) How far may advertising make it possible for a business to get an enlarged costing-margin apart from changes in the

---

[1] Short-run demands, according to the present theory.

quality of the product, thus resulting in higher prices which cover its costs and leaving the consumer paying higher prices than he would have had to pay for the same thing if advertising had not taken place? It will be remembered that *these questions arise only for the branded consumers' goods*; the analysis which has been made already for the other types of products, making up the bulk of the national output, implies that, for them, both questions must be answered in the negative; sheer persuasion will not increase the share of the market for any one product, and that product will compete with others according to the customers' valuation of the inherent qualities which it offers at its price.

The first question can be answered, for branded goods, in general terms. To the extent to which it is true that advertising easily persuades, then the business whose advertising is most persuasive will get the largest share of the market. But this can be only a short-run effect, for persuasiveness can be purchased at a price and is the product of a keenly competitive industry — that of the advertising consultant and agency. Moreover, in itself, one victory to pure propaganda makes it easier for the next, from whatever source it may come, and, accordingly, the more easily a business can increase its share of the market by advertising expenditure, the more tenuous its hold on its market; its competitors can restore the *status quo ante bellum* by a similar onslaught, and it will be able in the long run to retain only the share of the market which it gets on other, more rational, grounds. It is, therefore, considered that advertising brings only a short-term increase in the share of the market. Its use is thus analogous to price-cutting, which was discussed earlier; it is more obviously pernicious socially. In the case of price-cutting, the customer does get lower prices, temporary though they be, and the long-run level of price will come back to that determined by the normal costs of the goods.

The second question that has to be answered raises the possibility that the consequences of businesses fighting by advertising will be, not only that the share of the market going to any one good will revert to that determined by its real qualities, but also that the keeping of such a position will be at the cost of prices which cover rising expenditure upon advertising. The fact that the answer to the first question is negative in the long run, therefore, does not remove the possible objections to advertising — although it does affect the way in which the economic text-books represent the effect of advertising, in so far as we do not here recognize the possibility of a permanent increase in the demand for the product of an individual business being obtained solely on the basis of advertising.[1] The nice determination of output by balancing marginal advertising costs against marginal revenue from sales is, in any case, unrealistic.

The answer to the second question depends upon the type of consumers' good concerned. For all consumers' goods, persuasive advertising may make the consumer try the good with the best sales appeal, but, in many cases, his permanent pattern of expenditure will be decided by what he finds when he does try it. In so far as the natural turnover among the population will always be bringing into being consumers who are new to any particular type of commodity, advertising may be necessary to persuade the new generation to try particular commodities. Even so, for many goods the consumer will have had some experience in the household in which he was brought up before he decides his own consumption pattern, and is not entirely exposed to the influence of advertisements in deciding what field of choice is available to him.

However, the case of these more normal consumption goods may be referred to later. It will be convenient to start with the case of commodities which are purchased, to some extent or entirely, for reason of qualities other than those

---

[1] Those businesses which were first to exploit consumers' fears in the sales of proprietary medicines, for example, may have established themselves like this, but, once the industry settles down, the situation is as I describe it.

necessarily entailed by the physical specification. The leading
type of this class is the lucky charm or magic locket, although
it is not so important as the patent medicine which is normally
taken as representing the class (usually, indeed, as representing
the whole class of advertised commodities). The virtue of
the charm may be entirely in the mind of the consumer and
may be put there by persuasive advertising, which first arouses
the primitive fears which it will assuage. In a society which
runs at a high degree of nervous tension, and in times when
the content of the diet is restricted, the laxative in itself may
have value for those who need it. Advertising by informing
them that 'X' is a laxative, with the implied guarantee
attaching to all branded products that it is pure (does not
include powdered glass or other noxious ingredients!), will
have some informative value for those who need laxatives.
To the most naïve sufferers, indeed, a description of the symptoms which call for a laxative may enable them to recognize
what they suffer from, in which case the information given by
the advertisements has a definite value.

Of course, the advertisements of this type of product may
not end with pure information, but may paint the evils which
follow from the situation which they relieve, in such strong
colours, and describe the symptoms in such general terms, that
all who read will wish to avoid such a doom, and, equally, all
readers will at least be doubtful if they are not already
sufferers. (We are deliberately putting the case at its strongest,
and recognize that many advertisers of this kind of product
are obviously aware of some of the wider social obligations
that fall upon him who uses the powerful weapon of propaganda.) Such propaganda is necessarily powerful, and, other
things being equal, its use must entail some increase in the
demand for the particular product. If the advertisement
is powerful enough and sufficiently widely disseminated, it
will probably pay for itself, especially if the charm is an
inscribed piece of paper or stamped tin, and if the laxative is
a small quantity of pure soap. It is, however, a two-edged

weapon; not only will the other producers of similar goods be able to retaliate and get back some of the share of the market, but the creation of fears of one sort makes it easier to arouse fears of another, and the evils of constipation may be matched by the evils of sleeplessness. Since, however, there is no limit to the evils that men may dread, especially since they can be imaginary ones, the producers of this type of good may face an expanding market, although their individual shares may emerge constant from the battle between them.

It is not true, however, that the situation is as out of control as has been described. The code of conduct of those who control advertising agencies and those who control the media which they use has been improved, partly by legislative action, in the case of therapeutics, and partly by a greater consciousness of responsibility. When all this has been conceded, there is a lot in the text-book suspicion of this type of advertisement, and the theoretical diagnosis is correct in that, since what the consumer gets has imaginary qualities as well as real ones, he may be induced to pay the high price which covers the advertising costs which have created the qualities he imagines. As noted earlier, one relief to this situation has come about through the gradual emergence of big firms in the patent-medicine business, and the consequent beginning of a restraint in excessive competition through advertising, analogous to agreements against price-wars, however tacit it may be.

Although a prejudiced eye will see all advertising in terms of this type, that is not the case; it is merely that patent medicines make a large proportion of advertising expenditure. Such expenditure is perhaps capable of being further restricted and guided by legislative and other action, and the matter may be left here with the reminder that such goods form a still smaller proportion of the total national output, even, than do all advertised goods. We must not let the typical cases of economic theory be selected on the basis of the flesh-creeping opportunities which they offer to Fat Boys

among economists, but rather on that of their relative importance in the distribution of goods and the determination
of prices.

The great majority of the branded goods which are
advertised have intrinsic merits and are bought for the sake
of them. We may all enjoy Guinness advertisements,[1] but we
buy Guinness only because at the moment of purchase we
think we would prefer it to other drinks or to alternative ways
of spending money. Further, the costs of the manufacture of
the actual physical good, and the costs of the actual services
employed in its distribution to the consumers, are large in
relation to the advertising costs — in contrast to the proprietary medicine, where only a fraction of total costs may
be covered by the physical ingredients, and where the bulk
of the price may be represented by space in the ' Daily X ' or
by time purchased on Radio ' Y '.

The branding of the commodity consists, of course, in
its being named or marked in such a way that it can be
readily associated with the manufacturer.[2] Unless the product
is branded by the manufacturer, all the goodwill attaching to
its sale will adhere to the source from which the consumer
gets it. If that source changes its custom, the consumer has
no remedy — the change may not be obvious at first sight,
and the manufacturer's only incentive to drive for higher
quality lies in the goodwill of the wholesaler or retailer to
whom he sold the good.

Where quality is important but hard to detect in actual
use, there is a good case for making it compulsory to brand
all consumers' goods with the manufacturer's name, so that

---

[1] One point which should be made is that some advertisements have come
to be ' goods ' which are enjoyed for themselves. One can think of the case of
English women at the present time buying American papers for the sake of
advertisements of goods which they can never purchase, but in this country
Guinness advertisements are undoubtedly the example which comes first to mind.

[2] Or whichever link in the distributive process puts the brand on, although
we are here concerned only with manufacturers' brands as affecting the demand
for the manufacturers' goods. If the brand is put on by the wholesaler or the
retailer, the manufacturers' product will be undifferentiated, and the behaviour
of such a market has already been discussed at length.

the consumer may more successfully differentiate between the goodwill which properly belongs to the distributors, who may have designed the good and certainly will perform all the services associated with its sale, and that element which belongs to the skill and care of the manufacturer. The manufacturer will then get any extra demand due directly to the quality of his work, and there would be no harm if irate consumers could get directly into touch with him when they feel that defects in workmanship have let them down. However, this is taking us away from what it is strictly necessary to say about branding as affecting the determination of prices.

Branding has developed as a means whereby the manufacturer can make sufficiently direct contact with the consumer to develop his market there rather than at some intermediate stage of distribution. The motives for this are many. First, it does remove the manufacturer from the very keen price-competition which he has to face when he is selling through a wholesaler. He will not lose an order through a penny difference in price, where the penny cannot make any difference to the retail price (as already noted, many consumers' goods can be sold only at conventional prices) and may very well represent a real difference in quality. It also removes him from any danger of a chance loss of market through the whim of the professional buyer, when he is really as efficient as the alternative supplier.

Further, advertising makes it easier for a newcomer to set about establishing a market instead of waiting for the slow process of accretion of goodwill — in this case, of course, there will be heavy initial advertising expenses. It does not follow that the size of the market which will ultimately be created will vary with the size of those expenses. It is rather that a definite sum is required at any one time to open up a national market in a particular commodity with a manufacturer's brand, and that the tastes of the consumers and the quality which the manufacturer offers will decide the size of that market. Occasionally some novelty may sweep the country and establish a temporary market on the basis of persuasive advertising, but the large market of the initial developer of such a novelty will not last. If the commodity promises to stay, others will come in, without such heavy advertising, and the first product will have to hold its own with them.

The chief effect of branding, however, appears to have been the removal of limitations otherwise placed on the development of an individual business. If its goods are not identifiable by the consumer, to get a large output, it has to sell through many intermediaries, the commodity being modified a little perhaps each time to suit their desire to differentiate *their* market and offer something which is a little different and bears the stamp of their designing. Since the buying business will be able to get wholesalers' discount on relatively small-sized orders, it may well come to parcel up, between several manufacturers, orders which might have been planned as one. This limitation of the market may be important where the conditions of production offer scope for economies, provided that the goods could become more standardized than they would be if the business were selling generally to a wholesale market or, unbranded, to a retail market. In this way, whatever the costs of advertising, it seems probable that there have been quite powerful offsets to them in some industries through the reduction in costs of production.

Where such branding is adopted, as we have already noticed, fairly heavy initial advertising may be necessary at the time when the producer first enters on this method of distributing his product, but, as already said, the size of the consequent market will probably not be much affected by the size of that advertising expenditure, provided that it reached at least the minimum level — e.g. for a particular market it may be necessary to have fairly large advertisements in the daily newspapers, and so on. This advertising will be necessary to influence the retailers quite as much as the consumer, for they will regard it as some assurance that the manufacturer is going to create the demand which will justify their stocking the good, for an experimental period at all events.

Similarly, once a producer has been established, so long as he wishes to retain this method of distribution, there will be a certain minimum of regular advertising which he must do in order to keep his name in the market, but the bulk of his sales will come to depend upon the experience of those who have already bought the goods or have heard of them from other consumers. For the majority of consumers' goods of the type of which we are thinking, it is difficult to consider that advertising exercises so persuasive a function as it is thought to have in modern theory, and the picture that we wish to present is rather that of a business normally allocating a definite sum to its advertising, regarding that as necessary if it is to continue to distribute its goods direct to the retailer on a branded basis, and, subject to that, getting its share of the market.

Of course, it follows that this type of market is much less sensitive to minor changes in price — the typical branded good is at the rather better quality end of the market for the type of goods which a consumer purchases rather intermittently, and where, accordingly, he prefers to shop around, inspecting goods at about the same conventional level of prices rather than having to compare on both a price and quality basis — but it will still be true that competition will be necessary for a business to keep its share of the market, only it will tend to be competition in quality. The upshot of our theory will be the same: too high a gross profit margin will mean the entry of new businesses — who need not be completely new enterprises but may come from those who have up to now sold similar goods unbranded but are attracted by the larger gross margin in the branded market.

Accordingly, for these types of goods, it seems very unlikely indeed that the consequences of branding and advertising will be the simple ones described in some theories, of prices being high and yielding abnormal profits because of advertising. Further, in practically all these types of goods, there will be competing goods which are not branded by the manufacturers. The development of methods of mass selling of rather standardized products has been important here, and the advertised and branded goods have to stand up to the competition which is thus involved. Certainly, the normal position is not of advertisers competing in the extension of their market through advertising and, then, the price automatically rising to cover such excessive costs, or of the price being artificially held high above the level which would otherwise be reached on the basis of the sheer costs of production and distribution at the expanded level of the market. An abnormal gross profit margin, apart from advertising, will stimulate competition in this type of market just as much as in any other.

Of course, advertising wars can develop. A sudden burst of high-pressure advertising on the part of one manufacturer may well bring him in large returns, but there seems no reason to reject the view that these gains will be temporary. The consequence of such an advertising war seems more likely to be that the profits of the participants will be abnormally low in the end, but that their share of the market will be the same. Further, for the kind of product that is being considered now, it is unlikely that the total market will expand very much — i.e. the demand for any collective group of such goods tends to be as inelastic to advertising as to price changes. Businesses are well aware of this situation, and, generally, it is met by proper caution in the matter of advertising. Expenditure of this kind will run at a fairly regular level, given the type of market which the business is sharing. Furthermore, it is usually held in check by conventional rules that it should bear only a certain relation to sales, and that the resources for it should be provided out of profits rather than in expectation of profits.

It may here be noted that the efforts of the advertising industry often account for a war developing between advertisers of this type of good. There are few other industries where it can be at all true that the mere success in selling your product to one customer guarantees that another customer will call at your doors with an order: which is why the advertising journals devote so much space to reporting the details of the advertising campaigns of individual manufacturers *pour encourager les autres*. Once one particular manufacturer steps up his advertising, the others are forced to do the same. This is particularly likely to happen in moderately good times or when good times are just on the turn. It is then that some manufacturer is likely to be tempted to use some of the resources which he has in order to obtain extra orders, very likely with initial but temporary success in snatching a part of a rival's market, and then the chase begins. Bad times, however, generally cause the return to more rational conduct and to an acceptance of the share of the market which comes naturally.

This situation is much more likely to develop in the rather special markets for the classes of commodities where the market is always unstable, so far as the demand of the individual consumer, or of a large proportion of the individual consumers, is concerned. This class of products will be dominated by those cases where variety is demanded for its own sake; they vary from sweets and chocolates and toothpaste to goods whose chief attraction is that they conform to fashion, even though they may incidentally clothe the body. It cannot be said that these goods have little intrinsic merit; they cater for genuine needs.[1]

The producer who does not advertise cannot expect to keep his share of the market, for he must advertise in order

---

[1] And, incidentally, were it not for some of them, the inducement for the young female to work in factories and elsewhere for more than her strict living costs would be considerably weakened; the provision of these goods thus facilitates the manufacture of other goods welcomed by the most austere economist.

to keep the name of his product before the changing consumers. They will choose on the basis of the merits of the
goods as they see them, but advertisement widens the range of
goods at which they will look. If there were no advertising,
the product would almost certainly not be produced on the
same scale as it is now, or in some cases it would not be
produced at all, and advertising is certainly necessary to keep
some stability in the market for the individual business when
the demand of the individual consumer is so unstable.

Further, advertising will have to be very regular in this
type of market and will always be running at a relatively
heavy level. It will consequently be much easier for one
business, finding that an extended sales campaign appears to
be paying for itself, to step things up for the sake of the short-
period gain, which may be very important in what is a fashion
trade. If taste is swinging from boiled sweets to chocolates,
it can be encouraged to move the faster, and in the particular
direction of the advertiser. Advertising wars are consequently
as important in these industries as price-cutting would tend
to be if the normal pricing rules did not offer some restraint.
There would, in fact, be scope for agreements to keep advertising down in a similar fashion to those agreements which
have been developed to prevent simple price-cutting,[1] but it
is much more difficult to enforce, in so far as the market of
this type is peculiarly liable to be upset by the emergence of
new businesses, especially where economies of scale are not
very important.

It still seems likely that the normal consequence of excessive advertising will be abnormally low profits, or losses,
rather than prices which automatically cover the advertising
costs even when these are at a higher level than would enable
the business to keep its share of the long-term market. It
may, of course, happen that the risks of heavy advertising

---

[1] Such agreements have, in fact, developed between cigarette manufacturers
and between newspaper proprietors in the matter of gift-coupon advertising,
and tacit agreement has sometimes been reached in other industries.

necessary to force a larger share of the market will prevent businesses from growing in a way otherwise justified by the costs position, but such advertising as there is will have facilitated what growth has taken place.

SUMMARY OF CONCLUSIONS

In short, difficult though the subject is, our conclusion is that, in the normal types of advertised commodities, it is doubtful if advertising does result in excessive prices, and probable that it facilitates prices being lower than they would otherwise be. Certainly there is no question of their being used to bolster up a pricing policy of the kind described in the modern theory of monopolistic competition, where price is fixed so as to get maximum profits by producing only that output whose marginal cost equals its marginal revenue. The business man will still decide his price policy on the basis of his normal average costs, and, if these include more than the normal advertising costs for his market, he will have to lower his price to the normal level or lose his market.

The business man was, earlier in this chapter, described as determining his price on the basis of the normal costing rules and then simply producing whatever the market takes at that price. While it has become usual in economic theory to picture him as extending that market as far as he thinks desirable by means of the selling costs which he incurs, the broad conclusion of this part of the chapter is that the bulk of selling costs do not extend the market but are the service costs involved in selling the output which the market takes. Even in the case of advertising costs, it will very often be true that the *nature* of the market, and not its *extent*, will determine these costs, which should, accordingly, be seen as entailed in the business remaining in its market, however much it sells at the given price.

CHAPTER VI

MARKETS AND PRICES: PART II
THE FACTOR-MARKETS

(1) INTRODUCTORY

THE general conclusion of the theory which has so far been developed is that, *given* the prices of the factors of production, the price of a manufactured article will remain constant at the level determined by its average direct costs *plus* the competitively determined gross profit margin. At that price the business will produce whatever the market will take from it up to the limit of its capacity in the short run, but expanding in the long run to whatever scale is necessary to meet the demands of its market. It follows that the quantities of the various factors of production which the business will wish to employ will be determined by the demand for the product at the given price.[1] The next and final chapter of this book will be concerned with, amongst other things, what determines the demand for manufacturing products at any one time. The main question for this chapter to answer is to what extent manufacturing businesses' demand for factors of production will affect the prices which they have to pay.

The factors of production which a manufacturing business buys or hires may be classified into the services of employees and producers' goods bought from other businesses. In so far as the latter are the manufactured products of other

---

[1] Part of the total demand will come from the business itself in so far as it holds stocks of its own product, but this will not affect the theory of this chapter, and it will be convenient to postpone taking account of it until the next chapter.

businesses, it will not be necessary to pay special attention to the problem of their prices in this chapter, for that has been settled for this type of good, the resulting theory being summed up at the opening of this chapter. Accordingly, the present analysis will be concerned with the wages of labour and the prices of the strictly primary materials which enter into industrial production, and the relevant prices of these latter will be those which they fetch in their first form as the natural products of farms and mines.

These two types of factor markets will complete the analysis so far as real factors of production are concerned, but it will be necessary to analyse one more market for the sake of later theory — the market for loanable funds and for money capital. It was seen in Chapter I that the owners of a business are responsible for its financing, and will have to be the chief sources of the money which is used to buy the capital equipment and to provide circulating capital. In so far as they have not provided enough money capital to finance the business, they will have to induce other people to lend it money or to join them as owners. The business's effective demand for factors of production may, therefore, be limited by the resources which are available, even when the business's market might otherwise justify a larger employment of those factors. The final section of this chapter will, therefore, have to consider the capital market, which is the general source of funds for the financing of business.

Before turning on to the details of the particular markets which have been distinguished, it may be useful to give the explicit warning that we shall take into account only what are considered to be the broad essential characteristics of such markets. This is justified since the conclusions are wanted for the sake of the general theory of the behaviour of manufacturing business, and it will not be necessary to go into the details and peculiarities of special instances of any of the three broad classes of markets that are distinguished.

(2) THE PRICES OF PRIMARY MATERIALS

The primary materials of industry are bought for their inherent natural properties, and those properties can generally be measured and tested in one way or another. Of course, the supply of any particular material will not generally be of even quality, but this analysis need not be complicated by that fact; we may assume such differences in quality to be graded. The market will then come to deal in standard grades of the commodity, and may be assumed to use price differentials to reckon up the equivalence of the various grades. It will, therefore, be possible to speak as if the market were supplied with only one standard grade of quality and to analyse the market as if it dealt in that grade only.

The properties by reason of which a material is bought being capable of objective tests, there will be no room for the market of an individual producer being limited to a particular group of customers because of the confidence given by previous custom. Allowance being made for the effects of costs of transport and of any other hindrances to the movement of goods, a primary producer will not have to accept a price from any purchaser which is significantly lower than another is already paying to any other producer. Similarly, no buyer will purchase from any one primary producer at a higher price than would be quoted by someone else, allowance again being made for the costs involved in any transference of the materials. Such costs of transport apart, it follows that there can be only one price in the market at any given time, the market will be potentially world-wide, and, as was said in Chapter V, any individual producer of a primary product is better seen as selling to the market as a whole, rather than as possessing his own market.

It will also be characteristic of most primary materials that they come from many independent sources of supply

P

and that the total output of any individual producer will be too small in relation to the total quantity on the market for him to be able to affect the price which he is offered, by withholding supplies from the market, or by varying the output which he produces. Such producers will, therefore, tend to accept market price and to throw on the market at that price whatever output they may produce. Since we are concerned with the general theory of the activity of manufacturing business and not with the detailed theory of these primary markets, we need not pause to take into account the special cases where the concentration of the production of a particular material within a small area of the earth's surface has encouraged the banding together of producers, hoping by their union to get that control over their market which they could not hope to exercise separately. Similarly, it may generally be assumed that no single buyer in a typical materials market will take so large a proportion of the total supply that he can influence the market price which will be quoted to him.

Each producer of a given material will make plans to produce it only if he is reasonably sure that he will cover his costs and get a normal reward for his own exertions and expenditure. As far as existing producers are concerned, of course, we must draw a distinction between their total costs for the quantity which they are producing and the paying-out costs of that output. In so far as the start of production has involved the sinking of capital, they may find it worth their while to *continue* producing even if they do not get a normal return on such — in the circumstances — irrelevant expenditure. No such producer will, however, *extend* his supply, and no new producer will come into production, unless he expects to cover all his costs and make a normal profit.

The supply of any particular material will not all be produced at the same cost. There will be differences in the natural advantages of any source of supply and they will tend to lie at varying distances from the consumers. Some producers will, therefore, require higher prices at source than others if production is to be worth while; others will require higher prices for their product as delivered to the consumer than those with the same costs of production. Even in the case of the supply controlled by a single producer, it will often be the case that he can produce a smaller supply more cheaply than a larger one. For example, certain fields may be more suitable than others for the production of a particular crop, and a higher price will be necessary to justify its production from the other fields; or, again, in a certain mine some seams will be easier to work than others, and it will be profitable to work them at a lower price than would justify the opening of the others.[1]

There is another characteristic of the primary materials markets to which it will be necessary to make reference at some points of the analysis. It will be normal in many markets for the materials to reach the consumers through the hands of dealers who specialize in trading in them. This will tend particularly to be the case with the materials whose sources are especially numerous or scattered, so that dealers perform the function of collecting a material from its sources and selling it to the relatively fewer or concentrated — but generally numerous — consumers. The mere fact of such a market, in any case, tends to call into existence such a body of specialized dealers, making a living out of their trading in a commodity for which they have a greater specialized knowledge than either the producers or the consumers.

These dealers as a whole will hold stocks of the commodity, since this will be necessary if they are to be able to make deliveries despite any temporary breakdown in supplies.

---

[1] This calls attention to one point of difference between extractive industries and agricultural industries — that the production even of a constant supply of the former types of products will involve rising costs, the lower-cost sources getting used up and involving recourse to inferior sources of supply. This matter of long-term trends of prices is not relevant to the theory developed in this book.

In the case of agricultural materials, this stock-holding function will be especially important, because such materials will come on the market in great quantities at harvest-time, but will be consumed more gradually over the year. The convenience to the agricultural producer of having his output taken off his hands at harvest will leave a normal difference between the prices during the year and the price obtainable at harvest-time, out of which the dealer can recoup himself for the costs of storage.

In such a market the theory of the long-run equilibrium price is relatively simple. For any given supply the price cannot be lower than will just repay the costs (including normal profits) of the most expensive portion of the supply. A lower price will cause the more expensive producers to go out of production. Similarly a higher price will call forth an increase in supply by making it profitable for inferior sources of supply to come into production. If the demand for a primary material will not absorb the supply that is coming forward, price must fall to the level which will restrict the supply to the demand. If the demand is higher than can be met by the existing supply, then market price will tend to rise until once again it is such that a supply equivalent to the demand is coming forward. In the long run, then, an increased demand for a primary material will be met only at a rise of price, and similarly a falling demand for such a material will cause a fall in price. This generalization, like the analysis which it follows, presumes a given state of knowledge and technique, etc.

In the short run, a moderate increase of demand may be met at the expense of a fall in the stocks held by dealers, and market price may not rise. If the rise in demand is sustained, then dealers will wish to increase their depleted stocks as well as to meet the increased demand, and their competition will send up price, possibly very sharply as compared with the level at which price will settle down in the long run, which, as we have seen, will still tend to be higher than the level before demand increased. Before the short run merges into the long run, however, some oscillation of price is possible. The increased prices will act as a signal for increased output on the part of the producers, and, where there are very many of them, the total amount that is at first produced may be too large even for the increased demand, so that the dealers will have to absorb the excess in additions to their stocks. Any such increase in stocks will involve them in additional expenses and will be made only if the dealers think that price, when the extra stocks are sold, will repay them these additional costs as well as the actual price which they pay for the commodity. Any such excess supply will, therefore, cause a fall in the price of the commodity, since dealers will not buy unless the price is right, and it may even, temporarily, fall below the level which it had before demand increased.

In the event of a great excess of supply over demand, the dealers' capacity to absorb the extra stocks will be limited by one factor, quite apart from their ability to finance the holding of such stocks and their judgment that the difference in price will repay the costs involved in that finance; this will be the physical capacity which they have in which to place the extra stocks. If ever that limit is reached, and it certainly exists, then the dealers' demand will fall to the level at which they are actually selling out of stocks, and price will have to fall to a sufficiently low level to induce the producers to hold the additional supplies themselves. Any such serious discrepancy is likely to appear chiefly for agricultural products, where the time-lag between seed-time and harvest will lengthen the period before producers realize that they cannot in fact get the higher price which they counted on in order to justify the extra production.[1]

Similarly, any fall in demand will, at first, cause price to fall to a lower level than that at which it will produce a

---

[1] Note that for commodities like rubber and coffee the interval between planting and cropping may be as long as several years.

supply equal to the reduced demand. For the temporarily excessive supply has to be accommodated. Dealers will find that their stocks are increasing and will, therefore, reduce price to that level at which they are willing to hold the extra stocks. In the long run, as we have seen, this fall of price will discourage production and pull it down to a level at which it will equal the demand which is coming to the market. This fall may be especially sharp because it may take a long time to induce producers to curtail their output. This will be particularly the case for specialist products, such as some highly localized agricultural commodities. In fact, a specialist producer running into debt, but unable to produce anything else, may well react to a fall of price by increasing his output, trying, out of sheer desperation, to make the best of a bad job and knowing that his own small contribution to the total supply will not affect the price on the market. Something like the same phenomenon may also appear in mined products, where the producer who is committed to heavy paying-out costs may yet try to get back as much as he can by increasing his output.[1] Between the short-run level of price and its long-run level there may be oscillations of the kind referred to in the previous paragraph ; for a sharp fall of price may discourage production too much, as compared with the demand, and cause a rise in price until the higgling is done and supply settles down once more.

For the present theory we may leave out of account any oscillations of the kind referred to in the two preceding paragraphs, severe enough to reverse temporarily the tendency of price. These are unlikely, because we have rarely to deal with any sudden once-for-all change in the demand for a primary product in the real world, but rather with a general trend which is gradual and sustained over a period of years, or else, within any such trend, with the changes in demand over the trade cycle, where again the changes in demand,

---

[1] This type of reaction may provide a social justification for attempts at restricting the production of such commodities.

although relatively sharp, will continue for at least a few years in succession and will not manifest themselves all at once. With that exception, then, the conclusion is that a rising demand for a primary product will cause a rise in price in the short-run to a higher level than will be sustained in the long-run. Similarly, a fall in demand will cause a fall in price, and, once more, to a more extreme level in the short run than that at which it will be maintained in the long run. We shall use this general conclusion in later analysis whenever we are imagining such a change in the activity of manufacturing business as is likely to cause an appreciable change in the *total* demand for the primary materials of industry.

What is the effect of changes in the activity of individual manufacturing business on the prices of the materials which it uses? If such a business is imagined as growing so large and so rapidly that it comes to take a large proportion of the supply of any particular material, then its growth will entail a rise in the prices that it pays for its materials. In general, however, such a case will be rather rare. It will be met, in practice, chiefly where a business is localized near a cheap source of a particular material which is weight-losing (e.g. coal, which is destroyed in the process of production) or expensive to transport, but is producing a product which will stand any extra costs of transport involved in its location. The growth of such a business may well bring it to such a scale that it dominates the local supply and has to have recourse to more distant sources of supply, which, because of higher costs of production or transport, are more expensive. But it is suggested that, for our general theory, we can assume that the typical case is such that neither the growth in scale of such a business nor any normal fluctuations in its demand for its materials will affect the prices which it has to pay. In consequence, so far as materials are concerned, we shall not wish to modify the conclusions reached in Chapter III.

Quite apart from such market prices of primary materials, it is, of course, true that the cost of them to a business will be affected by the growth of that business. A very small business may get some advantages — to balance against any disadvantages in its position — because it can make use of any casual sources of supply — e.g. it may use the scrap thrown out by a bigger business. The size of business to which this economy will apply is necessarily very small scale, and, otherwise, as a business grows it is usually true that it will be able to make economies in its purchase and handling of materials. There will normally be discounts offered for the taking of certain minimum quantities, due to the greater economy to the trader of supplying these rather than smaller quantities — e.g. supplying in whole truck-loads. Also, the actual warehousing costs will fall if the business is large enough to provide specialized warehouses, etc., for its materials.

Although these economies exist, practical experience shows that they are *relatively* small, even over quite a big growth of a business, and we shall propose to ignore them in the later theory. We shall assume, therefore, that the costs of materials will not be affected by the conduct of any individual business, although they will be affected by the activity of any significant proportion of the manufacturing businesses using a given material. Once again, the earlier conclusions about the behaviour of costs of production are thought to be substantially unchanged.

Before we turn to consider the labour market, it will be convenient here to refer to the fact that changes in the activity of primary industries may have serious effects upon activity in manufacturing industries, due to the effect of the sharp changes that will be entailed in the prices of primary products on the incomes of their producers. The changes in the incomes of the primary producers will affect their demand for the products of manufacturing industry. This matter is not taken up in any detail, since it is not relevant to the main pattern of the analysis of this book, and, in our later theory, we shall simply be analysing the effect of changes in the activity in manufacturing industry upon the price of the materials which it uses.

(3) THE WAGES OF LABOUR

The analysis in this section will be much less subtle than it would need to be, if we were constructing a theory of wages for its own sake. For the theory of business activity we need only to answer the question : in what ways the wages of the labour employed by manufacturing industry will be affected by changes in the demand for such labour, either on the part of an individual business or generally. A quite broad answer will suit our purpose. The demand for labour in manufacturing industry will depend upon the total demand for the product, and this may be taken for granted in this part of the analysis. Our general question then becomes, what wage will the employer have to pay for a labour-force of the required size.

There is first the difficulty that labour of any class is certainly not naturally a homogeneous commodity, since the individual human beings will have very different potentialities and be of different grades of practical efficiency. We may evade this difficulty, by assuming that the employer pays differential wages or offers differential advantages which recognize the value to him of such differences in performance. Alternatively, if the terms of the wage contract are such that he pays a flat rate to each individual regardless of his performance, then it will not lead to any serious practical error if we assume that the employer will tend to get a more or less standard output per head. It will, therefore, be possible to speak as if any particular labour-market were, in fact, composed of individuals each of the same efficiency, and our theory will be in terms of the wage paid to such standard labour units unless specific notice is given to the contrary.

The General Demand for Labour

Looking first at the behaviour of wages in response to the changing demand of manufacturing industry as a whole — i.e. where the whole market demand for any class of labour is assumed to be affected — it is first necessary to recognize that the *whole* labour-force cannot be treated as homogeneous in the manner described above. It must be split up into a number of classes which are sufficiently distinct in type for the wages of each class to have some element of independent determination, even if only potentially. The principal basis for this splitting into economically distinct classes will be the exercise of different skills. These call for different types of training, and, at any one time, the demand for any one class of labour can be met only from those who have received the appropriate training. Only within each such class may the men be considered to be all alike.

The extent to which any such class can be increased by fresh recruits will be determined by a number of factors. The necessity of training them will impose a time-lag rather than cause any restriction of supply. The occupation may, however, require especial aptitudes or the training may be expensive either in actual money outlay or because low training wages are received for a relatively long time. The more expensive the training or the higher the abilities required from new entrants, the more difficult it will be to increase the supply of employees of a given class, and as a general, long-run fact, the higher will tend to be the average wage which will have to be paid for the class concerned, as compared with a class demanding a less restrictive sort of training. Otherwise, the occupation concerned would not be able to attract the new labour necessary to maintain its numbers in the face of the competition from those occupations with less onerous conditions of entry.

We may, in fact, lay it down as a general rule that, between successive levels of occupation graded according to the rarity of the natural aptitudes that they require or according to the expense of training, the normal wage which will have to be paid will rise more than in proportion to the apparent strength of these limiting factors. Thus, to take the monetary obstacles as being easier for quantitative demonstration, if we calculate the differences between the normal wage-levels for occupations graded according to the total costs of training, and calculate these as rates of interest upon the money which may be imagined as having been laid out in training, that rate of interest will rise progressively as we move to successively higher grades. Of course, in so far as an occupation is especially attractive, by reason of its prestige or because its other non-monetary conditions are especially attractive, it is to be expected that this will be reflected in a lessened difference between its level of wages and those applicable to another class of occupation.

In actual fact, of course, the entry into any occupation may be restricted by forces other than those of the quality required of the trainee or the expense which will have to be laid out on his training. The chief examples of such restrictions upon entry will come from the trade unions, whose job it is to organize the workers in particular occupations and to protect their interests. The desire of the trade unions to protect the wages of their members has naturally led them to seek to control the supply of future labourers by means of apprenticeships and traineeships. Such power is usually based, where it is important, upon the degree of skill required in some key positions filled by members of the trade union, so that their indispensability in the short run enables the union to insist upon the right to a say in the fixing of the number admitted to training. Of course, the position of the union will become weakened where technical changes reduce the importance of any particular skills, and it will be less able to insist upon any restriction of the numbers of new entrants, beyond that caused by forces outside its direct control.

Our relatively simple theory may, therefore, see the supply

of labour to manufacturing industry as divided into a hierarchy of groups or classes, according to the restrictions upon entry, however caused. The normal wages payable to any one class will rise with the relative position of that class in the general scale. At the bottom of the scale will come what are usually called the unskilled occupations — in fact this is rather a misnomer, since it is not true that their members are without skill, but their skill is rather of the kind that comes naturally on the job, without any especially long or expensive training. A better term is, therefore, the general-skilled occupations. As has been said, the normal forces operating in the labour-market will tend to cause settled differences to be established between the levels of wages in these different classes of occupations. It will be desirable for our subsequent theory to note that these differences will be especially clearly recognized as between any special-skilled grade of labour and the general-skilled labourers with whom it works. In time, this differentiation of wages becomes written into the thinking of all concerned, and is upset only with the greatest difficulty, after contrary economic forces have been in operation for a long time.

So far as the lowest class of general-skilled labour is concerned, it is especially important to note that its position will normally be weaker than that of the special-skilled occupations, not merely because there are hardly any restrictions on new entrants in the form of juveniles entering industry for the first time (which will be the chief form of entry into those other occupations), but also because it will tend to receive recruits from older people who have already been working in other occupations but have become displaced from them. The position of such labour will, accordingly, tend to worsen in a trade depression relatively to higher grades of occupation.

It may be taken for granted that workmen of any class will always desire to have their wages increased, and those who are employed may be thought of as always exercising some pressure in that direction. It will not give a correct picture of the position of the employers' side to say that they are *always* desirous of forcing wages down. Given the ruling rate of wages, prices will have been fixed so as normally to cover them, and the employer will accept the *status quo* unless he is in a period of falling output, so that the reduced coverage of overheads endangers his profit position. Certainly, if employers are not only making losses but are having difficulty in covering their paying-out costs, then they will seek to get relief from reduced wages. The bargaining pressure of employers should, therefore, be seen as usually devoted to restraining any tendency for wages to rise, becoming a positive pressure to get a reduction of wages only in times of falling markets.

To return to the position of labour: employees should be assumed generally to act through a trade union — in manufacturing industry as a whole, we can disregard the rare instances of the wages of labour being a matter of separate bargaining between individual labourers and their employer. The trade union as an organization representing its members, and the trade union leaders as individuals paid by the labour whom they represent, will always be conscious of the desirability of securing wage advances whenever possible. The ability of the trade union to secure higher wages rests, in the last resort, upon the right to strike, which means that conditions must be such that the body of employees in the particular occupation concerned will put up with the (possibly severe) short-run inconveniences arising from a strike in order to gain their day.

The power of organized labour, therefore, depends directly upon the difficulty which employers will have in finding substitute labour to take the place of the members of the union should they come out on strike. In the short run this will depend upon the degree of unemployment, both among the members of the particular occupation in question and in the country generally. The union will be especially conscious of a weak position if there is heavy unemployment among its members. The unemployed members will wish to secure jobs and will not be so keen to support an agitation for higher wages which will endanger their position. This balance, between the weakness arising from the fact of unemployed members and the strength of the pressure for higher wages from members who are in employment, will determine whether any particular occupation will be pressing for higher wages or not.[1] Accordingly, as a very simple statement of the position, we may imagine there to be a critical minimum level of employment below which the unions will not press for rising wages, although always prepared to resist any pressure from the employers for wage-cuts. After this degree of employment has been reached, there will be agitation to get higher wages, which will succeed in time and, thereby, cause costs and prices to rise for the products produced by the members of the unions concerned.

In the long run, the power of any union to maintain a given level of wages will also be affected by the relative attraction of that wage, given all the restrictions upon entry, to persons who would otherwise enter other occupations. Accordingly, it will be difficult for them to maintain a discrepancy in the level of wages which is greater than the facts of the case warrant. Sometimes the short-run indispensability of the skilled men enables the union to hold back the tide, but then there is a tendency for the ground to be cut from under the feet of the union, through the incentive which they are giving to individual employers to operate with a non-union labour-force, substituting, perhaps, less skilled labour working with more mechanical aids and with a greater subdivision of the actual tasks of production. Newer businesses will often be free to make such a fresh start and in time the position of the skilled craftsman will be endangered.

Quite apart from the effect of circumstances peculiar to

[1] This theory has been suggested by Mrs. Joan Robinson in her essay, ' Full Employment ', in *Essays in the Theory of Employment*.

the employment in the particular occupation concerned, there are two other sorts of influences at work, which tend to go the same way as the simple bargaining factors to which we have referred, given any general changes in industrial activity. The first is the fact that workmen, like other people, wish to maintain a given standard of life, once that has become sufficiently established for them to take it for granted. Rises in the general price level, therefore, tend to produce an increased pressure for higher wages. In many industries this has been explicitly recognized in the official rate of wages becoming tied in some way to a cost-of-living index number. The second factor is that, again like other persons, employees are brought up to the idea of a relative social status, and, in particular, they will get the idea of a normal difference between their standard of living, if they are special-skilled workmen, and the standard of the labourers who work with them. There will, therefore, be a general tendency for the more highly skilled workmen to increase their pressure for higher wages if circumstances result in the wages of general-skilled labourers being increased. Both of these factors, a rising cost of living and increasing wages for general-skilled workmen, will tend to be present in periods of increasing general industrial activity.

The wages of the normal type of general-skilled workmen are determined much more like the prices of a primary commodity, in so far as such workmen are difficult to organize in trade unions in normal times and are much more vulnerable to the presence of possible substitutes from outside any such union. In any large industrial area, the wages of such labour, even though employed in quite different industries, will tend to a general level, which will be quotable as the market-rate, and will become established through the bargaining of employers and of potential employees. This circumstance is mentioned here because it will be important in our later explanation of the course of activity and prices during the trade cycle. In our later theory we shall not pay much attention to the position of salaried employees. Here let it merely be said that their salaries will tend to move roughly with the wages of ordinary wage-labour but that they will move rather more slowly and with a time-lag.

THE INDIVIDUAL BUSINESS'S DEMAND FOR LABOUR

For the remainder of this section of the chapter we shall be concerned with the effects of the demand for labour in an individual business upon the wages which it pays — the demand for labour will be taken as given, since, as said before, we are not now discussing what determines the demand for the products of the business. Its demand for labour will simply reflect the demand for its products. Despite the general conclusion which has just been reached — that a rise in the general demand for any particular class of labour will make it necessary for employers to pay higher wages — and despite the fact that a typical manufacturing business will normally demand only a small proportion of the total supply of labour of a specified class — in spite of these we cannot dismiss the matter, as we could in the case of primary materials, and say that changes in the demand for labour in the individual business could exercise only a negligible influence upon price. Employees are not moved about as easily as physical materials, and, although it was quite legitimate to ignore this fact when discussing the effect of varying industrial activity and the consequent general demand for labour upon the general levels of wages, we cannot do so in the case of the individual business, where it is of crucial importance.

Workmen will reside in a particular area and will prefer to work near their homes. It will not be easy for them to move to another area. The actual costs of such movement will be a deterrent whose strength will be very great when once a man has become old enough to have his own household; but on top of that will come all the strength of the psychological factors which tend to root a man to his house and to the area in which he lives. It will be easier for a business to expand if it can get the labour which it wants from near by. Some examples can be given which show just how strong the preference for continuing to work in a given area can be; they are all the more impressive because each of them concerns the case of movement within the same town, and does not involve any great distances or the removal of the workers' households:

A textile business in the North of England owns two mills, each only a few hundred yards from the other. They are under the same general management. When, after the war, the firm decided to modernize its factories, it started first on one of the mills. In the course of modernization it made a good many improvements from the point of view of the working conditions of labour, which it could not make in the still unreorganized mill. When this case was reported, there was a great scarcity of labour both in the industry and in the town in which the business operated. At the time of the reconstruction of the first mill, the business was just emerging from war-time restrictions and from concentration. Its labour position was obscure, therefore, but it had always had a good reputation as an employer of labour, so it hoped that its improved conditions would enable it to hold its own. Its surprise can be imagined when it found that its reputation did enable it to hold its own and that it developed a queue of applicants for employment — but at the *older* mill! The matter was carefully investigated and the only reason seemed to be that the newly reorganized mill lay across the one side of a particular street and the available labour came from, and preferred to work on, the other side. A similar case was that of a small business in a large town in the Midlands which, de-concentrating after the war, had to take new but much better premises. Difficulty was found in getting labour. The reason appeared to be that the new location involved a walk from a bus stop, which was certainly less than half a mile, whereas previously the workers had been able to get off the bus at the factory gate.

The examples given in the previous paragraph relate to exceptional conditions from the point of view of full employment and labour scarcity, and, moreover, in each case the labour had already been displaced from the business and it was a question of getting it back. In normal circumstances, a man will prefer to continue working with the same business, and will not often be faced with the prospect of that business changing its location. The business in which he works is part of the life of the employee. He spends the best part of his waking hours there in the week, and it is not just the place where he works; some of his most important social relationships are at his work, and men do not like changing their society (this is one of the strongest factors making men disinclined to move their home).

When he has settled down in a particular factory, a man will also have got used to it, developing an intimate knowledge of the habits and requirements of the management under which he works.[1] All these consequences of familiarity combine in the end to make the work itself seem easier and make the performance of the daily duty become more of a routine. Working in a new business must bring enough preliminary trials and tribulations, but, however light these may prove in fact, there will be the added fears of the change, in prospect.

The upshot of all this is that an individual business cannot be supposed to draw on the whole labour supply in the occupations in which it is interested. It is much more near the truth to regard it as having its own supply of labour. The business which has established itself will have relations with a group of workmen whom it normally employs, and who will look to it for employment, even though at any one time they may be temporarily unemployed. If other busi-

---

[1] Just what a strange foreman means by a particular remark may be a mystery which causes a great deal of worry to a new man, until he gets to know the foreman and the way he sets about things.

nesses are operating in its area, the same will be true of them. There will probably also be a more floating body of persons who are not so clearly attached to any one business and who may be attracted by the prospect of employment in a business which is obviously growing, and, therefore, likely to offer more continuous employment than other businesses which are more stationary. In normal times, such a floating connexion will be dominated by older persons who have fallen out of employment, and by juveniles who have not yet settled in their job or in their employment. These classes of persons will be available to the business if it is expanding gradually and it will not be necessary for the business to offer increased wages in order to attract them at a gradual pace. In any large industrial areas, such as that around Birmingham, and especially for the lower types of skills, a business may have available a relatively large pool of labour, if enough time is given for workers to get to know the prospects.

If a business wishes to expand beyond this, or at a faster rate than the extra labourers will come to it at its existing wages, it will have to bid away workmen who have a preference for remaining where they are already. If it grows to the point where any further expansion will mean that it has to attract workers away from other areas, then the costs of so doing will rise markedly. This is especially likely to be the case with special-skilled workmen, of whom large numbers are not likely to be available, unless the business is expanding right against the general trend for the other employers of labour of this class in its area, so that it has a reservoir of unemployed on which to draw.

If, then, we stick to the strict letter of the case usually described in economic theory and ask what will happen to wages as a business grows at a given rate per unit of time, expanding its demand for labour correspondingly, the answer must be that, whilst the early stages of growth may not cause much trouble, at some stage it will have to bid away workmen from other firms or from other areas. Accordingly, if we made our later analysis on the basis of assuming a business to grow as rapidly as possible, irrespective of other factors, the growth in scale of a business must be seen as involving rising wage-rates, sending up direct costs of production and tending to cause total costs of production to rise, unless offset by technical economies.

It will be useful, however, to approach the problem a little more realistically. Let us first take the case of a business which is just starting up. Its founder will be well aware of the necessity of seeing that he has an adequate labour supply available and will not locate his business unless he thinks that he can get sufficient labour not only to start but to see him through the early stages of growth — i.e. to that scale to which he thinks his business will probably develop. Thus, if a business is of the modern technological kind, requiring a fairly large scale of production and number of men if it is to work at something like reasonable technical efficiency, it will usually locate itself either where there is a considerable volume of unemployment already, importing key personnel if necessary from other areas and paying them relatively high wages, or at least chose an area where the existing industries cannot afford such high rates of wages as it can.

Now let us suppose that the business grows, or wishes to grow, having found an expanding demand for its product. It will look at its wages policy from the long-term point of view and will not just rush into paying whatever rates are necessary in order to get the labour which its market demand would otherwise justify. It certainly will not act as supposed in the usual theory, continuously increasing its wages as it bids for an expanding labour-force. There is first the fact that such conduct on its part is likely to start wage-competition from other employers of the same type of labour in its area. If that develops, the business may be left with a labour-force which has expanded only slightly, but for which it has to pay very greatly increased rates of wages.

Such a situation bears resemblances to the price-cutting situation discussed in the previous Chapter. Its consequences will, naturally, deter the business man, in so far as he can foresee them. He will be especially reluctant to face them if, as will often be the case, other important units of his industry are located elsewhere, so that such a rise in wages will diminish his competing power.

The individual business, however, will have strong reasons against recruiting labour by means of naked wage-bidding, quite apart from this question of starting competition for labour which will frustrate itself in the long run. It will look at the matter from the point of view of a continuing business with an interest in settled relations with its workpeople. Too great a rate of growth is liable to bring disturbing factors anyway. The firm will wish the newcomers to settle down in the business and will wish to choose them carefully, bearing this in mind. If it gets its labour by snatching tactics based on the wage-packet, it will not only be liable to attract newcomers whom it will find undesirable in the long run, but it will also tend to unsettle relations with its existing workpeople.

In general, then, a business will be reluctant to grow at a faster rate than is suitable to its local labour conditions. No business minds having a moderately unsatisfied order book, so long as it is clearing the position in the long run. A business which sees that, as a long-term policy, it will need to grow at a very quick rate, will tend to offer a rate of wages which is rather higher than the district rate, and to maintain that rate, growing from the labour which comes to it naturally rather than forcing the pace by continually putting up wages. If it desires to grow at a faster rate than this, the normal tendency will be to put down another plant in a distinctly separate area from the point of view of labour supply. The weakening of technical economies with increasing size of plant will mean that the disadvantages of this policy grow less and there will be some compensating gain, in so far as the separate plants may compete one with the other so as to get maximum efficiency. A rapidly growing business thus tends to grow by establishing separate productive establishments. In general, whichever way it grows, a business will always prefer to grow by stages and to consolidate its position at each successive stage.

The theory of the behaviour of costs of production as a business grows in scale was discussed on the basis of assumed constant wage costs in the main part of Chapter IV. The analysis, there given, should be modified, if we stick to its strict terms. Costs of production would strictly tend to rise with a given rate of growth, once the business began to press on the reservoir of labour and to bid extra labourers from outside the normal channels. Our conclusion is, however, that it would be more realistic to regard the fact that such growth would cause higher wages, as entailing a restriction on the rate of growth rather than higher costs. The greater part of the later analysis, however, will be concerned with short-term changes in the output of an individual business, especially in the course of the trade cycle, and so will not be affected.

A business, in its initial planning, will try to ensure that it can meet any normal fluctuations and must make some allowance for, say, trade cycle or seasonal fluctuations. Certainly, then, if its output increases by an amount within this range, while other businesses are stationary, it will probably be able to get the extra employees that it needs. In any case, however, it will not at first try to make an expanded output on the basis of additions to its permanent staff. It will normally be able to meet extra output by working its existing staff overtime, and will always do this wherever possible, in addition to taking on any likely newcomers that present themselves at the given wage-rate. Similarly, it will tend to meet any short-term reduction of output by working short-time and thereby keeping its labour as a reserve against any later re-expansion. These cases have already been discussed at length in Chapter III, and they are merely mentioned now as part of a general statement. Later on, when we are discussing the independent growth of a business at a normal rate, or when we are discussing the effects of normal fluctuations in its output considered by itself, we shall assume that there is no serious pressure upon wage-rates, and can continue to use the analysis built up in the chapters on costs of production. When, on the other hand, as in the analysis of the trade cycle, we are concerned with a situation in which businesses generally are trying to expand, we shall assume (in accordance with the conclusions of the first part of this section) that the level of wage-rates will rise and that, accordingly, the level of costs, and particularly of direct costs, will rise.

(4) THE COST AND AVAILABILITY OF CAPITAL RESOURCES

As we know already, a manufacturing business will require capital resources for two main purposes: to acquire its fixed assets and to provide itself with sufficient floating capital (the latter being required to finance its current output, holdings of stocks, and debts, as well as to provide a reserve for any emergencies). The first questions to be answered in this section are, what determines the demand for such resources on the part of manufacturing businesses, and how far such demand may be expected to vary with the output of manufactured products? We shall later ask what determines the cost of any such finance and the extent to which it is available for any particular business. So far as the first questions are concerned, it will be convenient to consider a business which is already in existence, with sufficient finance for its existing activity, and to ask what will determine its current demands for fresh finance, whether it provides it itself or whether it has to seek it from outside the business. The case of the strictly new business may be left in the general terms in which it has already been discussed: such a business will come into existence, if the owners can provide or obtain sufficient funds, so long as, given their costing-rules and the consequent price, they can hope to sell an output sufficient in the long run to pay all their costs and achieve what the owners consider a satisfactory return.

THE FINANCING OF FIXED ASSETS

In a going concern the expenditure upon fixed assets will fall into three classes: (1) the simple replacement of worn-out equipment by others of exactly the same kind, so that the business remains equipped to produce the same output and by the same methods of production; (2) the purchase of additional items of equipment, so that the business may expand its output and produce at a larger scale; and (3) the replacement of existing equipment by more up-to-date, i.e. more efficient, types, so that the same output may be produced at lower costs. Dealing with (1) first, it is, of course, a very nice question exactly what constitutes worn-out equipment. If a machine is in such an advanced state of physical decrepitude that it cannot produce another unit of output, but is still needed for the production of current output, then it will obviously have to be replaced, if the current output is to be maintained, and a failure to replace it can only lead to the business losing part of what market it has, thus worsening its long-run position. A replacement which is so badly needed will always be made, no matter how bad the current position of the business, so long as it has sufficient cash or can get hold of it. There will be no nice calculation of profitability to sway the decision, for failure to act will jeopardize the whole business.

In fact, however, businesses will ordinarily replace long before this desperate position is reached, and will have an incentive to do so, in so far as the employment of worn-out equipment is not a costless affair. As machinery gets older, its repairs costs will rise, and there will be other costs, such as those associated with stoppages of production or with the necessity for closer supervision, etc., which may not appear so obviously in the profit and loss account but which will affect the profitability of the business none the less. A given individual business will replace its machinery as soon as it reaches a certain stage of the road towards complete wearing out, provided that it has the funds to do so. The actual point at which replacement occurs will vary between individual businesses even in the same industry, according to the policy of the owners and the general profitability of the business, but, given the business, there will normally be a consistent policy, and so, at any one time, there will be a definite demand for resources with which to replace equipment which the business regards as being worn-out.

This demand for the purposes of replacement will vary with output. In some industries, as where corrosion occurs, the mere fact of age will be sufficient to cause a machine to wear out and will thus give a minimum demand for replacement which will be constant with time. In all industries, however, the degree to which machinery wears out will tend also to be a function of the output which it has produced, and quite ordinarily the rate of wear and tear will go up disproportionately if the rate of output exceeds a certain figure and this is maintained for a fairly long period. When we are looking at manufacturing business as a whole, therefore, replacements may be thought of as rising with rising output, and as probably rising more quickly as the rate of output is stepped up. At a period of very great activity, however, actual replacement may be postponed, because new machinery will be difficult to get, and, once got, will be used to *increase* the output, and because the business will wish to avoid any interruption of output during the process of installation. As output falls off, the demand for replacement will fall too — probably more than in proportion to the rate of fall of output. Individual machines will be worked at a less intense rate, and, if output falls sufficiently, then some of them will be put out of commission, the question of their replacement not reviving until output recovers sufficiently to bring them back to work. In the case of a bad slump, businesses may well take up a more pessimistic position than they would normally adopt, and run their machinery a lot nearer to complete physical exhaustion, even deferring repairs — for, at such times, it may be thought better to maintain dwindling cash resources simply in order to carry the business through.

The other two types of demand for fixed assets may be thought of as involving new investment. The business man will be able to calculate the net earnings which any such asset will bring into his business, deducting any special costs that are involved, and, in the case of the replacement of technically inferior equipment, making allowance for the net earnings which he is already getting from the older machinery. He will have a minimum standard of earnings to which such equipment must conform if he is to think it worth while. This standard will be determined partly by the normal level of profitability in his business and partly by the type of asset (e.g. it will be higher if the asset is of a kind that wears out quickly or is especially liable to obsolescence than if it is long-lasting and not likely usually to be the subject of technical innovation). The rules can normally be expressed as requiring that a machine of such a type shall pay for itself in so many years on the basis of the earnings at the time of purchase. If it conforms to this standard, then the business man will invest in such assets up to the limit of the demand for his product.

In the case of the equipment required to effect a simple extension of output, the minimum-earnings requirement will ordinarily be met in any situation in which the existing equipment is being fully worked, or overworked. The extra investment may be especially justified through a net lowering of running costs, in so far as the business may be working its existing equipment overtime or at heavy repair costs, but it will presumably be justified any way, since the price fixed by the normal costing-rules will be based on the business working at less than maximum capacity, and the earnings of new equipment will generally be greater than the business man's required minimum before capacity output is reached. In such cases, therefore, when a business is producing at or near the limits of its short-run capacity and yet finds its market expanding, the earnings on the new equipment will tend to be higher than the minimum standard which the business usually requires.

The investment in newer types of machinery may take place at any time, but is less likely to be profitable in a time of general slump for the industry in which an individual business is operating. The motive to make the change will be stronger in times of rising output, especially in so far as the older equipment uses a larger quantity of labour or more highly skilled labour, and so will tend to become relatively more costly in times of rising wages.

In general, then, the desire to purchase new fixed assets will tend to rise with rising demand, provided that such assets are earning at least the minimum standard that each individual business will demand. This means that, taking manufacturing industry as a whole, the demand for resources for new capital investment should be seen as falling off drastically when output falls — the earnings of such assets will fall, and the lessened demand can be met with the existing capital equipment. Once demand rises sufficiently to employ the available equipment, then the demand for new machinery, etc., will rise and will be sustained so long as demand rises.

The Financing of Floating Assets

Turning now to floating assets, it will, of course, be necessary for a business to have sufficient resources to make a certain investment in these, if it is to maintain any given scale of output. It will have to wait a certain time for its customers to pay it, will have to provide the money which is locked up in the labour and materials used in current output, and will have to support its given level of paying-out costs, — all this implying the need for a certain amount of finance over the average period between the commencement of production and the receipt of the proceeds of sales. It will also require to maintain a given level of stocks, in order to meet the needs of the given flow of output. In addition to this finance, which is strictly called for by the level at which its sales are running, it may wish to vary its holdings of stocks for speculative reasons, to forestall any expected increase of prices (or to get something in hand against an expected continued rise of demand) or to avoid the losses in any current or expected price-falls. Increasing demand for the products of an individual business will naturally make it need extra circulating capital for the first group of reasons, but changes in its output will not necessarily be correlated with the changes in prices which will affect its holding of stocks for speculative reasons.

Taking manufacturing industry as a whole, however, all of these demands for floating capital will tend to increase at the same time. A rising demand for industrial production will make it necessary for businesses to increase their outlays upon current production, and will also make them desire to increase their quantum of stocks, since that will have to increase if it is to serve the needs of an increased output. Such a general movement in the demand for manufactured products, however, is usually accompanied by rising prices of materials, by rising wages, and hence by rising prices of products, and, accordingly, tends to cause a general desire to add to stocks. Similarly, falling industrial activity will cause a reduced need for resources to finance current production, and also tends to lead to a general desire to get stocks down even beyond the level which would otherwise be appropriate to the reduced demand (output, therefore, falling faster than sales). It is in this way that times of falling output generally lead to increased cash appearing in the balance sheets of industrial concerns, with the freeing of capital which has previously been locked up in floating assets.

The upshot of the previous argument is that the demand for capital resources on the part of manufacturing businesses will vary with the level of demand for the products, and that it will tend to increase more than proportionately in times of rising demand and to fall more than in proportion in times of falling demand, down to the low level necessary to keep the businesses ticking over. In so far as businesses provide all the finance that they need at an average level of activity, it will follow that the capital market will find a demand for extra finance only when activity is above the average, that such demand will then rise with increasing activity, but will fall to zero again once activity falls to its average level. In actual fact, activity will not simply fall and rise at the same rate and with the same timing in all industries, but this simple picture is near to the truth and will enable us better to understand what happens in the capital markets in conditions of fluctuating activity.

It will have been noticed that, in all this discussion of the factors affecting the demand for capital resources, there has been no mention of the effect of the rate of interest which a business will have to pay in order to get any such additional resources. This is contrary to tradition in economic theory, where the rate of interest is seen as the 'regulator of the capitalist economy', and where, in particular, the investment in any individual business is discussed as though it involved a careful balancing of the net yield against the rate of interest. Research during the last decade,[1] however, has shown that

---

[1] The pioneer research in this field seems to have been that carried out by the pre-war Oxford Economists' Research Group. The findings have been reported and discussed in ' The Significance of the Rate of Interest ', by (Sir) H. D. Henderson; ' Summary of Replies to Questions on Effects of Interest Rates ', by J. E. Meade and P. W. S. Andrews (*Oxford Economic Papers*,

the demand for capital resources on the part of *manufacturing* businesses will not be affected by the changes in the level of the rates of interest that have to be paid for those resources. Business men do not pay attention to changes in the rates of interest in assessing the desirability of a given piece of investment, because such changes are small against the necessary charges for depreciation and obsolescence, and against the uncertainties which make all calculations of future earnings liable to a wide possible margin of error.

Sources of Business Finance

A business which has sufficient resources of its own to make all the investment which it desires and to leave it with spare cash (which it may leave on deposit with its bank or invest in securities) will have no special problems about the making of further investment, or growing, until such spare resources have been used up. It will simply use its money as it sees fit, and will increase its investment within the business so long as it can earn the required minimum on the new investment. If, however, the business needs additional finance, it will either have to get more from the existing owners or to persuade outsiders to let it have what it needs; failing this, it will have to put up with its restricted position and will be able to grow only at the rate corresponding to that at which it accumulates resources out of profits.

In general, a business which borrows will get a lower rate of net earnings than another which is in the same expansionary situation but which grows by the use of its own resources, previously invested outside the business; for the rate of earnings on securities will ordinarily be lower than the rate of interest for industrial finance. It follows that it will be easier for a business, which starts on an expansion by

No. 1, October 1938); ' Business Men and the Terms of Borrowing ', by R. S. Sayers; ' A Further Inquiry into the Effects of Rates of Interest ', by P. W. S. Andrews (*Oxford Economic Papers*, No. 3, February 1940). It should be said that my later studies of business behaviour have not led to any doubts about the accuracy of the Research Group's conclusions.

using its own finance, to continue getting the resources towards further expansion, than it will be for a business which has to borrow initially. It should be mentioned that practical research has shown the existence of a considerable reluctance to borrow on the part of business men, quite apart from any question of the rate of interest which has to be paid. The chief reason seems to be the fear of a loss of control over their business in difficult times, but this is reinforced by a general prejudice in favour of a business looking after itself, and a general tendency to spend one's own money more freely than borrowed money (i.e. one's own money will be used as soon as its earnings stand at a satisfactory level; in the case of borrowed money, however, the cautious business man will require other conditions to be satisfied).

(a) Short-term Finance

The sources from which a business can get extra resources may be divided according to the extent to which they are willing to lend or to invest for long periods. For the purpose of our theory, it will be simplest to speak as if there were only two sorts of capital markets — making short-term and long-term loans respectively. The leading type of short-period loans is that provided by joint-stock banks in the form of overdrafts and advances. Such borrowing will be for only a relatively short term — e.g. up to three months — being formally repayable after that period on notice from the lender. It follows that such credit will be used only for temporary purposes, such as to provide funds for the purpose of investing in fixed assets for a short period while more permanent finance is being arranged, or to meet the need for circulating capital, since that can always be liquidated when the output is sold, provided that prices have not fallen.

In this country, short-term finance is usually readily available, provided that sufficient security is offered. The degree of security will vary with the chance that, if the worst came to the worst, the business could pay off any creditors which ranked before the loan in question and yet have sufficient resources to pay off the loan itself. The lender of such short-term capital will not be very willing to see his loan covered by fixed assets, for their value in a forced sale is always very problematical and may take a fair time to be realized. Banks and such-like lenders will like to be able to get the total of their advances down fairly quickly, if monetary policy should make that desirable. Accordingly, the security to which they will look first will be the extent to which, even if the business's circumstances should worsen, there will still be sufficiently valuable marketable assets to make repayment possible. Accordingly, it will be difficult for a business to borrow more than a proportion of its total needs by way of circulating capital. It will have to provide the rest from resources which are more permanently invested in it, so that, if it wants to expand even its circulating capital beyond a certain rate, it will have to arrange for an increase in its longer-term finance.

In addition to bank finance, there is, as we have already seen during the analysis of accounts, also the possibility of using trade credit from the business's suppliers. That is very expensive as compared with other short-term credit, and businesses will tend not to use it except for temporary finance in very busy periods, unless they are very pressed for current resources. Generally speaking, it will be true for manufacturing businesses in this country that they will not like to borrow up to the hilt from their banks, except on a purely temporary basis, such as to meet exceptional seasonal needs which are self-liquidating. Such borrowers themselves will wish to be sure that they could at any time repay the bank without any great inconvenience. It is too well known that in bad times the banks will take quick action to protect their advances and will try to call in a sufficient proportion of their loans to leave the relative security unaffected.[1] It will be just

---

[1] I.e. it should be clear that I am not disputing the banks' statements that they do not vary their criteria of the soundness of any loan.

at such times that it will be most inconvenient for businesses to repay such loans, at the expense of cutting down the easily saleable assets that they have. The experience of manufacturing industry of the emergencies which could be created by such banking policies, especially during the period of the 1921 slump, seems to have strongly reinforced the sentiments in favour of caution in borrowing short-term for manufacturing business. Accordingly, the typical business will prefer to call a halt in normal times long before its bank would do so, and will prefer to substitute some more permanent basis of finance for bank overdrafts, if it appears that the business is going to need such extra finance at a permanently higher level. Only a business which is desperately short of capital will go as far as it can by way of short-term borrowing.

(b) *Long-term Finance*

The supply of longer-term loans and share capital is more the concern of the capital market proper. A long-term lender will have the same concern about the security for his loan as will a short-term lender. He will wish to be reasonably sure of two things : that the business will, in fact, be able to pay the stipulated rate of interest ; and that the business will be able easily to realize what is required, if it becomes necessary to enforce the recovery of the sum lent, or when such a loan becomes due for repayment. The first requirement will mean that such a lender will not like to see the interest which is due to him stand at too high a proportion of the normal earnings of the business, and the second that the value of the business's assets should be considerably greater than the value of the loan at the time when the loan is made. All this implies that the extent to which a business may borrow extra resources will be limited by the extent of the resources put permanently into the business by its owners. When that limit is reached, a business which wishes further to expand will have to find more permanent finance.[1]

[1] The significance of the proportion between ' own ' capital and borrowed capital is discussed at length in J. Steindl, *Small and Big Business* (Blackwell, 1945).

R

If a business is doing reasonably well, it may be attractive to its owners to raise *some* of its finance by means of long-term borrowing, since a sound business may be able to raise debentures at a lower rate of return than would have to be assured to new shareholders, and, in so far as the money will earn more than the debenture interest, the surplus will go to swell the income accruing to the existing shareholders. At all times, however, there will be a limit to the amount which owners will wish to borrow. They will have incurred fixed obligations to make the regular interest payments and may also be obliged to set aside regular sums for the redemption of the loans.

Such fixed paying-out costs will cause the income accruing to the shareholders to fluctuate more than the income of the business before paying the loan interest, etc. The income of the shareholders thus will become more highly geared than it would be if all the capital were raised through shares. There may be positive dangers in this if income falls, for then the fixed paying-out costs will make it more difficult for the business to accumulate reserves of profits. There is, therefore, normally a limit to the extent to which a business will seek permanent finance by long-term loans, unless it is forced to do so by its needs for finance being too great to be met by increases of share capital, and a business which can avoid it will usually not borrow as much as it might from the point of view of the lenders. A business which is struggling to get extra capital may very well find that, because of the limits to the resources which the owners have provided themselves, it needs even more capital than it can get by way of loans, and so may be borrowing up to the hilt. The basic fact in any study of the capital market, therefore, is the extent to which the size of a business's share capital is limited.

The Problem of Small and Medium-sized Businesses

The preceding paragraphs show that the extent to which a business can get new capital by way of permanent investment in its shares will be one of the factors most severely limiting the extent to which it can grow. The market for long-term capital is, in fact, so constituted that the availability of further finance of this kind depends upon the size which the business has already attained; it is a case of unto him that hath is it given. For a business to be able to get complete strangers to invest in its shares, it must be sufficiently large to be able to use one of the organized stock exchanges. If it is too small, then the amount of its capital will be too small for its shares to become marketable and so dealt in on such an exchange, and unmarketable investments are not easy to sell. Further, because of the relatively heavy weight of the part of the costs of making an issue which do not depend upon its size, share issues have to be of a certain size before the costs of making the issue cease to be relatively prohibitive.

A small business will be able to get new capital only from those who know it very well. At its start, the main capital will have to come from the business men who are actually going to run it, or from their families and friends; no-one else will be able to gauge the true worth of the main asset of the business — the personalities of such business men. Once this circle has been fully tapped, the business will have to approach persons who are more truly outsiders. In a large industrial area, where business men easily get to know one another, a successful and growing small business may be able to get other business men to take shares in it — these will know the personalities with whom they have to deal and will be used to sizing up the potentialities of a business proposition. That is an important reason why, in the past, small business has been able to grow fairly vigorously in such industrial areas as those around Birmingham and Manchester. Outside this sort of contact, the business will have to depend upon the services of such persons as local solicitors and bank managers for introductions to clients who wish to make suitable investments in profitable businesses. Here it will be quite usual for the capital to be available only by way of loan on mortgage or debenture terms or, at the best, in the form of an investment in preference shares, carrying the right to fixed prior dividends and possibly subject to other safeguards to protect the investors.

Whichever way the small business secures its capital it will be relatively expensive, i.e. the net profitability to the business of the extra resources will be less than they would be for a bigger business, and it will be relatively difficult for it to grow by this means. Any such investor will have to make rather expensive special inquiries and will be left with an investment which will, therefore, not be easily marketable. He will expect to be compensated by a higher yield than he could get on more marketable forms of investment. Even with this, there will be a limit to the total amount of resources which can be raised at any one time, and that limit will largely be determined by the security offered by the resources which the existing owners have already put into the business. It is also the case that the availability of such extra investment will depend upon the general industrial condition. It will be difficult to find such extra capital at all unless the potential investors are in a prosperous condition.

As already indicated, its circumstances will be greatly improved once the business has grown large enough to be sufficiently well known and to require capital of such a size that it can be got through one of the stock exchanges. The local exchanges play a much more important part here than is generally recognized, for they can specialize in local businesses too small to be attractive to the London Stock Exchange, but well enough known locally for investors to consider them. Even so, it will be difficult for a business to use them unless it wants something like £100,000 in new resources, and, disregarding the case of a business which is simply being sold out to new owners, this means a much larger size of business. Once a business is large enough, not only will it be able to tap a market where the provision of capital is relatively cheaper, but it will be able to vary the way in which it seeks its new resources to suit the needs of the moment, and thus get capital over a bigger range of economic conditions. When times are good, it may raise capital through ordinary shares; in worse times, it may still be able to get resources through preference shares or debentures. Further, the increased marketability of its shares will enable it to get capital more easily from the shareholders who are its owners.

As we have described it, then, there is a 'gap' in the facilities offered by the English capital market. At the one end, the very small business will be able to raise sufficient capital through the savings of its owners and from the rather restricted circle of persons with whom the business is in sufficient contact. Its pressure for capital, if it is a growing business, will tend to cause it to borrow more than it would like to do. In particular, its need to get resources to invest in the fixed assets, which will form the basis of any growth, will tend to leave it short of circulating capital. In consequence, it tends to borrow up to the hilt from short-term lenders and to make use of expensive trade credit. This increases the vulnerability of the business if bad times come, but does enable it to grow bigger than its position in the long-term capital market would allow.

At the other end of the size-scale, a large business will be able to use the excellent facilities offered by the stock exchanges. Once a business has reached a sufficient size, then, the capital market will cease to restrict its growth through the sheer difficulties of getting extra capital, and with extra capital will go, as we have seen, extended facilities for raising money through borrowing. The capital market, as described, will not be able to help the small business which finds that it could grow and extend its market quite profitably if only it could get more capital. This was broadly the situation when the Macmillan Committee reported in 1931, and it is only in recent years that there has begun to be any significant change. How, then, did British businesses grow over these intermediate stages ? The answer is, by ploughing back into the business a large proportion of the profits which they made, and growing on the basis of such self-finance until they were able to take advantage of the stock markets. Even in the early stages of growth, the help of other local business men meant that they were growing on the savings from the profits of other businesses which their owners could invest according to their foresight.

In the last two or three decades the situation has changed recognizably for the worse, in so far as the stream of undistributed profits available for these purposes has tended to become considerably shrunken. The chief cause has been the heavy rise in the incidence of taxation upon business profits and of surtax upon their owners — it is not irrelevant that the law now treats the whole income of a business with relatively few owners as if it were personally distributed to these. The new level to which such taxation has risen appears to make it virtually certain that the stream is as near dry as makes no matter. This is a serious matter for British industry, which has gained most in the past through the uprising of new businesses, nourished by the enterprise of vigorous founders with the full control that comes through their providing the bulk of their own finance. If the gap were not filled, the larger businesses at the top would be exposed to a good deal less competition than hitherto (such competition does not come only from minnows growing up to fight directly with the tritons for their existence, but through the smaller fry developing the new product that turns out to be a powerful indirect competitor). In these circumstances the smaller business can grow only at a much slower rate, and, to make any progress at all, will have to be much more dependent upon loans, which stifle the freedom of the business.

Recent developments in the capital market have done something to help this situation of the medium-to-small business whose circumstances would justify its growth. Quite obviously, it ought to be a good business proposition to help at least the most promising of such smaller businesses by providing the long-term finance that is needed as a basis for growth, and the first development came from private enterprise in the form of finance companies such as the Charterhouse Trust, which provided money for companies which were small but which were likely to develop rapidly. The essential feature of this sort of financing operation was that money was provided at moderate rates of interest, the financiers retaining certain rights to subscribe for share capital in the event of the business making further development. Since the war, the Government has sponsored the Industrial and Commercial Finance Corporation, and the vigorous start which this has made has shown how great a need existed for this sort of finance.

It is, however, doubtful whether these corporations can ever fully meet the need of the medium-sized business. They are likely to be most successful in the case of the business, e.g. in the engineering field, which is developing a brand new product, whose ultimate success may be speculated on, and where there is some basis for estimating the results if the success occurs. It will not be so easy to spot the winner in a small business developing an *existing* product, which could make its way by fighting existing large businesses — a circumstance which may not appear very promising to an outside investor of capital. Also, it is the essence of this sort of investment that the decision must largely turn upon the judgment of the personalities involved in the particular business, and it is not easily made. Any error must be on the side of caution. In the business which is developing out of its own profits, however, success brings the automatic permission to have a shot at a larger size ; the business man may fail to make the grade, but it is his own money that he risks and he is free to back his own judgment.

There is one final point which makes it doubtful, granted that these new financial institutions will do a lot of good work, whether they will ever really fill the gap : there is a lot of difference between the feel of a business which is expanding on the basis of assets at the free control of the business man and one which is expanding on the basis of borrowed money. In the first case the business man can follow his own judgment, and, in some of the most important examples of industrial development, it may be very difficult to justify that judgment to an outsider, correct though it is. If there is any disagreement, he who pays the piper will expect to have the tune varied. It is, frankly, impossible to imagine such a business man as William Morris (now Lord Nuffield) being able to make the vigorous but risky investment that characterized the early stages of the development of the modern motor industry in circumstances which necessitated his justifying his main decisions to outsiders, who, try as they will, must have some regard to the apparent security of the capital which they lend, but which the type of personality that we are imagining *must* wish to risk on bold ventures — and it is to the social interest that he should be able to do so.

The type of personality that contributes most to industrial development appears to need full control of his businesses ; in fact, such a personality will develop only in the fullest possible freedom to take responsibility and to suffer and learn from his own mistakes. Useful though the new financial institutions may be, there is, in our opinion, then, still a very important gap, and, if it remain unfilled, then British industry is not going to present the same picture in the future as in the past. It is true that this ignores the fact, to which we have earlier called attention, that the bigger businesses are not without the spirit of enterprise and that they are always looking for the opportunity to develop still further. We owe a lot of new development to this, but it really is not enough. The developments that such established businesses will make will naturally tend to be complementary to themselves, and they will not tend to develop rivals to themselves, which is what an efficient industrial situation calls for.

The suggestion is sometimes made that the development of trading estates, where state-assisted organizations provide premises and services on a rental basis, will help the solution of this problem, in so far as a small business will now be able to economize in the limited resources that it has available for the investment in fixed assets, and thus grow more easily. It is true that such schemes help new enterprise to get started, but the argument misses the point — they do not necessarily help it to *grow* as substantial undistributed profits would have done. For one thing, the importance of premises and other facilities will tend to be greatest in assembly and packing industries. These developments, therefore, especially encourage enterprise of one sort. But, in any case, they may make growth of any enterprise more difficult. It is the essence of the trading estate that a number of small businesses are located together, drawing upon a common labour supply. If one of them shows anything like the vigorous development that has, in the past, characterized the sort of business of which we are thinking, it will soon press too hard upon the available supplies of labour, and may, in fact, not be able to grow on the estate, by reason of the size of premises that it will want in one spot. It will, therefore, have to go elsewhere and lose the advantages of the estate. In any case, as has already been said, the advantages of such estates are especially in the encouragement of the *starting-up* of small-scale businesses, their facilities are less likely to be important to a growing business.

The only remedy that the author can suggest is a bold one — that of a change in the income-tax law whereby *undistributed* profits — possibly up to a certain size of business in terms of employment, or some other criterion which did not directly bring in profits — were totally exempt from income taxation. Of course, in so far as the owners drew out any sums from the business, they would have to pay income-tax. It might be more practical to confine this suggestion to

private companies, since it is here that the difficulty of getting
new capital is so much more serious. In the case of public
companies, such a change in legislation might merely lead
to unnecessary disputes between directors and shareholders
about the dividend policy which is adopted.

To prevent any evasion, it might be necessary to refuse
to recognize capital payments but to treat all payments to
owners as income. If this were done, the Inland Revenue
need not suffer — the tax on *distributed* profits from exempted
businesses could go up in proportion and strict interpretation
of the suggested law would make evasion difficult. There
would be a complete change in the mental climate of industry
as we have come to know it, and the way would be open for
the development of much more vigorous competition in
manufacturing industry, such as would not be developed by
any other means.

The last paragraph has taken us into industrial politics,
and it is time we got back on to the path and considered the
main questions that are more relevant to theory. So far as
the first question is concerned, the conclusion that we have
reached is that up to a certain size the individual manufacturing business will have access to only a limited amount
of capital resources, and the price that it has to pay for such
resources, whether directly in the rate of interest or indirectly
in the effect of the other terms to which it may have to agree,
will tend to fall with increases in the scale of business, provided that the business can get sufficient resources to make the
growth over the intervening points in the scale.

EFFECT OF CHANGES IN GENERAL INDUSTRIAL ACTIVITY

The whole of the previous discussion has been in terms
of the individual manufacturing business, and of the difficulty
of its getting new capital at the given rates of interest. We
have left open the question of the effect upon rates of interest
of changes in industrial activity as a whole, and it will be

convenient to refer briefly to this here. Any rise in interest rates must affect the net profitability of manufacturers who have borrowed money, even if their investment decisions are unaffected. The whole complex of rates of interest will tend to move upwards, if there is a sustained general increase in the industrial demand for financial resources. In the market for short-term capital, this will occur quite simply because the banks, meeting additional demand for industrial advances, will tend to curtail somewhat their loans and investments elsewhere. They will, in particular, tend to sell some of their investments and to raise the rates of interest charged in the shortest term money market. All their rates and charges will move in sympathy. The tendency will be accelerated in so far as an industrial revival will tend to cause increased calls upon the cash resources of the banking system through the withdrawal of funds for the payment of wages. As industrial activity goes on it will, therefore, tend to be accompanied by rising rates of interest.

The rates of interest charged in the long-term market will also tend to move upwards. The selling of securities which will take place, both by existing businesses realizing their reserves and from the banks redistributing their investments and advances, will tend to depress the prices of securities — especially gilt-edged securities in the first place — thereby raising the rate of interest on them. Other rates of interest will tend to rise in sympathy. The long-term rates for industrial finance will also tend to rise with the appearance in the market of new demands for resources, calling for a redistribution of the flow of loanable funds in favour of industrial investment. The revival of the profitability of industrial shares will tend to cause some funds to be diverted from other long-term securities into this market, with, once again, a raising of the rates of interest which are quoted. In such conditions, however, it will be easier for industry to raise new capital (for the businesses which are large enough to have access to the markets) even if the earnings prospect which they have to show in order to get the new resources is also larger.

As has already been said at the beginning of this section, the rate of interest which manufacturing industry has to pay for capital resources will not generally affect its demand for them, which is better thought of as determined by the current level of industrial activity.

CHAPTER VII

THE THEORY OF BUSINESS ACTIVITY

(1) INTRODUCTORY

THE production and marketing aspects of manufacturing have been considered quite separately in the four preceding chapters. So the first task of this final chapter is to bring the conclusions together into a general view of activity in an individual manufacturing business. This will round off the main purpose of the book, which is to develop the pattern of ideas which seems most useful for the study of businesses engaged in manufacturing industry. The analysis will necessarily be made in as simple a form as possible, since a general theory which is not simple is useless, and it is necessary to concentrate on the essential factors which are common to all manufacturing businesses, as such.

The present analysis will, however, lead us directly into a wider field; activity in a manufacturing business depends most directly upon the demand for its products, and it will, therefore, be necessary to go on and to ask what determines the level of the demand for the products of manufacturing industry. This will lead into the general theory of business activity and particularly into a discussion of the trade cycle. The main conclusions that will be reached there will not have any great novelty, since they must follow the lines laid down by the late Lord Keynes in his *General Theory of Employment*. There will, however, be some advantages in the form of the present exposition, since it will make it possible for the theory of general business activity and employment to be much more closely tied in with the theory of price-determination and with the theory of the individual business than has been possible so far; in recent years the theory of the trade cycle has been far too separate a topic in economics. The method of analysis will also make it possible to take a more realistic view of the difficulties in the way of ensuring full employment with a rising standard of living.

(2) ACTIVITY IN THE INDIVIDUAL BUSINESS

THE EFFECTS OF FLUCTUATING OUTPUT

In this section of the chapter we shall be considering the theory of changes in the activity of an individual business. Throughout the section we shall assume the business to be changing its output independently of what other businesses are doing, for it is desirable not to confuse the issue by introducing the effects of general changes in industrial activity; these will be considered in the following section of this chapter, which will be concerned with the trade cycle. This part of the present section is intended to provide the basic theory of the simple effects of fluctuating output for an individual business. It will then be possible to graft on to this an account of the effects of changes in general activity, as such, when the trade cycle theory is being constructed. All questions of continuous growth and related matters are, therefore, held over until the next part of this section. Here we shall be concerned mainly with the effects of fluctuations of the order normally experienced during the trade cycle.

For the present purpose it may be assumed that the changes in the level of activity in the individual business, with the consequent changes in its demand for its factors of production, will not affect the prices which it has to pay for those factors. This will be the typical case, and even if there were some effect, it would almost certainly be very small beside the changes in factor prices, which will accompany changes in general activity, with which we shall be concerned when we come to the trade cycle.

At any given time, an individual business will be producing a given range of products with a given investment in equipment and with a given overhead organization (i.e. with a given complement of indirect labour and of office and managerial staffs; ref. Chapter III). In what follows, we shall speak for simplicity's sake as if the business produced only a single product, and as if the specification of that product were rigidly determined.

In the assumed conditions, the business will be offering its product for sale at a fixed price which will remain unchanged despite the fluctuations in output. That price will equal the average direct costs of production for the normal range of output plus the normal costing-margin adopted in the business (which, as explained in Chapter V, will give the business the highest level of price that it can expect to maintain against competition in the long run, and will be revised downwards at once if the business, in fact, meets competition at a lower level of price).

Over any period, the level of the business's costs of production will depend upon the size of the output that it has produced. The variable part of its sales costs — all of which will be included in the profit and loss account charges — will, of course, vary with its sales. To get our conclusion in as simple a form as possible at first, it will be useful to assume that the level of output is equal to the volume of sales. This means assuming that there is no change in the volume of the stocks held by the business, or rather it means that we ignore, for the moment, any change that does take place. In fact, of course, its output will be affected by the extent to which the business is adding to its stocks of its own products (or is cutting them down) as well as by the current level of sales. Similarly, its expenses will be affected by the extent to which it is varying its holding of stocks of materials. The leaving out of account of any change in the size of the business's stocks will enable us to get a picture of the effect upon the general position of a business of changes in its sales, apart from any complications due to changes in stocks.

Diagrams III and IV have been constructed to show the effects of changing sales-outputs in these simple conditions. On the revenue side, as has just been said, the business is to be thought of as selling its current output at a constant price. It will be very useful to think of its price as its average revenue, which, of course, it is. Since this is thought to be constant, the line in Diagram III, which shows it, is drawn at a constant height. The total revenue of the business will increase proportionately to its sales-output, and, therefore, in Diagram IV, where the situation is shown in the form of a ' break-even ' chart, and in terms of totals rather than averages, the line showing total revenue is drawn with a constant slope (which will equal the assumed price, since each additional item sold will add that amount of money to the total revenue) showing that the total revenue increases at a constant rate in proportion to sales-output.

The discussion of costs of production in Chapter III will have made it clear that, before the effects of a change of output upon costs can be specified, it is necessary to state within what limits the output is supposed to be fluctuating. Average direct costs of production will be constant per unit of product, so long as the business is producing within the limits given by its ability to vary the employment of direct labour at the given wage. This will, of course, cover a wider range of output when a single business is varying its output independently than it will if such a variation is part of a general change in industrial activity — the latter case is, as already indicated, reserved for discussion in the second section of this chapter, which is concerned with the trade cycle. The diagrams restrict themselves to this simple case, showing the direct costs situation up to the point at which the business would find it necessary to work its direct labour overtime. Average direct costs will be constant over the indicated range of output. In Diagram III the average direct costs of production are, accordingly, drawn at a constant height, which is equal to the assumed level of those costs. Diagram IV shows the total direct costs, for the range of sales-outputs covered by the diagram, as a straight line with a constant slope

DIAGRAM III

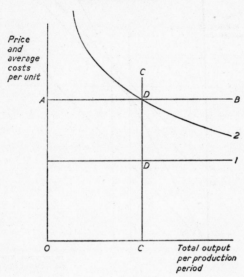

NOTES

(1) = average direct costs per unit of output.
(2) = average total costs per unit of output.
    = (1) plus average indirect costs.
AB = average revenue per unit when price is OA.
OC = ' break-even ' level of output when price is OA.
DD = average gross profit margin per unit when price is OA.

corresponding to the constant average direct costs (for simplicity, the line of total direct costs, like the corresponding average direct-costs line in the companion diagram, is drawn right back to zero output, although the significant part of the range of output will almost certainly stop short at some positive level of output).

In Diagram III the vertical distance between the average

S

revenue — price — line and the average direct-costs line will equal the average costing-margin (and, since we are assuming a constant price and ignoring the effects of changes in stocks,

DIAGRAM IV

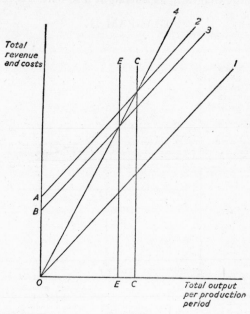

NOTES

(1) = total direct costs of output.

(2) = total costs of output.

　 = (1) plus OA (total indirect costs).

(3) = total paying-out costs = total direct costs plus OB (total paying-out indirect costs).

(4) = total revenue when price is constant at average direct cost plus costing margin.

OC = ' break-even ' level of output with given price.

OE = ' current solvency point ', given price.

it will also equal the average realized gross profit margin as shown in the trading account) and this, according to the assumptions that have been made, will be constant whatever the level of output. In Diagram IV the distance between a point on the total revenue line, corresponding to any particular sales-output, and that on the total direct-costs line will, similarly, equal the total gross profit shown in the trading account for the period covered by the total output; this will, given our assumptions, necessarily increase in direct proportion to the total sales output.

So long as the business does not have to add to its overhead organization and equipment, its total indirect costs (the profit and loss account expenses) will remain constant, apart from the effect of changes in its output upon the variable selling costs, if any, charged in the profit and loss account (e.g. salesmen's commissions and packaging charges, etc.) and the current repair costs of machinery, etc. The variable sales costs will merely increase the height of the average indirect costs by an approximately constant amount, or the height of the total indirect costs by an amount which will approximately increase in proportion to sales-output. Its effect is ignored in the diagrams but could, if preferred, be taken into account by an appropriate deduction from the realized price. It is convenient also to ignore the effect of increasing activity upon repair costs — in the case of a fluctuation of output to a high level they will be relatively small and they will increase to a substantial extent only if the output remains at an unusually high level for a considerable period.[1]

So far as the diagrams are concerned, indirect costs are taken as constant in total, and the range of output is assumed to be within the maximum capacity of the plant and organization. As shown in Diagram III, average indirect costs will, therefore, fall with increasing output, but at a slackening rate (as explained in Chapter III), and will, similarly, rise at an increasing rate for decreasing outputs. The curve showing average total costs per unit of output is obtained by adding the average indirect costs to the — constant — average direct

---

[1] Although these costs are ignored in the diagrams, it will be useful to remember them later as one of several factors tending in the same direction — increasing the amount of paying-out costs as output increases, and also as making the investment in new equipment more attractive.

costs. In Diagram IV the line showing total costs for any particular output is similarly obtained by adding the — assumed constant — total indirect costs to the line showing the level of total direct costs, thus, in effect, stepping up the whole level of the total direct costs line by the extent of the indirect costs.

In Chapter III, attention was called to the fact that some, and usually a large proportion, of total indirect costs were paying-out costs, involving the current payment of money to the factors entitled to them. On our assumptions these may be assumed to be constant. In Diagram IV, total paying-out costs are, therefore, shown by a line drawn at a constant level above total direct costs and lying at a constant level below total costs.

Diagram IV is perhaps the most useful for reference when we are discussing the effect of a particular change in the activity of the individual manufacturing business under the assumed conditions. Two critical levels of output stand out. The first is the output at which, given the price, the total revenue line crosses over the total costs line. This is the ' break-even ' level of output, and shows the lowest level of output at which the business will cover all its costs ; at, or above this level, the net profit shown in the profit and loss account cannot be less than zero, and, beyond this level, its net profit will increase in proportion to the increase in total output. For any output less than the break-even point, it will be making a net loss, and the amount of the loss will again increase proportionately to the reduction of output. The income earned for shareholders as a whole must, therefore, fluctuate in a more extreme manner than total output.

It follows that for any output less than the break-even level the owners will not earn any income, their income rising above that point, whilst below that point losses will be accumulating in the accounts and then may have to be cleared before future incomes can be paid. If they are, in fact, paid a steady minimum, then the maintenance of their income will involve a continuous depletion of the business's cash balance as soon as the output falls below an appropriate level above the break-even point. Similarly, if some of the owners are entitled to a fixed preference income, the income shown as earned for the residual owners will be negative at a point which is above the break-even level of output, and their income will fluctuate more widely than the total shareholders' income. These remarks refer to income earned for the respective classes of owners; so far as non-preference shares are concerned, the extent to which that income will, in fact, be distributed will depend upon the policy of the directors, and, although something can be said about this when we are thinking of industry as a whole, the precise policy which will be adopted in any individual business will be uncertain.

Whilst referring to the owners' incomes, it will be useful to call attention to one important point of difference between them and all other incomes arising from the business's activities: the other income recipients will have to be paid fairly near to the production of the particular output considered, but the income of the owners will not be known until the accounts are made up at the end of the year, and this will be, on the average, roughly six months after the output which has produced it. There will be a further delay for the preparation of the accounts and the calling of the meeting authorizing the dividend payments. An interim payment may be made on account six months before this date, but it will have to be made cautiously, lest the final accounts show it not to have been covered by the actual profits of the period. Not only, then, will the incomes of business owners fluctuate more sharply than the total revenues of a business, but they will tend to lag behind any changes in those revenues by a fairly long period. It will tend to be at least six months after a rise in revenue before the income of the owners will be affected. Similarly it will be at least six months after a fall of revenue before its effect on profits becomes visible to the owners.

Referring to the time-lags discussed in the previous paragraph, the present author, when a young graduate, was amused to construct what he called the company-board theory of the trade cycle. The tenor of this was that any directors would be allowed one bad set of accounts; if they produced a second the shareholders would wish to know that something was being done about it, particularly in the matter of cutting overheads rendered redundant by any fall of output. In a world of public joint-stock companies, it would follow that the worst cuts in the expenditure of such companies might be delayed for up to eighteen months, on the average, after a down-turn had occurred in sales. As we shall see in the theory of the trade cycle, this would cause the worst period of the slump to tend to have a similar timing. This theory is no longer believed in with any degree of rigidity, but the factor to which it calls attention is worth mentioning.

The second of the critical levels of output to which reference was made on page 258 is that at which the line of total revenue crosses the line showing total paying-out costs (total paying-out indirect costs plus direct costs). Diagram IV shows this as the ' current solvency point '. So long as the business is producing at least that amount of output at the given price, it will at least be getting all the cash that it needs for its minimum current cash expenditure. If output runs at below that critical level, the business will have to make inroads in its cash balances in order to carry on producing the given level of output, or borrow money from outsiders (in which case the interest payments will subsequently have to be added to its paying-out costs). If this situation goes on long enough, the business will have to close down. The lower output falls below this level, the more desperate will be the position of the business.

In industries where overhead costs are a high proportion of total costs and where paying-out overheads are a high proportion of total overheads (which is the case with many heavy capital-goods industries) this situation is especially likely to lead to desperate attempts to regain revenue by price-cutting. So long, on the other hand, as the business is increasing its cash reserves as a result of current sales-output, it will have extra resources available for any expenditure that it wishes to make, since it will nearly always be able to defer part, at least, of its financial costs. It may, accordingly, be able to improve its position, temporarily at least, even when its accounts show a net loss. This is the usual explanation of a situation which is sometimes found puzzling, where a business carries on for years although its accounts show the piling up of heavy losses. In this case, the cash receipts are often sufficient to pay for necessary repairs, the capital equipment may have a long life, and the business can manage without making good all the depreciation charged as a current cost.[1] Meanwhile the weight of such charges will cause the accounts to show a loss.

The simple diagrams that have been prepared have now served their immediate purpose, and it is time to modify the conclusions that have been drawn from them, in the light of the more complex facts to be met in reality. The first, which has already been referred to, but which was ignored in the diagrams, is that, at some output, the business will be able to produce still more only if it works its direct labour-force overtime. As was shown in Chapter III, the average direct costs of production will rise as output increases beyond this point, and will rise at a steadily increasing rate towards the higher level of the rate of pay for overtime. Repairs costs will also tend to increase more sharply with increasing output. These factors will reduce the rate at which profits will increase for further increases in output — it is relevant to remind ourselves that the factor making for an increase in profits, the proportionate saving in total indirect costs, will also tend to be relatively less important for successive increases in output. Both these increases in costs will also raise the level

---

[1] In the end, of course, these costs will have to be covered, and, failing the necessary resources, the business will have to go out of production.

of paying-out costs, and these also will tend to have a reduced rate of fall once output has reached overtime level.

Similarly, if the output gets to the limit that can be produced with the existing overhead organization without extending equipment, or extending (or working overtime) the overhead man-power, then the business will have to extend its organization. Additions to the non-equipment element in this organization must cause both total costs and total paying-out costs to rise to a new level. At the same time, the business will normally wish to add to its equipment in this situation. It will want extra cash resources for this; these may be available from the extra cash resources which the additional sales are tending to produce, or from its cash balances accumulated in the past. If these are not sufficient, then it will have to get extra resources, and, in the short-run at least, it will tend to increase its short-term borrowings (the first available source of extra funds), thus freeing resources previously used to finance circulating capital and investing them in fixed capital. In this case, its interest payments on current account will rise and constitute a further factor making for a further fall in its current net additions to its cash balances. The contrary argument applies to the case of a falling output; the business may be able to save paying-out costs through cutting down its overhead personnel, and it will get additions to its cash resources through the decrease in its investment in circulating capital.

The general conclusion from the above paragraph is that, whilst the early stages of industrial recovery will bring increasing cash resources, the rate of increase of cash will tend to fall off once output gets to a sufficient level. In the slump, on the other hand, the cash brought in by current trading will fall off, but there will be some relief through the freeing of circulating capital and the reduction of paying-out overheads. When the fall in output is bad enough, the net liquidity of the business may increase, despite any loss that it may be suffering on current account, especially if stocks are normally held at a high level. The special circumstances arising from the fact of businesses holding stocks have yet to be analysed, however.

Given the assumption that prices do not change, the size of the stocks of finished goods which a business wishes to hold will normally vary directly with its sales (and the size of its holdings of work-in-progress or semi-finished goods, with which we are not now concerned, will vary with its output). Its output over any given period, therefore, will equal its sales, plus any increase in holdings of its own products, or minus any decrease in such stocks. If its sales rise to a new level, the business will normally wish to hold a higher level of stocks; the fall of its sales to a lower level will similarly enable it to manage with smaller stock-holdings. A sudden increase of demand will, of course, be met out of stocks and a sudden decrease of demand will cause them to pile up temporarily. Disregarding such temporary effects, a rising demand, if maintained, will tend to cause output to rise still faster, provided that the business has sufficient productive capacity both to meet its market and to add to its stocks. A falling demand will similarly be generally accompanied by a more rapidly falling output, since the getting-down of its stocks will enable the market to be met from stocks instead of from current production.

Output will, therefore, generally vary in a more extreme way than sales. A similar argument will show that, when the business's products are sold to dealers who hold stocks rather than direct to the final ' consumer ', the output will fluctuate even more out of proportion to the changes in the demand coming from the final consumer. If that consumer himself carries stocks, then his demand will fluctuate more extremely than his actual usage. We thus get a chain of increasing order of fluctuations as we move, from the ultimate demand for any particular product, through the stages at which stocks are carried, back to the stage at which production takes place.

It may be argued, in a similar manner, that the business's

holdings of stocks of materials will also tend to vary in proportion to the size of its output, and that a rising output will, therefore, tend to cause the demand for materials to rise faster, whilst a falling output will tend to cause the demand to fall more quickly. The demand for materials will, therefore, tend to fluctuate in a more extreme manner than the output in which such materials are used. This again provides one reason why the farther back we go in the stages between the emergence of an ultimate product towards the first stage of the production of the original raw materials, the more extreme will tend to be the gearing of the demand for the intermediate products in relation to that for the products at a higher stage.

Since we have assumed prices to be unchanged, any changes such as have been discussed in the holdings of stocks of finished products or of materials will not affect the business's total profits. Stocks will be brought into the accounts at cost, and so any addition to the stocks on the revenue side of the accounts will be counterbalanced by an increase in the costs on the other side. Any such increase will, however, as we have already seen, cause an increased locking up of the business's cash resources, and any decreased holding of stocks will cause a release of such resources. This reinforces the general argument that times of expanding trade will cause increased strain on the cash resources of manufacturing business. There will be one certain consequence for the trading accounts of such businesses — since stocks are brought in at cost, the gross profit margin realized per unit of output will tend to fall in a period when increasing stocks are being built up.

Although it is excluded by the assumptions that have been made in this part of the chapter, it will be useful to insert at this point an analysis of the effect of changes in prices of materials and of finished products. If, in fact, prices are rising, businesses will have a strong motive for adding to their stocks, even if there is no change in their sales (and materials stocks will tend to be increased even if there is no change in output). The business will wish to get the extra profits from selling at higher prices goods which have been produced, or bought, at lower costs. Since, as we shall see, times of increasing industrial activity are usually accompanied by rising price levels, and times of falling activity by falling prices, this will cause outputs to fluctuate in an even more extreme manner than justified by the changes in the demand which business is finding, and once again these changes will be more extreme the farther back we go from the stage of ultimate consumption — especially since, at each stage, there will be more difficulty in adding to output, and hence to the stocks of finished goods, than there will be in piling up stocks of materials. The effect of such speculative changes in stocks will, therefore, be especially concentrated upon the materials used at any one stage of production, and these are, of course, the products of the previous stage.

Rising prices will tend to increase the average gross profit margin shown in the accounts, since the business at any one time will be selling at a higher price-level goods which were produced at the lower costs corresponding to a lower level of prices, but which have since been passing through the stocks of the business. Falling prices, because of the writing-down of stock-values, will, similarly, tend to reduce the gross profit margin which is realized, and to reduce the net profit of the profit and loss account, quite apart from the effects of any changes in industrial activity in themselves. Any change in prices will tend to cause a more extreme change in industrial activity and in business profits than is justified by the contemporary situation, but the effect of falling prices will be particularly drastic. It is for this reason that some accountants are beginning to press for a new method of taking stocks into account. They would prefer it to be assumed that the stocks which are sold have always been produced at the current price levels, so preventing any writing down in values from reducing profits and accentuating the effects of a trade depression, and, also, preventing the profits of a boom being magnified by the profit realized on stocks taken in at earlier price levels.

THE THEORY OF GROWTH AND OF SCALE

This part of the present chapter will round off the theory of the individual business with a discussion of some aspects, first, of the continued growth of the individual business, taking into account the ways in which practical considerations limit the freedom of a business to grow in a simple or continuous fashion, and, second, of the factors affecting the survival of businesses of different sizes. This discussion will be shorter than the importance of its subject would warrant — not because there is little that could be said, but because it is here that the theory of business behaviour is most in need of enrichment by the details of actual cases. The relative strengths of some of the factors which are considered will vary greatly, not only between different industries but also as between individual businesses which are producing substantially the same type of product.

Since some of the theoretical factors operate in contrary directions, it is impossible to produce systematic generalizations of the kind that are possible in price-theory or in the theory of the effects of fluctuating outputs. A fruitful theory has usually to be *ad hoc* in nature and needs the examples of live businesses in terms of which it can proceed. Case-studies are, therefore, extremely important in this sort of analysis, but none of them can be conclusive. To get a general theory, it is necessary to abstract from the practical details of the cases that have been studied, and one is then left with an extremely generalized argument. It is for a similar reason that large-scale statistical inquiries into such matters as business efficiency are often so inconclusive; their interpretation demands detailed data, which they cannot provide, about the situation of the individual businesses.

(a) *Limitations on Growth*

Given the product, or range of products, which a business is producing, its growth will be limited fundamentally by its market. A business can sometimes change the nature of its market by a deliberate decision so that it is *possible* for it to sell more than would have been likely in its former kind of market. This type of situation arises where a particular type of product is being distributed through a number of channels, e.g. through wholesalers and retailers. A business with only a certain size of output will have to sell through wholesalers or take the risks of selling through a relatively small number of retail outlets (its selling costs will tend to be higher, in that case, than the margin which a wholesaler would take and it will be difficult for its goods to compete). When selling through a wholesaler, its goodwill will end with its wholesaler-customer, and he will be buying its product against those of a number of others.

At, or beyond, a certain size, the business could sell direct to retailers and will be large enough to be able to enter into competition with the wholesalers, and to offer its retailer-customers the sort of service that they would expect from a wholesaler. Granted that it has reached such a minimum size, instead of waiting for its market to expand through the growth of the demand from its wholesale customers, it may decide to take what must be to some extent a leap in the dark, and sell to retailers direct. Its gross margin will now go up, for it will get the wholesaler's mark-up, but so will its costs, not only because it will have to bear the costs of carrying out the wholesaler's functions, but also because, as a manu-facturer-wholesaler, it will have to incur the special selling costs of advertising to the ultimate consumer in order to get the retailer to stock its goods.

Once it has taken the plunge, the business will be in the same fundamental type of position as before; it will now have the *possibility* of growing to a larger size than it could have done with its old method of marketing, but what it *actually* sells will depend upon the response in the market, and its rate of growth will be determined, as before, by the demand which it meets — the larger sales will not come automatically nor because it has incurred the extra selling costs. Cases are not rare of businesses finding that such a change of policy has not paid, and of its being reversed. Given the use of a certain system of marketing, the level of a business's selling costs is more determined by, than it is a factor determining, its sales.

In general, the market of an individual business will expand only because it proves to be more efficient than its rivals — we are not now thinking of the spectacular increases that may occur in the market for a brand new type of product, after the slow initial stages of introducing that product and as the appreciation of its possibilities becomes more widely known. Thus, the pioneer producers of, say, nylon would expect to have such a rising demand when once its peculiar virtues began to be appreciated. The established business's market will expand or decline at the average rate for that type of product (e.g. if it makes medium-grade men's worsted suitings) unless it can produce the good cheaper than its competitors or offers a better quality of product at the same price — it being understood that any reference to quality includes the standard of associated services such as promptness of delivery, etc.

It is necessary to take up this question of price competition again, even at the cost of some repetition of our previous discussion, because the position is so frequently misunderstood. It is quite true that a price reduction, *if* it were not followed by competitors, would give a business a very rapid expansion of its market. If there were any significant difference in its price, then, in the case of most manufacturing businesses, its competitors would not sell anything at all (allowance being made for any special delivery costs, etc.) so long as it could deliver the goods, and its expansion would be limited only by the physical rate at which it could grow to meet its market. The other businesses, however, would cut their price to meet it, and the business would then continue to get only its share of the not very greatly expanded total market. How it fared in the long run would depend upon its relative ability to survive at the lower price, as compared with its competitors. If the price were too low to enable the latter to pay their way and meet all their costs, whilst being sufficient to enable it to meet all its costs and yet get the resources which would be necessary for growth, then the price reduction would pay it. It would grow and they would decline.

A price reduction, therefore, always pays in the long run, if it is justified by the cost position, but it will essentially pay through the operation of rather long-run factors, unless the business can offer so substantial a price reduction that its competitors find it difficult to meet it in the short-run. This will be the case if, at the new level of price, the other businesses cannot cover all their paying-out costs, so that their survival will depend upon the length of their purse. Even then, the driving out of the competitors will take a little time. A price reduction will force a competitor out of business at once only if the new price is below the level of average direct costs, so that they had better go out of business at once. So substantial a price reduction would imply that the business initiating it had first access to the results of what must be no less than a technical revolution. In an industry which has at all settled down, there is a limit to the possible reduction of price and it will, in fact, be difficult for a business to find that normal circumstances, such as growth, will enable it to make a significant reduction in price at one go, although it may be able to make successive shadings of price which add up to something in the end. Alternatively, it may successively improve the quality of its product, and grow for that reason.

The way that the business man typically fixes his price recognizes this, and operates against price reductions which

will not be justified in the long run. As we saw in Chapter
V, the price will be fixed according to the Normal Cost
Principle, and will tend to settle down at the level which
yields the most efficient businesses a margin sufficient to
cover their costs and to give them what they regard as normal
profits for their type of industry. In so far as the normal
level of profits is not more than sufficient to enable the
industry to attract capital in the long run, and to cover
any risks that are peculiar to it, any reduction below the
level of the normal cost price will prove unjustified in the
long run.

If an industry is especially difficult to enter, then its
normal prices may yet yield the typical business a higher level
of profits than could be obtained in other industries with the
same sort of situation so far as risks, etc., are concerned. In
the author's opinion, the importance of this has been greatly
exaggerated. Manufacturing industry is much more competitive than economists are prone to believe. The business
man's pricing policy takes account of the long-run danger of
competition emerging if he sets too high a gross profit
margin. Some industries are more sheltered than others,
and the rates of net profit made by the most efficient businesses in each will reflect that fact, but, even in the extreme,
the rate of net profit does not usually appear excessive.

Economic theories of business behaviour have so far been
much too short-term in their outlook, seeing the business man
too much as a ' spiv ' — to use the word which has emerged
precisely in order to denote an entrepreneur, with an essentially
short-run outlook, of a type which is characteristic only of
conditions of extreme scarcities during war-time and the
immediate post-war period. The whole approach to the
theory of the demand for the products of a manufacturing
business is too short run; the sensitivity of demand is
calculated too much on a short-term basis more appropriate
to a robber baron than to a man who has sunk a lot of capital
in a business (and this is especially true of some of the most

'monopolistic' businesses) which will justify itself only in the rather long run.

In any case, since the normal margin in an industry will be settled by the policy in the more efficient businesses, and since they will have already settled what they regard as the normal rate of profits which they should get in the long run, they will not revise it downwards for the sake of short-run advantage any more than they would revise it upwards. The other businesses' price policies will reflect the fact of the superior long-run competing power of the more efficient businesses and will be set to yield them a lower net profit. The typical business will, therefore, stick to its pricing policy and will change its price only to the extent to which an actual or clearly foreseen change in costs would justify it. Given the degree of efficiency of the management, and existing technical knowledge, such a reduction of costs can only come about through the technical economies of scale arising from growth.

Economists generally seem to have too short-term a view of the economies of scale.[1] It is true that, in the short run, if a business can use its spare capacity, its costs of production may decrease quite sharply. Over the trade cycle, when output may rise from, and fall to, a level of output which is seriously below the normal productive capacity,[2] the changing weight of overhead costs may make for a relatively drastic fall in costs with increasing output, and it is this sort of change of costs that can most easily be reckoned from common knowledge. Even then, the notions of a student of economics tend to be too much affected by the diagrams used to illustrate this point in the text-books (this book as well) where it is necessary to make overhead costs

[1] The parallel fact that purchasing economies are much less important than is generally believed, and that they decrease in importance at an early stage of growth, has been stressed earlier, and it is not repeated here.

[2] It is interesting to note, for example, that the output of the United States Steel Corporation ranged between 18 per cent and 90 per cent of 'capacity' over the period 1927–1938.

relatively important in order that their characteristic effects may be most clearly seen. Overhead costs are seldom so sensational in their effect, even in the short run, as they appear in text-books diagrams, and long-run economies are much less important. The business man will have to take the normal long-run situation into account and will make some allowance for the fact of the trade cycle in his planning.

The short-run costs of an output which is greater than normal will, as we saw in Chapter III, be lower than the cost of a smaller output, but the business could not continue to produce that output at so low a cost in the long run. For the reasons that we have previously discussed, it would need to have a greater reserve of overhead organization and equipment in the long run, than that with which it could manage during a purely temporary increase of output. It will be expected that costs would be lower for an increased output even when all long-run readjustments had been made, but they will not be so sensationally lower as they can be, in the short run, for a business where overhead costs are an extremely high proportion of total costs.[1]

As it grows, a business will let any actual fall in costs influence its price through the operation of the normal pricing policy. As was seen in Chapter V, an expanding business will tend to fix its costing margin on the basis of average overheads in the last accounts plus an allowance for normal profit. It will, therefore, tend to reduce its price. Granted a rapidly expanding market, it may even look ahead a little and take account of the lower costs which it expects at the larger outputs; but the extent to which costs will actually fall in subsequent periods will depend upon the net

---

[1] In technical language: short-run costs will equal long-run costs when the business is running at its planned capacity; the short-run cost-curve will run steeper than the long-run cost-curve, lying above it for outputs below the scale-output and below it for larger outputs. This will be true of those curves even on the normal theoretical definitions, in so far as the business men must be presumed to plan for repairs reserves; it is the more valid on our definition, in so far as we also recognize the existence of strategic reserves not relevant to the strictly static case of orthodox theory.

balance between technical and managerial economies.

In so far as a business expects a sharp fall of technical costs, if it could expand significantly above its present scale, it will usually give full effect to this in its policy, since it will not normally expect its management to become less efficient. A growing business may well be too small to get the full technical economies which it knows exist. This will tend to be reflected in its *existing* price policy — i.e. it will tend to set a price which it will expect to be fully justified only when it has grown sufficiently. If it is up against larger, more efficient, businesses, it will have to do this anyway, in order to meet their price.

An abnormally efficient growing business will tend to set a lower price. In so far as its extra efficiency is associated with the special energy of a founder launching his business, it may slacken as the business grows and may revert to a more normal level on his decease or retirement. Growth will tend to come quite as much because of service to the customer as because of lower prices. A more efficient business man may be better than others in finding out and catering for the special needs of a section of the market hitherto rather neglected. In that case, his business will grow, and may grow rapidly. So long as his price is still set on a competitive basis, having regard to the service which he gives, he will preserve his goodwill and be protected from the competition of others in the markets which he has discovered.

It is often the case that the price which a small and growing business can get will be lower than that which it would like to see set in its industry (or, indeed, than it will consider 'fair' having regard to the 'work involved' in its product). This is especially likely in an industry with heavy technical economies, so that there is a relatively great discrepancy between the costs of the small and of the large business. The relatively great need of the smaller firm to get sufficient net profits to be able to grow, or even to hang on, in its industry will make it tend to adopt a much shorter-term point of view than that of the larger, more efficient, business. The larger firm, taking the longer view of its own interest, but also in conformity with the long-run interest of the industry taken as a whole, will hold the price down to that level which will yield it a safe profit in the long run, and will wish to maintain its normal price policy in good years and bad years alike.

In good years the small business will be well aware that the industry could temporarily set a higher margin, and that that would give it the extra resources which it will need to grow, or to keep in being during the next recession. This attitude has on occasion been forcibly expressed in public when the advent of technical change has caused the larger business to enforce a lower level of normal price when the technical change occurs, even in relatively good years (and such major changes are especially likely to be introduced in good times). In bad times, the small business will be well aware that, if it could make a price-cut which was not noticed at first by its bigger brethren, it would get a very greatly increased share of the trade that is going. If it is very small, it may be able to count on a breathing space, before the other businesses find out and retaliate. Inability to meet its paying-out costs and the apparent certainty of disaster may then lead to price-cutting, even against its long-run interests, assuming its survival. It is for this reason that the price-leadership may pass from the large business to the small, during a depression.

(b) *The Survival of Small Businesses*

The previous paragraph introduced indirectly the wider problem of just how smaller businesses survive against the competition of large businesses. There will, of course, be no problem where the technical economies of increased scale are slight, and it must first be said that the economies of large-scale production are often not so sensational as they are generally assumed to be; the folk-lore on this subject is dominated by the cases of assembly industries, where the processes are very repetitive and where designing the task for mass-production can make so much difference to the total costs. In any case, as was said earlier, technical economies often have their greatest force during the early stages of growth and, in consequence, in a given industry, despite the known importance of technical economies, even the smaller firms may be working comparatively near the scale after which the relative incidence of technical economies becomes much less sensational. So the medium firms, at all events, may not be so far from their potential target as may be assumed. Further, it is frequently the case that the layman's notions of the strength of technical economies of scale are derived from evidence of the fall of short-run costs with increases in output, or still more the rapid rate at which they rise with falling output.

Even so, it is remarkable, at first sight, just how small a small business can be, in an industry where technical economies are known to be important, and yet apparently survive, making heavy losses perhaps in bad times but scraping by in better times. Sometimes appearances are deceptive. The stage is indeed set for the long-run disappearance of the smaller business, and the long run is merely a matter of time. In industries where the capital investment required is very large, so that the financial costs of providing for the replacement of capital are relatively heavy, the bigger business may adopt a depreciation policy which facilitates the short-term survival of a smaller business.

The bigger business will tend to be especially subject to obsolescence, and it will have to make sufficient provision for its equipment to be kept up to date. It will have a position to maintain as a technical leader, etc. The small man may simply not have got into a sufficiently profitable position to get ideas about making such provisions and may only be able to reckon on covering depreciation and repairs, if that. There may also be an irrational element here, in so far as a big business will not be able to resist the attractions of even wasteful technical investment, and so may make excessive provisions for obsolescence. The smaller business will see *its* problem much more in terms of hanging on, and of replacing the equipment that it is using. A price which yields the large business its obsolescence charges plus a normal profit may well enable a small business to survive, to replace its equipment on a less generous basis and to make a moderate profit — or, at the worst, to survive until its capital equipment really has worn out. In such cases, the desperation of the small business may lead it to experiment, and to find that its equipment lasts for a much longer time than the better-provided big business would believe!

The characteristic of technical economies of scale, that they are more important in the early stages of growth, means that at a comparatively modest scale of plant, a business may be able to compete effectively with a much bigger rival, simply by adopting a less stringent depreciation policy, which is not so absurd for it as it would be for the larger business.

Another point which is applicable in some cases is that the bigger business may not be so big in the size of its plant, which is the most important factor from the point of view of technical economies. Where the size of the plant runs to a large figure, further growth might bring more technical economies, but these might be offset by the effects of the pressure that growth would bring in the local labour market. In such cases the big business may become multi-factory, and the size of any one factory may be much nearer that of a smaller business, which may, therefore, not be in so bad a position as might be thought from the naïve technical facts.

The multi-factory business has both advantages and disadvantages from the point of view of management. Sometimes there is an advantage in having several factories under the same control virtually competing one with another, but it would be still better if they could be in the same area. It is frequently necessary for the main administration to be

separated geographically from the factories, and, in consequence, the business's policy may be too much dominated
by policy on the sales side — which easily tends to over-
variety of product — and the factory may suffer from too
great a feeling of remoteness from the central office, which
itself becomes an ' outside ' transmitter of orders. Spreading
the work between a number of factories must limit the
extent to which the business can take advantage of technical
economies, excepting in such ancillary departments as may
be concentrated. It will, on the other hand, as we have seen,
perhaps be able to specialize much more in a single factory
than can any independent producer, and will have some
advantage in the long run through the ease with which it
can introduce technical change in a piecemeal fashion.

Sometimes a small business may be able to compete with
a larger business because its small size will enable it to start,
or to remain, in an area where labour is not so well organized,
or where the predominant industry is low-wage, whereas a
larger business would make too many demands on the local
labour market, or would have to face a union which it has
recognized elsewhere and which will not take too good a view
of local discrepancies in wage-rates. The larger business is
naturally much more vulnerable to the pressure of trade
unions, who will frequently leave a small business alone,
since it is obviously just making out, so long as it is offering
an agreed minimum wage, but who will have a strong inducement to ' keep the pot boiling ' in a large business, and to try
to get better than the minimum terms. The large business
will find it politically difficult to resist paying a higher rate of
wages, if it could afford to pay them and yet could charge a
price leaving it strongly competitive with smaller businesses.

Where special reasons of this sort do not apply and
where, nevertheless, the smaller businesses are surviving
relatively profitably, the reason will usually be found to be in
the fact of the smaller business being able to specialize more
effectively than the bigger business is able to do, in effect

concentrating more upon the sections of the market which are relatively more profitable for it. In this connexion, it is necessary to recognize that what is ordinarily and conveniently thought of as a single industry is usually producing a group of products, which are alike in that they emerge from the same sort of technical processes, but yet differ significantly in quality (the innate capacity which they have to render services in use) and in the ' external ' factors of the associated services which are sold with them. The smaller business is frequently a lot freer to ' go for ' a particular section of the common market than is the big business, whose very position will make it necessary for it to sell to the market as a whole, taking what orders come its way.

The problem of the smaller business is that (just because its scale limits its capacity to earn profits) it can recover its relatively heavy overheads only by putting up its turnover through specializing in those parts of the market where it can get a higher gross profit margin either in the price directly, or, indirectly, in a reduction of quality. In general, the parts of the market with a higher gross profit margin will call for special services. It will be easier for a small business to provide these, since its management may have relatively a good deal of spare capacity, than it will be for the big business to whom the trouble involved may be more costly. In so far as this will be reflected in the gross margin which the bigger business sets, the small firm may find that it can provide those services relatively cheaply, and get by.

One obvious instance of this is in the matter of repairs ; in many industries the very small businesses are repairers rather than manufacturers. They may, similarly, specialize in the type of product which needs special fitting and has to be produced much more to the individual order of the customer. Further, the small business will tend to get rush jobs, and will find these profitable just because it can and will turn around more quickly than a large business, whose plant is much more usually set to work on large runs. In many industries the small businesses play an important part as sub-contractors to the large; their relationship thus being complementary rather than competitive in this respect.

Even where the business does not become an absolute specialist in a line which is not touched by the larger business, its relative technical disadvantage may be greatly reduced by its picking a part of the market and setting up to cater for that specially. Thus in the hosiery industry a small firm may be able to concentrate entirely upon one sort of article whereas the large business may have to produce anything that is ordered.[1] The large business may still reach a scale big enough in each line to be more efficient than the small business, but because it is relatively less specialized it will not have the same order of reduction in its relative costs as if it had been able to concentrate to the same extent as the smaller business.

It is an axiom that a single plant can have only one standard of workmanship. Its products may differ in quality because of clearly defined differences in the quality of the materials, but they must not differ because of less careful work going into their construction. In so far as a large business is selling to the national market as a whole, it will have to maintain a standard of quality which is appropriate to the part of the market where quality is most important.[2] Any products which do not come up to that standard will have to be sold quite frankly as ' seconds '. At the same time, it may not pay the business to produce at the very high quality which is required for a special, but small, section of the market. It may serve that section by sorting out appropriate grades from its standard products, at a cost.

The smaller business, however, can specialize in its quality at a different level from the big business. Thus, it

[1] As just noted, it may employ the small business as sub-contractors for very inconvenient orders.

[2] A large multi-factory business may, of course, be able to produce to different standards in separate factories. Quite commonly, however, it then tends to use different selling machinery, and thus the factories become more nearly separate businesses.

may select a part of the market where the quality required is lower, and sell to that as a speciality, but at a price which is only a shade below, if at all below, the price charged by the bigger business for better quality. Its market may never have occasion to discover the inherent, but irrelevant, difference in quality, and the small business may never have to classify its output as the ' seconds ' that they are, but will profit from the lower costs. Similarly, a small business may go all out for quality, special testing, etc., and get a firm hold on the appropriate part of the market for the product of its industry.

A similar factor which is sometimes found to operate is that the small business, in its zeal to get its cost down, may take risks and make experiments, discovering that some process which the larger businesses insist on to maintain their quality is not really necessary, or can be covered by some much cheaper method, so far as its customers are concerned.

In any industry the bigger business will have to pay more attention to the question of research, since it will be much more vulnerable to the effect of any major technical changes and has to keep its position against international as well as national rivals. It will, accordingly, have to set a price which covers its research costs. This is one of the reasons for some cases of non-combine firms being able to produce at a lower price than ' the ring ' — they specialize rather more upon bread-and-butter lines, but the big business has to be up to date and spend a lot of money upon technical development, which will justify itself in the future but which adds to costs now. Not only will the smaller business not have the costs of research, because it is too small to do any, and because it can go for that section of the home market where it does not matter so much being a little behind-hand in technique, but also it will very often be able to rely on the larger business doing its research for it, in so far as that may result in additions to technical know-how which are not patented. In any case, the larger business may be training the technicians, etc., which the small business later employs.[1] Such training costs have to be covered by the margins of the bigger business.

It may be amusing to recount a minor example of this. A relatively small-scale business was, so its manager told the author, very attractive to the office staffs of a larger business in the same town, so that, at a time when there was a shortage of trained typists, the small business could rely on an intake from the bigger. The big business, in order to get around the shortage, introduced an expensive training school, and, said the man from the smaller business, " It is a very good training school; we much appreciate it ". In this particular instance the businesses were not in the same industry, but it illustrates the point.[2]

Where the technical economies of scale are largely in the basic service departments, such as the tool-room, or in the making of special parts of the product, the business otherwise being an assembly shop, a big business may be driven into producing a relatively large variety of products all stemming from the same processes. This leads to management difficulties as a rule, and a small business may very well compete quite effectively with the bigger business by concentrating on a narrower range of product but exercising a closer supervision over it.

The larger business may be especially likely to develop in this way if a heavy depression, in what have hitherto been its main products, causes some of the overhead departments serving those products to become under-employed, when the taking on of a new product may seem a good way of keeping those departments going, especially if they are important

---

[1] To some extent there is a two-way traffic in British industry: ambitious younger men coming to the large business with the benefits of the more all-round experience of the small firm, and older technicians seeking in a small business the responsibility they cannot get in the large.

[2] Training costs are particularly important in industries employing female labour (where there is normally a fairly large turnover, due to girls leaving to get married). Smaller businesses thus tend to cluster around a larger one. In one case, a large clothing manufacturer removed to an area where the labour supply was relatively undeveloped and started training labour, as he thought, for himself, but in a short while the smaller businesses had moved out too.

features of the organization of the business.

It has also to be recognized that a progressive business of any size will have another driving force making for this sort of expansion in the young up-and-coming men, pressing for promotion and looking for ways in which to achieve it. If they see a job which would be likely to be profitable and which they could add to their department, they will press for the consequent extension. This will make management more complex, will make the business less easy to control, and will, granted any inefficiencies involved in such a spread of activities, make the economies — which might be available, if the energies of the management were directed more narrowly at fewer products — less attractive. It may very well tend to make the business less efficient in some directions than smaller specialist rivals.

This is perhaps rather a static view; if a business really stands still it dies, or rots alive. The new departments facilitate the training of the next generation of responsible managers — and the problem of the succession is a real one in big business; the business does at least keep its live young men whom it may attract just because of the opportunities it gives them; and in a dynamic world the consequent reduction in the risks of so large a business being completely dependent upon a single market (especially in an industry where the vagaries of foreign trade have to be met) brings some off-setting advantages, which are worth paying for in the long run.

We have been speaking so far as if it is only the survival of abnormally small businesses that presents a problem, and the disabilities of big business have been mentioned only incidentally. It is worth noting that in some industries where the technical economies of scale are not very important and are exhausted at a relatively small scale, and where at the same time managerial diseconomies would be expected to be important (as where a fairly close supervision of the product is necessary), it is sometimes possible to find surprisingly big businesses. In some cases it has been found that they have come into existence because of the development of large-scale customers, who find it inconvenient to place orders on a small scale, and whose normal order may be far beyond the capacity of a small business, or far larger than the clutch of eggs which it is prepared to put into the same basket. This may happen during a war, when some of the army contracts are more suitably placed in a piece, but the *general* development of large business has encouraged this. A large business, e.g. a large retail chain, is a large buyer and will not like to parcel its orders up too much. A business may thereby be encouraged to grow very rapidly and to a relatively great size. It may well be maintained afterwards by the convenience which it offers to other large businesses.

The whole of the previous discussion has left the managerial factor out of account, except for its incidental introduction into the last paragraph. There is a disadvantage, generally believed in, that large-scale management may become too much of a routine, perhaps resting too much on the technical economies that it has achieved. It may be careless about costs ; not that it does not get good value for what it buys — good managers and the best equipment, etc. — but it may, in fact, invest in them too easily, not finding it easy to exercise the detailed control over day-to-day expenditure that is possible in the small business, or, if it attempts it, again piling up costs in the ' red tape ' that entangles such decisions. There is no doubt that it is easy for lethargy of this kind to come into a large business, but equally it is easy for a vigorous newcomer to management to spot it, and sooner or later there tends to be a day of reckoning, although that may take some time to arrive.

It may be argued that standards of managerial efficiency will be the same in all *established* businesses, or that the advantage may be with the bigger business, which will be able to develop its technique of management more fully and with greater continuity. But this is to overlook the fact that in any industry new enterprise will tend to be *relatively* small. Now, it is among the newcomers that we can expect to find especial keenness and new ideas. There is no care like that of a vigorous founder of a business, with a fresh mind, looking, as he will do, at his business as a whole, and usually seeing it much more freshly than a manager will who has been brought up in a particular business; such a man will usually be more efficient and have more ' drive '.

This brings up the whole problem of industrial growth from the social aspect. In such a case as this, the small business may well survive by reason of making abnormal profits for a business of its size. In the past it has also contributed to the efficiency of its industry by growing and giving those ' up at the top ' something to reckon with. In the previous chapter it was seen how difficult it is for the smaller business to grow except out of profits, and this factor reinforces our remarks there about the social disadvantage of the effects of present high taxation. Social devices such as trading estates may help small firms to establish themselves, but they will not help them to grow, as small businesses have grown in the past, out of initial specialization, into the more mass-production markets, the whole growth being financed out of accumulated profits and sustained by the surging energy of the founder-type of personality.

At the present time, large-scale new enterprise can come only through the special finance agency, and this is more likely to back a completely new product than it is to help a small business to take the chances of a fight with the established big business. Reference was made in Chapter V to the competitiveness in modern industry which comes from the big business. That is correct, but it is natural that the big business should expand into other lines, producing a larger variety of different products. It will presumably be as efficient as it knows it can be in its own line, where its market will limit its expansion, and the resources which it gets from the undistributed profits which it makes in that market, plus the drive for expansion from its up-and-coming young men, will naturally tend to make it spill over into new lines, in which it may compete with established business, but never directly in its own line. In other words, just as the pressure for growth will make the small business tend to produce a relatively great variety of the same type of product, the same force operating in the big business will make it tend to produce a greater variety of different products.

It is on these grounds that it seems worth urging that an experiment should be adopted which would enable at least the smaller businesses to retain a larger proportion of the profits which they earn, so long as they are genuinely invested in the business. The general picture of smaller business must be of a struggle for existence, and in normal times we should expect them to have a larger mortality than the bigger businesses. Those which survive, however, will contain the newer personalities, and the growth of these businesses should be encouraged in the social interest.

(3) GENERAL INDUSTRIAL ACTIVITY—
THE TRADE CYCLE

Previous analysis has shown that output and activity in an individual business will depend upon the demand for its product. The level of its demand at any time will, of course, be affected by many circumstances which are peculiar to the business, but it will also share in the recurring fluctuations in general industrial activity which are the trade cycle. Even a rapidly expanding business will do worse than it would otherwise have done if there is a general slump in industry as a whole, and even a business which is declining will improve its position to some extent in case of a general recovery. Established businesses will generally find that their output fluctuates from year to year much more because of their share in this general rhythm than it changes because of circumstances which are peculiar to them.

The general pattern of the trade cycle is of periods of rising output and prices succeeded by periods of falling outputs and prices. Within this general pattern, there are significant differences in the experience of particular groups of industries. In particular, activity in the industries making producers' goods — i.e. products which are used by other manufacturers in order to facilitate their own production — tends to change first, and such industries tend to have a greater fluctuation in prices and outputs than do the industries making consumers' goods for the home market. In this country the export industries tend to have a similar pattern to the capital goods industries, but this is to be expected since our exports are dominated by capital goods and by semi-manufactured goods (in the sense of goods which have to undergo further processing and stocking before reaching the final consumer).

The reference to exports reminds us that the trade cycle has become an international phenomenon with the spread of trading relations between countries and the general development of industrialization. Although particular countries may experience differences in the timing and degree of the fluctuations in their activity, which will be affected by circumstances peculiar to them, they nevertheless share in the fundamental rhythms. In the present simplified explanation of the trade cycle, however, it is not necessary to take account of its international aspects, since it is possible to argue in terms of a self-contained country, as if it were isolated from the rest of the world.

Let us first consider a country producing at a definite rate of output at a given time, all prices being constant, and then ask what is the condition of that output remaining unchanged; it will then be possible to proceed with the further question of what happens when the balance of output changes. So far as the individual business is concerned, the value of its output over any period will equal its sales plus any change (positive or negative) in the value of its work in progress and stocks of finished goods. The amount of work in progress and the size of its stocks, given stable prices, will depend upon the level of its sales, and so in stable conditions the value of its output will equal its sales. In the same conditions, its demand for the products of other businesses which are used in its own processes will equal its usage, and so will also be stable. It follows that, for the output of the country as a whole to be stable, the final demand for the finished goods in the form in which they are sold to their ultimate user must remain unchanged. If this is so, then even a business which is a long way back in the chain of production (and whose products, therefore, have to undergo a number of processes before they reach their final stage) will find that its demand will be stable.

The problem can now be seen in terms of the expenditure upon finished products, and this may be related to the national income. The country's national income over a period will equal the value of its output of finished goods, plus any change in its output of semi-finished goods, plus the value of personal services performed during that period other than those of persons employed on production. If we value the finished goods at the point where they are sold to the user (i.e. by the retail shop in the case of consumers' goods), the services whose value is to be added to the value of the total output will consist entirely of personal services to consumers. Those rendered to producers or traders as such will already have been taken into account. It will then be possible to leave the expenditure on consumers' services on one side and to discuss the national income as if it were entirely made up of the output of manufactured products.

The value of the national output, as defined, will then equal that of the national income over the period during which the output is produced; the value of the national income will, therefore, equal the value of the outputs of finished consumers' goods and of finished producers' goods (the 'finished' output being that of the last stage in the

U

chain of production and distribution at which they are handed over to the final user) plus or minus the net change in the value of stocks of semi-finished goods of either class.[1] The level of such stocks will, given that prices are not changing, depend upon the rate at which outputs are running, and so, given stable conditions, there will be no change in stocks. In stable conditions, therefore, the demand for finished goods of either class will equal their total output.

We may now turn to the other side of the counter and think of the customers' side of the situation, i.e. in terms of expenditure rather than of income. The total national expenditure for the period in question can be divided into expenditure upon consumers' goods and expenditure upon producers' goods, correspondingly to the analysis of output. The expenditure upon consumers' goods will generally depend upon the personal incomes of members of the community. For a time a man may draw upon savings to maintain his expenditure when he has a period of low or no income, but there will be a limit to this. Equally, he may borrow from others, or receive gifts; in either case he will be spending income or savings transferred from others. Finally, in our community, unemployed persons are entitled to social service income, either by way of unemployment insurance, as of right, or by way of public assistance, according to need. These payments will be properly regarded as income payments by the recipients, but they are not formally included in the national income as we have defined it. They may be regarded as paid for out of the taxation which is included in the income figure, and which covers the costs of the state's activities, including dispensing charity and providing social

---

[1] It is a consequence of the decision to value output at the last point of distribution that the stocks of ' semi-finished ' goods will include the stocks of technically finished goods in the hands of producers where, as in the case of most consumers' goods, they are finally sold through retailers or other intermediaries. Similarly, the output of such a pure distributor will be his sales, his stocks being regarded as ' semi-finished ' since the whole of his productive process, if it may be so called, is to perform the service of holding and selling the goods.

services. The fact of such extra personal incomes is, as we shall see, important in the analysis of what happens in a depression, but it will first be necessary to follow out the results of fluctuations in incomes and outputs, as already defined, and to regard the effect of such payments as additional.

The general assumption for the moment, then, is that the personal expenditure of consumers depends upon their money incomes. There is one point of difficulty here which will be avoided, but which should not be glossed over — there is a lag between the earning of income by services rendered to contemporary output and the corresponding payment to the persons who have earned that income. This lag will be only three days on the average for weekly wage-earners, but it will be considerably greater in the case of salary-earners and property-owners who are paid at longer intervals, and may be well over six months in the case of business owners, including shareholders, whose incomes cannot be known until after the close of the annual accounting period. The complications that arise from this lag can be avoided in the present discussion because we are presuming stable outputs, which in turn implies stable incomes, given that prices have not changed. In these conditions, it follows that current expenditure may be regarded as related to the current level of income, which will equal the value of current output.

Given the assumption that prices are not changing, and ignoring the effects of any technical change — which will always increase the demand for capital goods in the sort of period with which we are concerned — the expenditure upon producers' goods will depend upon the level of output which they help to produce, as stated earlier in this chapter, and the chain of dependent outputs will end with the output of consumers' goods which is the ultimate justification of all business activity. If, therefore, we assume a stable rate of expenditure upon consumers' goods, it will follow that the amount of investment that producers wish to make currently will also be stable, remaining at the level which corresponds to the rate at which the producers' goods, used in order to get the current rate of output, need to be replaced.

The national income can now be looked at from another point of view — as the total of personal expenditure on consumers' goods plus savings. It follows that, for the output situation to be stable, the expenditure upon consumers' goods should equal the value of the current output of such goods, and hence that savings — the amount of income not spent upon consumption — should equal the value of the current output of producers' goods, i.e. the current amount of investment.

If savings exceed the value of current output of producers' goods, or, to look at it another way, if total consumers' expenditure falls below the value of the current output of consumers' goods, then the total amount of consumers' goods bought will be less than the current output of such goods and there will be an increase in the value of stocks of such goods held. Those producing consumers' goods will find that they have sold less than they expected to sell, and, until output is reduced, there will be an undesired piling up of stocks of finished consumers' goods, since less will be required at the lower rate of sales. On balance, then, not only will such stocks have increased to a level which is greater than will be desired by the business men who hold them, but, at the lower rate of output, they would prefer to have their stocks standing at a lower figure than before. The effect of savings being larger than the current value of producers' goods is that total investments will be larger than producers will like at the given rate of output of consumers' goods — for, of course, any addition to such stocks will be just as much an investment as will the production of producers' goods.

This situation cannot last, even in its present form. When they can do so, those who are left holding unsold stocks will curtail their orders for consumers' goods, or, in the case of manufacturers' stocks, they will cut down their output directly. This fall of output will lower the national income simultaneously. It will also cause the production of producers' goods to fall off, since, at a lower level of final outputs, less of these will be required. In fact, as we have already seen, in the short period, the production of such goods may be far less than the amount that will normally be required for replacement purposes at the new, lower, level of output. In this way businesses will be cutting down the proportion of their income retained by them which they reinvest in capital goods, even though they may still be earning a profit (in which case the proportion of undistributed profits invested in outside securities will rise). This curtailment in the output of producers' goods will further reduce the national income and will cause the total of consumers' expenditure to fall still further. This, in turn, will cause a further reduction in the output of consumers' goods, and so the process goes on.

The preceding paragraph has not referred to any changes in prices, and the effects described would follow even if prices remained unchanged. That, however, is impossible, since we are thinking in terms of industrial activity, and the changes in prices that will occur will, in fact, accelerate the process of contraction. Falling industrial activity will, as explained in Chapter VI, tend to cause the prices of primary materials to fall at once, thereby reducing the level of the prices of the goods which are made with them. The reduction in employment which will accompany a shrinkage in industrial output will also tend to cause wages to fall; there may be more of a time-lag in this case, since labour will resist wage-cuts as strongly as it can, but, with increased unemployment, the strength of the resistance will be diminished, the fall in bargaining power being most marked and occurring first in the relatively less skilled occupations. Equally, on the employers' side there will usually be some reluctance to propose wage-cuts, but in the end the inducement to do so will become stronger, as the reduced outputs cause the increased weight of the overhead costs to cut into profits, with actual losses appearing in the accounts of the businesses in the weakest positions. The falls in the level of wages and in the prices of materials will, in accordance with normal pricing policy, cause the prices of manufactured goods to fall. The reduction in profits, or increase in losses, will grow as output falls, and will be worsened by any price cutting which causes an industry to depart from its normal price policy.

Such falls in prices will further accelerate the process of contraction, since both stock-holdings and investment in producers' goods will be cut down even faster than they would have been in consequence of the falls in output, taken by themselves. Falling prices, with the losses that they cause to be charged to the trading account, will make businesses cut their stocks to the minimum, until they are sure that prices have become stabilized. The stocks of materials purchased from other businesses will tend to be affected more than the stocks of their own products, since the needs of the market will set some limit to the fall of the latter type of stocks, and buyers will, in fact, expect very prompt deliveries in bad times. Stocks of materials can be cut to the bone, further supplies being bought on a hand-to-mouth basis.

Although stocks of capital goods will not be so important as stocks of materials and consumers' goods, since so many of them are made to specifications, their producers will ordinarily keep substantial stocks of parts and these will be affected in the same way as other stocks. The effect of price-falls will be most marked from the demand side, however. We have already seen that any reduction in output, since it will free capacity, will enable normal replacement demand to be avoided. The investment in capital goods will be further postponed, if falling prices make it seem likely that, by waiting, the investment can be made even more advantageously. Businesses will, therefore, tend to make do with machinery, etc., which they would otherwise have replaced, putting up with any temporary rise in repairs costs.

Although it falls outside the assumptions on which we

are arguing at the moment, it will usually be the case that even in a depression there will be some forces making for increased capital investment; there will normally be some industries whose secular trend is upward, as was the case with the motor industry in the depression of the 1930's. In so far as falling prices of capital goods cause such industries to delay the extensions that they would otherwise have made, they must seriously delay the recovery, and prevent such industries from mitigating the severity of the slump.

The analyses which have just been given of the cumulative effects of falling outputs, once they have occurred, will raise the question why an industrial society which behaves in this way does not go down in the slump to the *Ragnarok* of zero output; why is it that slumps come to an end and that industrial activity at the lowest level is still not negligible? The answer can be found in the very factors responsible for the possibility of the decline taking the form that it does — there is a limit to the extent to which the total expenditure will fall, even in bad times.

If the previous analysis is retraced, it will be seen that the principal cause of the vicious nature of the decline in industrial activity is the progressive contraction in investment, through the cutting down of stocks and the curtailment of orders for capital goods. There will be a limit to this. Some stocks must be held and some capital investment must take place. Once this rock-bottom level has been reached the position will tend to become more stable, with a continuously maintained demand for new output corresponding to the rate at which output is tending to run. Further, the reduction in consumers' incomes due to increased unemployment will be offset to some extent by the fact of social security payments and other factors which have previously been mentioned. The reductions in the prices of materials and in the levels of wages will also set in motion forces working towards a stoppage of the decline. There will be some tendency for the supplies of primary materials to be cut, and, in so far as their producers have managed to carry on for a time, producing in the aggregate an excessive supply of their products, the correction that comes on this account may be sharp. Also, the lower the levels to which wages fall, the more surely there will come a point at which the resistance of labour to further cuts will increase. This will certainly be the case in a country like ours where unemployment benefit will give a minimum income available to a man who is not working. If the wages of lower skilled labour get sufficiently near to this, it will be more possible for trade unions to stand out against further cuts.

The rapid downfall of the slump, therefore, tends characteristically to end in what Mr. Oscar Hobson aptly called the ' sloom ', where industrial activity runs at a low level but, at that level, the current level of investment is sufficient to take up the difference between consumers' expenditure and total national income. This lower-level stability may last for a long time, especially if the depression has been particularly severe, but its continuance will, in the end, be terminated by factors making for a revival of industrial investment and a recovery.

One factor will be the effect of the rate of interest. Not much attention has been paid to this so far, because it is not thought to have an important direct effect upon industrial investment; there are other effects, however, and these may be important if the rate of interest falls very low, and continues low for some time. The onset of depression will tend to cause a reduction in rates of interest. The demand for loans and advances on the part of business men will fall off, and, at the same time, the proportion of cash in hand in the bank balance sheet will tend to rise, because the weekly call for cash to pay wages will be running at a lower level. The banks will, therefore, have to rely upon investment in securities, for a larger proportion of their income. The increased relative pressure upon the market for Government securities, in particular, which will be reinforced by businesses reinvesting any working capital which has become temporarily surplus due to the decline in output, will cause the prices of such securities to rise,[1] thereby reducing the effective rate of interest which they earn. Similarly, the banks will be more anxious to make very short-term loans to the money market, despite the low earnings, and these rates of interest will also fall. In the end there will be a general reduction in rates of interest, including the charges upon advances, in so far as these latter stand above their minimum levels.

Such a fall in the rate of interest may well have a stimulating effect upon the construction of houses; owing to their relatively long life, with the consequently long period of repayment allowed by building societies, etc., a reduction in the rate of interest will permit of charges made by lenders on house property getting considerably nearer to the ordinary level of rents. This may stimulate the demand for new houses (as it appears to have done in the last depression) which will affect directly only the building industry, but, indirectly, it will have a much wider effect, not only through the revival in demand for building materials, but also in the increased consumers' expenditure due to the revival in employment, and the latter may be very widespread in its effects.

The low rate of interest may also encourage persons or institutions with postponed investment, or investment which they can anticipate as likely to be needed in the near future, to borrow money while rates are low. Local authorities, for example, will appreciate the reduction in the loan charges which will be made possible. The same considerations may affect businesses which are large enough, and sufficiently well thought of, to be able to borrow even in a slump. A good deal of extra investment seems to have taken place in the

---

[1] This will give capital gains to the holders of such securities, and if the rise in values is sharp enough, as with a *sudden* readjustment of rates of interest, they may be induced to spend more freely. This, however, will usually be a minor effect. It should be noted, of course, that the values of ordinary shares will still be falling.

later stages of the 1930–33 'sloom', but it should not be overlooked that costs of construction were then low. This fact of low cost of construction may well be more important than low rates of interest in the slump.

Any such extra demand will be reinforced by the fact that there will be some investment which was postponed in the early days of the depression, but which it becomes increasingly difficult to postpone, so that, sooner or later, some increase in the demand for investment goods must occur. We have already mentioned the fact that, in a normal society, there will also be some industries which are meeting a long-term increase in demand, and these will maintain or increase their investment once the first shock of the slump is over. In modern times the government, also, will tend to act deliberately in order to increase employment by means of public works and other projects. These characteristically take a little time to get going, and their pace tends to be increased for political reasons the longer the slump has lasted.

Any depression will, therefore, tend to stabilize itself in the end and will then germinate the seeds of future recovery. These characteristically show themselves by increased production of investment goods — i.e. their products are not of the kind that go into ordinary consumption. Once any increase of this type has occurred, it is bound to cause a cumulative upward movement in activity. Its direct effects will be to increase activity in the industries making the products which are used by it, but it should also be noted that, in so far as such investment does not provide goods for personal consumption, the increased personal incomes which it will give to the re-employed men will cause a net increase in consumers' expenditure, and thus increase the demand for the industries making consumers' goods.

Just as, in the decline, the repercussions on stocks and the demand for capital goods accelerated any tendency to a fall, so now they will accelerate the tendency to rising output. The initial rising demand will cause a depletion of stocks in the first instance, as producers find their output rising beyond what they expected. They will, therefore, increase their output, not only to the level of the higher demand but also to meet the depletion of stocks. At each stage of increased employment, the consumers' goods industries will find an increased demand. This will be selective in its effects. The demand for the staple — 'fodder' — type of goods will not change very much, since very much the same amount will be consumed per head whether a man is employed or unemployed. The increased income will first affect the industries producing consumers' goods, whose demand is more postponable, such as footwear and clothing, and will affect the better types of these more and more as the revival goes on, so stepping up the labour content of such goods, and causing increased demand for labour. When incomes have risen sufficiently, the demand for consumers' capital goods (those goods which are relatively expensive, are bought infrequently, etc.), such as motor-cars and radio sets, will tend to be greatly affected, as will the demand for luxuries generally.

The demand for capital goods will, perhaps, take a little time to be affected, for there will be a fair amount of excess capacity, and the first increase in demand — apart from the stimulus of rising prices, to be referred to later — will accordingly come from accelerated replacements. As soon, however, as recovery causes the rate of output to get sufficiently near the existing capacity (and this will ordinarily have been reduced during the depression by such goods being worn out rather than maintained or replaced), then the demand for *extra* capacity will appear.[1] Any further expansion will cause at least a proportionate increase in the demand for capital goods. It follows that the demand for capital goods during a recovery will tend to increase in proportion to the rate of increase in output, and hence more than in proportion to the

---

[1] Since capital goods cannot easily be installed in small units, the demand will, in fact, tend to increase rather discontinuously and to anticipate further output.

actual level of output. This will also apply to the increases in stocks.

In the first stages of a recovery, there may not be any great rise in prices. The pressure on materials may be able to be met by the excessive stocks whose size has caused the abnormal depression in their prices, and there will be reserves of unemployed and under-employed labour. Gradually, however, the position will be reversed and there will be a general tendency to rises both in wages and in prices. The rises in wages will tend to lag behind the rise in the demand for labour, until employment has reached the critical levels in each class of labour at which the bargaining power of trade unions is greatly strengthened. At that point wages may begin to move sharply upwards. When these rises in prices have occurred, they will affect prices generally, in the same way as their falls did in the slump. The later stages of a recovery tend, therefore, to be accompanied by rising prices, which will tend to rise rather more sharply as the recovery goes on.

There will be other factors which will tend to cause prices to rise as compared with their slump levels. First, in so far as depression has brought the cutting of any prices below the level at which they would be set on the basis of normal pricing policy, the normal relation of prices to costs will tend to be restored. Secondly, less efficient businesses, which in times of normal pressure on their markets cannot get a price which would yield them a normal profit, may well find in busy times that they can get their price, even if it is dearer than their competitors', in so far as they can supply goods which their competitors are going to take a considerable time to deliver. It should be mentioned that one characteristic feature of the later stages of a boom is the sharp rise in the time taken to give delivery of goods that have been ordered, especially in the capital goods industries, whose output will press most severely upon their capacity. This leads to a false optimism in industry, in so far as there is a natural tendency to over-order in order to make sure of delivery from one source or another. The swollen order books contain a lot of 'water' of this sort, and, when the break comes, this will be drained away suddenly in cancelled orders, thus accelerating the spread of any pessimism.

Rising prices will lead to an increased desire to hold stocks, especially of materials, in order to secure the extra profits through rising prices of the products. The effect of this will also tend to be magnified with the distance of a business down the chain of production from the final product, and will produce its maximum effect in the market for primary materials, where it will tend further to maintain rising prices, so sustaining itself. Rising prices will similarly give a strong inducement to increase the capital equipment of industry. The earning power of such new equipment will be higher than the minimum level which the business man will demand, and he can look forward to increased output and will be induced to replace capital which would otherwise have been kept in use. So, once again, the effect of the induced rises in prices will be to cause a sharper rate of increase of output, and the rate of such increase will be magnified the farther we go back from the consumers' goods stage, having the maximum effect upon industries producing heavy capital goods.

The upshot of the previous analysis is similar to that of the analysis of the downward movement of the slump. Once a revival of demand has occurred, the increased desire to invest in stocks and capital goods will be the causal factor making it become a cumulative movement, especially under the stimulus of rising prices. The upward movement of the recovery (and the boom) must come to an end finally, however strong it may be, for it, too, will generate the seeds of its own destruction. It has been noted that, in general, the increased capital investment will rise at a faster rate than output, since the real factors behind it depend upon the rate of increase of investment. It follows that if the rate of increase of output slackens off, the demand for capital goods, etc., will cease to rise and may even fall.

Such a slackening in the rate of increase of output will be caused by many factors. As recovery goes on, the productive capacity of industrial equipment will be continuously being increased by the coming into use of new equipment whose construction was started previously. This will affect the production of capital goods especially, since the equipment to make such goods will usually itself take an especially long time to make. The delay in the delivery of such equipment will, therefore, tend to lessen, and the manufacturers will find that they are beginning to make some reduction in their swollen order books, which will reduce the apparent pressure on them. That pressure will be still further reduced by cancellations of excess orders as buyers see the possibility of getting delivery from particular manufacturers at an early date.

The actual need for capital will probably begin to fall somewhat. As has already been said, it will be usual for those making extensions of equipment to look ahead a little, especially in the heavier types of equipment, so that previous expansions will have anticipated some rise in output. The importance of purely replacement demand will naturally have diminished during the progress of the boom. This, taken together with the increased availability of capital goods, will mean that the bottle-necks of productive capacity will tend to become less important than they were during the early stages.

In the later stages of the boom, the limitation on output, due to the capacity of equipment, will be less important than the limitation due to the dwindling reserves of labour. The pool of available lower-skilled labour will have been cut down, not only by the employment of such persons on the lower-skilled jobs, but also by the increasing possibility of their securing more attractive employment. The scarcity of this type of labour (which, although poorly paid in times of low employment, is yet essential to the working of industry) will tend to cause a marked rise in its wages, and, since such labour is much more likely to move about after better wages, it is so much more easy for wage competition to appear in its market. Rising wages of this class of labour will affect the wages of other classes, since these will tend to move in order to preserve the customary distance between them and lower-skilled wages.

There will also be other classes of labour, the supply of which will become progressively an important limitation on output as activity increases, and the capital goods industries are likely to be particularly affected. These industries will have suffered from especially low employment in the slump, which will have encouraged their skilled labour reserves to move into other employment where this was obtainable. The labour reserves of such industries will, therefore, tend to have disappeared by the time that they get to the high level of activity caused by the boom. The wages of such labour will, therefore, tend to rise faster than the general wage level. The labour costs of the industries that employ them will tend to rise faster, in so far as they are having to use less skilled labour in order to eke out their supplies of the more highly skilled.

As the boom goes on, the overhead costs of salaries will tend to rise. Salaries naturally lag some time behind wages, but they will have to be readjusted at some point. As tenancies fall in for renewal, rents will tend also to be revised upwards. In this way, the costing-margins for overheads will tend to rise and will be still another factor making for rising prices.

The later stages of a boom are, therefore, characterized by very little increase in the physical rate of output, but by continuous pressure upon materials and labour — especially labour — in order to maintain the rate of output which is available from the existing equipment. Not only will wages and materials prices tend to continue to rise, and to rise more sharply as time goes on, the actual costs of production will be tending to rise independently and for other reasons. It will not be so easy to enforce an economy in the usage of materials. The discipline on the factory floor will tend to deteriorate. Workmen who have been under heavy pressure for a considerable period will be more tired and less enthusiastic about their job. Newcomers will tend to be less efficient than the existing staffs, and will, perhaps, pull down their efficiency as well. In such conditions it will also be easier for restrictive practices to be enforced by workers — especially in the operation of new machinery. The efficiency of management will also tend to be lower. A factory which is working hectically in order to catch up with arrears of orders will not run so efficiently. All these factors will make the rise of prices tend to become progressively more sharp, whilst the rate of increase of production slows down.

The slowing down in the rate of growth of real output must in itself produce a factor making for a turn-down in industrial activity. Although there will be less addition to stocks called for by the actual rate of output, it is true that the rising prices of materials may still provide a stimulus for additions to their stocks, but the stimulus of rising prices will begin to lose its effect in the presence of the well-known signs of a boom that is coming to an end. Once business men begin asking themselves if prices have not gone too high, the falling rate of growth of output will produce its effect. Its depressing effect will not be weakened at all by the continued rise in prices so far as capital goods are concerned. These are not traded in by the buyers, and their rising prices will increase the cost-charges of the profit and loss account without affecting the revenue side as stocks will do. Such goods will not be ordered unless they are thought to be required for production in the near future, either as a replacement of older equipment or as an extension. The latter purpose will have become more important, and a slackening growth of output will tend to cause an actual fall in the rate of orders for this type of good. It is for this reason that the turn-down will come first in the capital goods industries, and may develop in them whilst the rate of output at higher stages of production is relatively unaffected. But the end is inevitable from that point, the falling output in the capital goods industries causing the symptoms of reduced incomes, reduced consumers' expenditure, reduced production, reduced investment, etc., and the situation will then proceed into the continuous decline that we have analysed previously.

The slackening of output during a boom will also be reinforced by another factor which has not been introduced into the analysis so far — the tendency for expenditure by consumers not to keep pace with income, once that has risen to a certain level. This will operate even with wage-earners. In the first stages of increased incomes they will spend more upon the products of manufacturing industry than they will at a later stage, when they will wish to spend more upon service industries such as entertainments, including gambling. These industries can provide extra output without it being much reflected in extra demand for productive equipment, and the extra receipts will go into the profits and salaries of those engaged in them. In so far as these are likely to save some of their incomes, and to spend part of them again upon personal services, it follows that the expenditure upon ordinary goods and services will slacken. There will have been some important shifts within the total expenditure that wage-earners do make, away from weekly wage-goods to goods of a capital nature, such as radios and cars, which require the expenditure of the savings made from wages over comparatively long periods of time. These may well be bought by hire-purchase, in which case the goods may be produced first, the savings coming later. There will, in any case, be a limit to the expenditure of this kind, and at some point the rate of savings will increase, so that expenditure ceases to rise in the same proportion to wage-earners' income.

The shift towards savings will, however, tend to be

especially important so far as profit receivers are concerned. It will be readily seen from our previous analyses that profits will increase in a boom and will form a progressively larger share of the national income. The fact that there is a long lag before the amount of this income can be known will be one factor making for the expenditure of the recipients not rising so fast as their incomes. It must also be borne in mind, however, that not all of this income will be distributed to persons, a proportion being retained for reinvestment in the business. The amount of such retained profits that is spent is especially likely to fall off as the boom gets near its final stage. In the early stages of recovery, businesses will tend to be spending upon new equipment, etc., more than the current rate of undistributed profits, for it will pay them to use any free money capital that they have. In the later stages, as we have just seen, the inducement for extra investment will slacken. Also, the charges for depreciation with the introduction of new equipment will have been rising, and these funds also will not necessarily be reinvested at once in new equipment. So we have here another factor making expenditure slacken below the rate of increase of income, thus contributing to the likelihood of the turn-down.

The general conclusion that we have reached is, therefore, that the industrial system is inherently unstable, in so far as any advance in the general rate of output will lead to a rate of capital investment which is too great to be sustained, and the consequent slackening in investment that must occur at some point or another will lead to falling industrial activity. The fluctuations that would result from this are reinforced by the working of the pricing system in the markets for primary materials and for labour. It may, indeed, be this which is responsible both for the unhealthy character of the boom, which ordinarily develops in the later stages of a period of advance, and for the morbid nature of the depression. In this way the industrial system of the world tends not to produce a steady level of output, or an output which grows steadily according to the rate of technical progress, but to suffer the fluctuations of the trade cycle.

Many writers have pointed out that the trade cycle is not without its advantages, in so far as it forces economic society to develop at a much greater pace than it would do otherwise, and until recent years slumps have been too easily regarded as the price of economic progress. With an increased knowledge of how slumps might be mitigated — a consequence of all the work on the problem of the trade cycle which culminated in the theories of Lord Keynes — there has grown up an increased desire to avoid the stagnation of the depression by the use of planned social action. This desire has been greatly strengthened by the experience of the last depression, which was made so much worse by the great distortions and over-expansions in industrial capacity caused by the 1914 War and by the beggar-my-neighbour restrictions on international trading which were also a consequence of that war.

The trade cycle is, then, a disorder of the economic system, but industry cannot help itself in this matter. What is required is to stabilize the expenditure of the community, and particularly the expenditure not going to personal consumption, so that other uses for productive resources may take up the slack when the replacement and reinvestment needs of industry fall off. This can be done by governmental action, which can plan public works and other useful projects to be introduced in times of falling activity and postponed when the ordinary needs of industry revive. Industry itself could co-operate, given such a system of planned public investment, and given an understanding of what it is trying to do.

The co-operation required from industry is that, so far as possible, it should itself refrain from postponable capital investment in times of great pressure on the capital goods industries, introducing them when activity is less. This is the more feasible, in so far as many important industries, from

the point of view of the demand for capital goods, are dominated by relatively large businesses who can take a longer
view, and would do so, given the encouragement. Further,
with the recent nationalization of transport and coal, the
Government itself will have under its control two very
important spheres for a planned investment programme —
just as the Government-sponsored project of modernization
and improvement in the electricity industry with its heavy
expenditure in 1930–32 was, almost accidentally, a factor in
the timing and extent of the recovery.

All this need not be laboured, for it has been the subject
of a good deal of attention in recent years. If the State really
set out to work an anti-cyclical policy, it could do a great deal
of good even within one country. In fact, until now, the State
has rather aggravated the slump, the principle of balancing
the Budget leading to the cutting down of state expenditure
just at the time when private expenditure was falling most
rapidly. Any relief through public works has traditionally
come rather late in a depression. It would certainly be
possible to achieve a much more steady level of output and
employment.[1] Too much should not be expected of this,
however. There is, first, the minor point that the State can only
act on signals which will not be clearly seen until the down-
turn in industrial activity is in sight, and that plans for public
investment, even if they are as ready as they can be, will take
a little time to bring into effect. Some instability must be
expected in any case, therefore, unless we abandon altogether
the private enterprise system on which our society has
developed.

A major point for this country is its dependence upon
international trade. If we are to maintain anything like our
present standard of life, we must get the maximum benefit
from international trade. It will, therefore, not be possible
for us to insulate ourselves from the trade cycle, in so far as

---

[1] *Public Investment and the Trade Cycle*, by Bretherton, Burchardt and
Rutherford, Oxford, 1940, contains a good study of these possibilities.

that is a world phenomenon. In a depression our export industries at least will face a decline in output, and that will not be fully compensated by home investment. Labour, in particular, is too localized, and the products of the investment industries are too specialized, for the home market to be able to absorb them, or for the sort of goods which can be produced under a state programme of home investment to take up all the productive facilities which a depression will show to be redundant. The trade cycle can be fully removed only by international action of a more complete kind than we can foresee at this time.

If we cut ourselves off from the rest of the world, we could, of course, maintain a steady level of employment, and that at a high level — it would need to be! For a withdrawal from the knocks of international trade would be at the cost of a considerable reduction in our standard of living. The loss of our imports would mean that we should all have to work so hard for what standard was available that we should have little resources left for investment and, in consequence, the need for an anti-cyclical programme would disappear in the misery of our poverty.

This has been overlooked by the enthusiastic champions of the new economics, who speak as though full employment and a rising standard of living were fully compatible in one country, such as ours, acting by itself. An attempt to sustain a genuinely full employment programme in this country must mean, in a slump, an immense diversion of resources away from the channels in which we ordinarily earn our living overseas and into those which can more easily be the subject of Government encouragement. Such a programme, further, raises many difficulties with regard to the location of industry, since so many of our export industries are concentrated and localized away from the industries making more directly for the home market. Further, recent experience has shown that it is difficult to maintain productivity in conditions of continued over-full output, in view of the frustrations due to bottlenecks and to the immobility of labour. Full employment with rising productivity, even in the home industries, could not be achieved without a complete change in the policies of organized labour and some sort of wages policy, for which the time does not seem to be ready.

Even if we cannot go all the way with those who argue that full employment is achievable by administrative action, the fact remains that a much more stable level of industrial activity is possible. Within that framework, manufacturing business would be much more free to develop, and economic progress would be greater, because more certain.

THE END

PRINTED BY R. & R. CLARK, LTD., EDINBURGH